D1370665

2013 | World Development Indicators

THE WORLD BANK

Preface

Welcome to *World Development Indicators 2013*, the World Bank's premier compilation of relevant, high-quality, and internationally comparable statistics about global development.

The first edition of *World Development Indicators* in 1997 included this forecast: "The global economy is undergoing an information revolution that will be as significant in effect as the industrial revolution of the nineteenth century." At that time the number of mobile phones worldwide was estimated to be less than 2 per 100 people, with eight times as many telephone mainlines. *World Development Indicators* has tracked the revolution: this edition reports that mobile phone subscriptions in 2011 grew to 85 per 100 people—a more than fortyfold increase.

This is just one example of how people were communicating and acquiring knowledge and how information was changing. But in addition to measuring the change, *World Development Indicators* has felt it directly. Use of the online database and the tools that access it—particularly the Open Data website (http://data.worldbank.org), the web-based DataBank query application (http://databank.worldbank.org), and applications for mobile devices—has increased dramatically.

And so we have refined and improved the presentation of this 17th edition. Our aim is to find the best way to put data in the hands of policymakers, development specialists, students, and the public, so that they may use the data to reduce poverty and solve the world's most pressing development challenges. The biggest change is that the data tables previously published in the book are now available online (http://wdi.worldbank.org/tables). This has many advantages: The tables will reflect the latest additions and revisions to the data. They will be available to a far greater audience. And they will be free for everyone.

World Development Indicators 2013 is organized around six themes—world view, people, environment, economy, states and markets, and global links. Each section includes an introduction, a set of six stories highlighting regional trends, a table of the most relevant and popular indicators, and an index to the full set of tables and indicators available online. *World view* also reviews progress toward the Millennium Development Goals.

Other companion products include *The Little Data Book 2013*, which provides an at-a-glance view of indicators for each economy, and a new version of the DataFinder mobile application, available in Chinese, English, French, and Spanish and designed to reflect the structure and tables of *World Development Indicators 2013,* for both tablet and handheld devices and for all major mobile platforms (http://data.worldbank .org/apps).

World Development Indicators is the result of a collaborative effort of many partners: the United Nations family, the International Monetary Fund, the International Telecommunication Union, the Organisation for Economic Co-operation and Development, the statistical offices of more than 200 economies, and countless others. I extend my gratitude to them all—and especially to government statisticians around the world. Without their hard work, professionalism, and dedication, measuring and monitoring trends in global development would not be possible.

We hope you will find the new *World Development Indicators* a useful resource, and we welcome any suggestions to improve it at data@worldbank.org.

Shaida Badiee
Director
Development Economics Data Group

Acknowledgments

This book was prepared by a team led by Soong Sup Lee under the management of Neil Fantom and comprising Azita Amjadi, Liu Cui, Federico Escaler, Mahyar Eshragh-Tabary, Juan Feng, Masako Hiraga, Wendy Ven-dee Huang, Bala Bhaskar Naidu Kalimili, Buyant Khaltarkhuu, Elysee Kiti, Alison Kwong, Ibrahim Levent, Hiroko Maeda, Johan Mistiaen, Vanessa Moreira da Silva, Maurice Nsabimana, Beatriz Prieto-Oramas, William Prince, Evis Rucaj, Rubena Sukaj, Emi Suzuki, Eric Swanson, Jomo Tariku, Rasiel Victor Vellos, and Olga Victorovna Vybornaia, working closely with other teams in the Development Economics Vice Presidency's Development Data Group.

World Development Indicators electronic products were prepared by a team led by Reza Farivari and comprising Ying Chi, Jean-Pierre Djomalieu, Ramgopal Erabelly, Shelley Fu, Gytis Kanchas, Siddhesh Kaushik, Ugendran Machakkalai, Nacer Megherbi, Shanmugam Natarajan, Parastoo Oloumi, Manish Rathore, Ashish Shah, Atsushi Shimo, Malarvizhi Veerappan, and Vera Wen.

All work was carried out under the direction of Shaida Badiee. Valuable advice was provided by Tito Cordella, Doerte Doemeland, Zia M. Qureshi, and David Rosenblatt.

The choice of indicators and text content was shaped through close consultation with and substantial contributions from staff in the World Bank's four thematic networks—Sustainable Development, Human Development, Poverty Reduction and Economic Management, and Financial and Private Sector Development—and staff of the International Finance Corporation and the Multilateral Investment Guarantee Agency. Most important, the team received substantial help, guidance, and data from external partners. For individual acknowledgments of contributions to the book's content, see *Credits.* For a listing of our key partners, see *Partners.*

Communications Development Incorporated provided overall design direction, editing, and layout, led by Meta de Coquereaumont, Jack Harlow, Bruce Ross-Larson, and Christopher Trott. Elaine Wilson created the cover and graphics and typeset the book. Peter Grundy, of Peter Grundy Art & Design, and Diane Broadley, of Broadley Design, designed the report. Staff from The World Bank's Office of the Publisher oversaw printing and dissemination of the book.

Table of contents

Partners

Defining, gathering, and disseminating international statistics is a collective effort of many people and organizations. The indicators presented in *World Development Indicators* are the fruit of decades of work at many levels, from the field workers who administer censuses and household surveys to the committees and working parties of the national and international statistical agencies that develop the nomenclature, classifications, and standards fundamental to an international statistical system. Nongovernmental organizations and the private sector have also made important contributions, both in gathering primary data and in organizing and publishing their results. And academic researchers have played a crucial role in developing statistical methods and carrying on a continuing dialogue about the quality and interpretation of statistical indicators. All these contributors have a strong belief that available, accurate data will improve the quality of public and private decisionmaking.

The organizations listed here have made *World Development Indicators* possible by sharing their data and their expertise with us. More important, their collaboration contributes to the World Bank's efforts, and to those of many others, to improve the quality of life of the world's people. We acknowledge our debt and gratitude to all who have helped to build a base of comprehensive, quantitative information about the world and its people.

For easy reference, web addresses are included for each listed organization. The addresses shown were active on March 1, 2013.

International and government agencies

Carbon Dioxide Information Analysis Center

http://cdiac.ornl.gov

Centre for Research on the Epidemiology of Disasters

www.emdat.be

Deutsche Gesellschaft für Internationale Zusammenarbeit

www.giz.de

Food and Agriculture Organization

www.fao.org

Internal Displacement Monitoring Centre

www.internal-displacement.org/

International Civil Aviation Organization

www.icao.int

International Diabetes Federation

www.idf.org

International Energy Agency

www.iea.org

International Labour Organization

www.ilo.org

International Monetary Fund

www.imf.org

International Telecommunication Union

www.itu.int

Joint United Programme on HIV/AIDS

www.unaids.org

Partners

National Science
Foundation

www.nsf.gov

The Office of U.S. Foreign
Disaster Assistance

www.globalcorps.com/ofda.html

Organisation for Economic
Co-operation and Development

www.oecd.org

Stockholm International
Peace Research Institute

www.sipri.org

Understanding
Children's Work

www.ucw-project.org

United Nations

www.un.org

United Nations Centre for Human
Settlements, Global Urban Observatory

www.unhabitat.org

United Nations
Children's Fund

www.unicef.org

United Nations Conference on
Trade and Development

www.unctad.org

United Nations Department of
Economic and Social Affairs,
Population Division

www.un.org/esa/population

United Nations Department of
Peacekeeping Operations

www.un.org/en/peacekeeping

United Nations Educational,
Scientific, and Cultural Organization,
Institute for Statistics

www.uis.unesco.org

United Nations Environment Programme

www.unep.org

United Nations Industrial Development Organization

www.unido.org

United Nations International Strategy for Disaster Reduction

www.unisdr.org

United Nations Office on Drugs and Crime

www.unodc.org

United Nations Office of the High Commissioner for Refugees

www.unhcr.org

United Nations Population Fund

www.unfpa.org

Upsalla Conflict Data Program

www.pcr.uu.se/research/UCDP

World Bank

http://data.worldbank.org

World Health Organization

www.who.int

World Intellectual Property Organization

www.wipo.int

World Tourism Organization

www.unwto.org

World Trade Organization

www.wto.org

Partners

Private and nongovernmental organizations

Center for International Earth Science Information Network

www.ciesin.org

Containerisation International

www.ci-online.co.uk

DHL

www.dhl.com

International Institute for Strategic Studies

IISS

www.iiss.org

International Road Federation

IRF

www.irfnet.org

Netcraft

http://news.netcraft.com

PwC

www.pwc.com

Standard & Poor's

www.standardandpoors.com

World Conservation Monitoring Centre

www.unep-wcmc.org

World Economic Forum

www.weforum.org

World Resources Institute

www.wri.org

User guide to tables

World Development Indicators is the World Bank's premier compilation of cross-country comparable data on development. The database contains more than 1,200 time series indicators for 214 economies and more than 30 country groups, with data for many indicators going back more than 50 years.

The 2013 edition of *World Development Indicators* has been reconfigured to offer a more condensed presentation of the principal indicators, arranged in their traditional sections, along with regional and topical highlights.

- World view
- People
- Environment
- Economy
- States and markets
- Global links

Tables

The tables include all World Bank member countries (188), and all other economies with populations of more than 30,000 (214 total). Countries and economies are listed alphabetically (except for Hong Kong SAR, China, and Macao SAR, China, which appear after China).

The term *country,* used interchangeably with *economy,* does not imply political independence but refers to any territory for which authorities report separate social or economic statistics. When available, aggregate measures for income and regional groups appear at the end of each table.

Aggregate measures for income groups

Aggregate measures for income groups include the 214 economies listed in the tables, plus Taiwan, China, whenever data are available. To maintain consistency in the aggregate measures over time and between tables, missing data are imputed where possible.

Aggregate measures for regions

The aggregate measures for regions cover only low- and middle-income economies.

The country composition of regions is based on the World Bank's analytical regions and may differ from common geographic usage. For regional classifications, see the map on the inside back cover and the list on the back cover flap. For further discussion of aggregation methods, see *Statistical methods.*

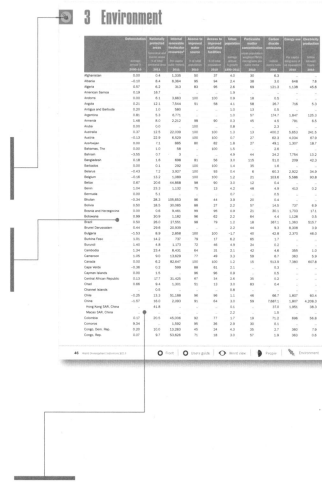

Data presentation conventions

- A blank means not applicable or, for an aggregate, not analytically meaningful.
- A billion is 1,000 million.
- A trillion is 1,000 billion.
- Figures in orange italics refer to years or periods other than those specified or to growth rates calculated for less than the full period specified.
- Data for years that are more than three years from the range shown are footnoted.
- The cutoff date for data is February 1, 2013.

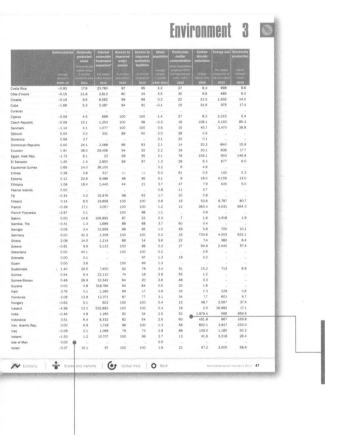

Classification of economies

For operational and analytical purposes the World Bank's main criterion for classifying economies is gross national income (GNI) per capita (calculated using the *World Bank Atlas* method). Because GNI per capita changes over time, the country composition of income groups may change from one edition of *World Development Indicators* to the next. Once the classification is fixed for an edition, based on GNI per capita in the most recent year for which data are available (2011 in this edition), all historical data presented are based on the same country grouping.

Low-income economies are those with a GNI per capita of $1,025 or less in 2011. Middle-income economies are those with a GNI per capita of more than $1,025 but less than $12,475. Lower middle-income and upper middle-income economies are separated at a GNI per capita of $4,036. High-income economies are those with a GNI per capita of $12,476 or more. The 17 participating member countries of the euro area are presented as a subgroup under high income economies.

Statistics

Additional information about the data is provided in *Primary data documentation,* which summarizes national and international efforts to improve basic data collection and gives country-level information on primary sources, census years, fiscal years, statistical methods and concepts used, and other background information. *Statistical methods* provides technical information on some of the general calculations and formulas used throughout the book.

Symbols

..	means that data are not available or that aggregates cannot be calculated because of missing data in the years shown.
0 or 0.0	means zero or small enough that the number would round to zero at the displayed number of decimal places.
/	in dates, as in 2010/11, means that the period of time, usually 12 months, straddles two calendar years and refers to a crop year, a survey year, or a fiscal year.
$	means current U.S. dollars unless otherwise noted.
<	means less than.

Country notes

· Data for China do not include data for Hong Kong SAR, China; Macao SAR, China; or Taiwan, China.
· Data for Indonesia include Timor-Leste through 1999.
· Data for Mayotte, to which a reference appeared in previous editions, are included in data for France.
· Data for Serbia do not include data for Kosovo or Montenegro.
· Data for Sudan include South Sudan unless otherwise noted.

User guide to WDI online tables

Statistical tables that were previously available in the *World Development Indicators* print edition are now available online. Using an automated query process, these reference tables will be consistently updated based on the revisions to the World Development Indicators database.

How to access WDI online tables

To access the WDI online tables, visit http://wdi.worldbank.org/tables. To access a specific WDI online table directly, use the URL http://wdi.worldbank.org/table/ and the table number (for example, http://wdi.worldbank.org/table/1.1 to view the first table in the *World view* section). Each section of this book also lists the indicators included by table and by code. To view a specific indicator online, use the URL http://data.worldbank.org/indicator/ and the indicator code (for example, http://data.worldbank.org/indicator/SP.POP.TOTL to view a page for total population).

 Front | User guide | World view | People | Environment

Breadcrumbs to show
where you've been

Click on an indicator
to view metadata

Click on a country
to view metadata

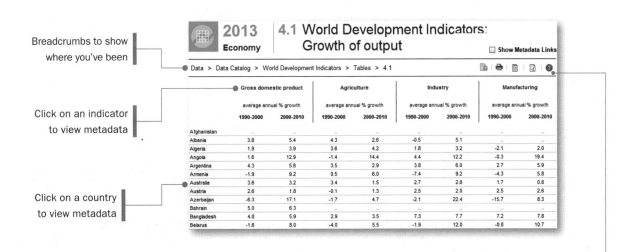

	2013 Economy	4.1 World Development Indicators: Growth of output						Show Metadata Links

Data > Data Catalog > World Development Indicators > Tables > 4.1

	Gross domestic product average annual % growth		Agriculture average annual % growth		Industry average annual % growth		Manufacturing average annual % growth	
	1990-2000	2000-2010	1990-2000	2000-2010	1990-2000	2000-2010	1990-2000	2000-2010
Afghanistan	..	..	..	..	..	..	..	..
Albania	3.8	5.4	4.3	2.6	-0.5	5.1	..	..
Algeria	1.9	3.9	3.6	4.2	1.8	3.2	-2.1	2.0
Angola	1.6	12.9	-1.4	14.4	4.4	12.2	-0.3	19.4
Argentina	4.3	5.6	3.5	2.9	3.8	6.0	2.7	5.9
Armenia	-1.9	9.2	0.5	6.0	-7.4	9.2	-4.3	5.8
Australia	3.6	3.2	3.4	1.5	2.7	2.8	1.7	0.8
Austria	2.6	1.8	-0.1	1.3	2.5	2.0	2.5	2.6
Azerbaijan	-6.3	17.1	-1.7	4.7	-2.1	22.4	-15.7	8.3
Bahrain	5.0	6.3	..	..	..	..	..	..
Bangladesh	4.8	5.9	2.9	3.5	7.3	7.7	7.2	7.8
Belarus	-1.6	8.0	-4.0	5.5	-1.9	12.0	-0.8	10.7

How to use DataBank

DataBank (http://databank.worldbank.org) is an online web resource that provides simple and quick access to collections of time series data. It has advanced functions for selecting and displaying data, performing customized queries, downloading data, and creating charts and maps. Users can create dynamic custom reports based on their selection of countries, indicators, and years. All these reports can be easily edited, shared, and embedded as widgets on websites or blogs. For more information, see http://databank.worldbank.org/help.

Actions

	Click to edit and revise the table in DataBank
	Click to print the table and corresponding indicator metadata
	Click to export the table to Excel
	Click to export the table and corresponding indicator metadata to PDF
	Click to access the WDI Online Tables Help file
Show Metadata Links	Click the checkbox to highlight cell level metadata and values from years other than those specified; click the checkbox again to reset to the default display

User guide to DataFinder

DataFinder is a free mobile app that accesses the full set of data from the World Development Indicators database. Data can be displayed and saved in a table, chart, or map and shared via email, Facebook, and Twitter.

DataFinder works on mobile devices (smartphone or tablet computer) in both offline (no Internet connection) and online (Wi-Fi or 3G/4G connection to the Internet) modes.

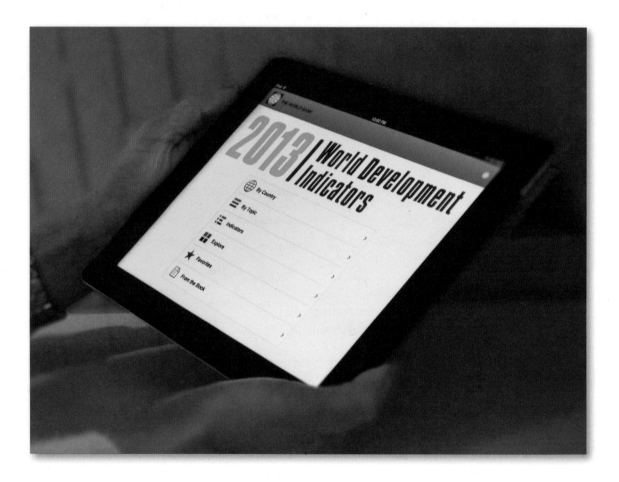

- Select a topic to display all related indicators.
- Compare data for multiple countries.
- Select predefined queries.
- Create a new query that can be saved and edited later.

- View reports in table, chart, and map formats.
- Send the data as a CSV file attachment to an email.
- Share comments and screenshots via Facebook, Twitter, or email.

Table view provides time series data tables of key development indicators by country or topic. A compare option shows the most recent year's data for the selected country and another country.

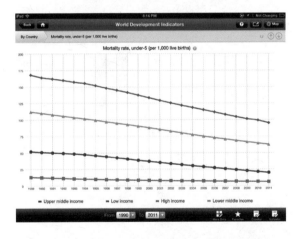

Chart view illustrates data trends and cross-country comparisons as line or bar charts.

Map view colors selected indicators on world and regional maps. A motion option animates the data changes from year to year.

WORLD VIEW

The Millennium Declaration adopted by all the members of the United Nations General Assembly in 2000 represents a commitment to a more effective, results-oriented development partnership in the 21st century. Progress documented here and in the annual reports of the United Nations Secretary-General has been encouraging: poverty rates have fallen, more children—especially girls—are enrolled in and completing school, and they are—on average—living longer and healthier lives. Fewer mothers die in child birth, and more women have access to reproductive health services.

The indicators used to monitor the Millennium Development Goals have traced the path of the HIV epidemic, the resurgence and retreat of tuberculosis, and the step-by-step efforts to "roll back malaria." More people now have access to reliable water supplies and basic sanitation facilities. But forests continue to disappear and with them the habitat for many species of plants and animals, and greenhouse gases continue to accumulate in the atmosphere.

From the start monitoring the Millennium Development Goals posed three challenges: selecting appropriate targets and indicators, constructing an international database for global monitoring, and significantly improving the quality, frequency, and availability of the relevant statistics. When they were adopted, the target year of 2015 seemed comfortably far away, and the baseline year of 1990 for measuring progress seemed a reasonable starting point with well-established data. As we near the end of that 25-year span, we have a better appreciation of how great those challenges were.

Already there is discussion of the post-2015 development agenda and the monitoring framework needed to record commitments and measure progress. The Millennium Development Goals have contributed to the development of a statistical infrastructure that is increasingly capable of producing reliable statistics on various topics. The post-2015 agenda and a well-designed monitoring framework will build on that infrastructure.

The international database for monitoring the Millennium Development Goals is a valuable resource for analyzing many development issues. The effort of building and maintaining such a database should not be underestimated, and it will take several years to implement a new framework of goals and targets. To serve as an analytical resource, the database will need to include additional indicators, beyond those directly associated with the targets and the core data for conducting these indicators. New technologies and methods for reporting data should improve the quality and timeliness of the resulting database. The quality of data will ultimately depend on the capacity of national statistical systems, where most data originate.

When the Millennium Development Goals were adopted, few developing countries had the capacity or resources to produce statistics of the requisite quality or frequency. Despite much progress, the statistical capacity-building programs initiated over the last decade should continue, and other statistical domains need attention. Planning for post-2015 goals must include concomitant plans for investments in statistics—by governments and development partners alike.

The effort to achieve the Millennium Development Goals has been enormous. The next set of goals will require an even larger effort. Without good statistics, we will never know if we have succeeded.

Goal 1 Eradicate extreme poverty

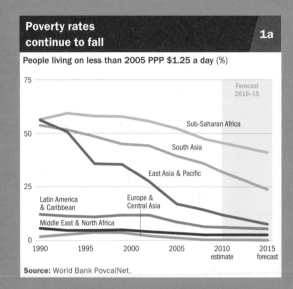

Poverty rates continue to fall
1a

People living on less than 2005 PPP $1.25 a day (%)

Source: World Bank PovcalNet.

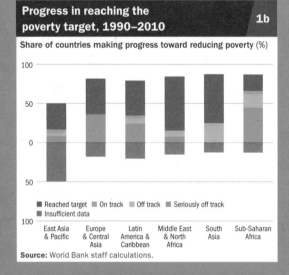

Progress in reaching the poverty target, 1990–2010
1b

Share of countries making progress toward reducing poverty (%)

Reached target ■ On track ■ Off track ■ Seriously off track
■ Insufficient data

East Asia & Pacific · Europe & Central Asia · Latin America & Caribbean · Middle East & North Africa · South Asia · Sub-Saharan Africa

Source: World Bank staff calculations.

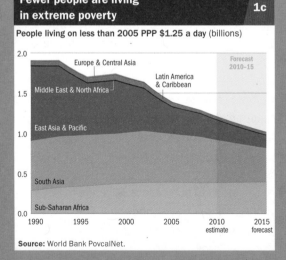

Fewer people are living in extreme poverty
1c

People living on less than 2005 PPP $1.25 a day (billions)

Source: World Bank PovcalNet.

The world will not have eradicated extreme poverty in 2015, but the Millennium Development Goal target of halving world poverty will have been met. The proportion of people living on less than $1.25 a day fell from 43.1 percent in 1990 to 22.7 percent in 2008, reaching new lows in all six developing country regions. While the food, fuel, and financial crises over the past five years worsened the situation of vulnerable populations and slowed poverty reduction in some countries, global poverty rates continued to fall in most regions. Preliminary estimates for 2010 confirm that the extreme poverty rate fell further, to 20.6 percent, reaching the global target five years early. Except in South Asia and Sub-Saharan Africa the target has also been met at the regional level (figure 1a).

Further progress is possible and likely before the 2015 target date of the Millennium Development Goals. Developing economies are expected to maintain GDP growth of 6.6–6.8 percent over the next three years, with growth of GDP per capita around 5.5 percent. Growth will be fastest in East Asia and Pacific and South Asia, which still contain more than half the world's poorest people. Growth will be slower in Sub-Saharan Africa, the poorest region in the world, but faster than in the preceding years, quickening the pace of poverty reduction. According to these forecasts, the proportion of people living in extreme poverty will fall to 16 percent by 2015. Based on current trends, 59 of 112 economies with adequate data are likely to achieve the first Millennium Development Goal (figure 1b). The number of people living in extreme poverty will continue to fall to less than a billion in 2015 (figure 1c). Of these, 40 percent will live in South Asia and 40 percent in Sub-Saharan Africa.

How fast poverty reduction will proceed depends not just on the growth of GDP but also on its distribution. Income distribution has improved in some countries, such as Brazil, while worsening in others, such as China. To speed progress toward eliminating extreme poverty, development strategies should attempt to increase not just the mean rate of growth but also the share of income going to the poorest part of the population. Sub-Saharan Africa, where average income is low and average income of those below the poverty line is even lower, will face great difficulties in bringing the poorest people to an adequate standard of living (figure 1d). Latin America and the Caribbean, where average income is higher, must overcome extremely inequitable income distributions.

Two Millennium Development Goal indicators address hunger and malnutrition. Child malnutrition, measured by comparing a child's weight with that of other children of similar age, reflects a shortfall in food energy, poor feeding practices by mothers, and lack of essential nutrients in the diet. Malnutrition in children often begins at birth, when poorly nourished mothers give birth to underweight babies. Malnourished children develop more slowly, enter school later, and perform less well. Malnutrition rates have dropped substantially since 1990, from 28 percent of children under age 5 in developing countries to 17 percent in 2011. Every developing region except Sub-Saharan Africa is on track to cut child malnutrition rates in half by 2015 (figure 1e). However, collecting data on malnutrition through surveys with direct measurement of children's weight and height is costly, and many countries lack the information to calculate time trends.

Undernourishment, a shortage of food energy to sustain normal daily activities, is affected by changes in the average amount of food available and its distribution. After steady declines in most regions from 1991 to 2005, further improvements in undernourishment have stalled, leaving 13 percent of the world's population, almost 900 million people, without adequate daily food intake (figure 1f).

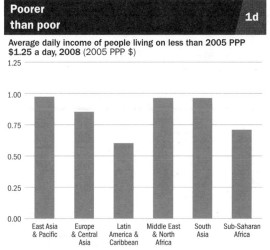

Poorer than poor 1d

Average daily income of people living on less than 2005 PPP $1.25 a day, **2008** (2005 PPP $)

Source: World Bank PovcalNet.

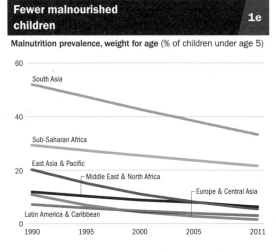

Fewer malnourished children 1e

Malnutrition prevalence, weight for age (% of children under age 5)

Source: World Development Indicators database.

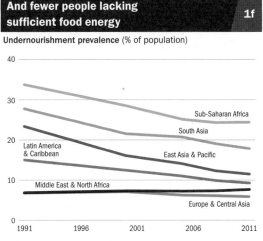

And fewer people lacking sufficient food energy 1f

Undernourishment prevalence (% of population)

Source: Food and Agriculture Organization and World Development Indicators database.

Goal 2 Achieve universal primary education

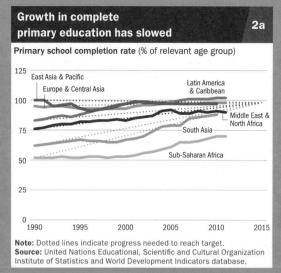

Growth in complete primary education has slowed `2a`

Primary school completion rate (% of relevant age group)

Note: Dotted lines indicate progress needed to reach target.
Source: United Nations Educational, Scientific and Cultural Organization Institute of Statistics and World Development Indicators database.

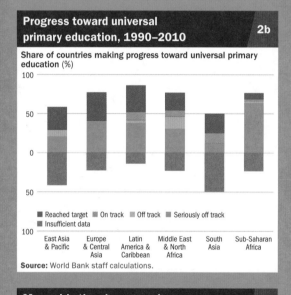

Progress toward universal primary education, 1990–2010 `2b`

Share of countries making progress toward universal primary education (%)

■ Reached target ■ On track ■ Off track ■ Seriously off track
■ Insufficient data

East Asia & Pacific | Europe & Central Asia | Latin America & Caribbean | Middle East & North Africa | South Asia | Sub-Saharan Africa

Source: World Bank staff calculations.

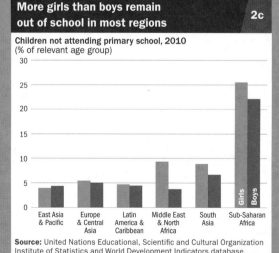

More girls than boys remain out of school in most regions `2c`

Children not attending primary school, 2010 (% of relevant age group)

East Asia & Pacific | Europe & Central Asia | Latin America & Caribbean | Middle East & North Africa | South Asia | Sub-Saharan Africa

Source: United Nations Educational, Scientific and Cultural Organization Institute of Statistics and World Development Indicators database.

The commitment to provide primary education to every child is the oldest of the Millennium Development Goals, having been set at the first Education for All conference in Jomtien, Thailand, more than 20 years ago.

Progress among the poorest countries has accelerated since 2000, particularly in South Asia and Sub-Saharan Africa, but full enrollment remains elusive. Many children start school but drop out before completion, discouraged by cost, distance, physical danger, and failure to progress. Even as countries approach the target, the education demands of modern economies expand, and primary education will increasingly be of value only as a stepping stone toward secondary and higher education.

In most developing country regions school enrollment picked up after the Millennium Development Goals were promulgated in 2000, when the completion rate was 80 percent. Sub-Saharan Africa and South Asia, which started out farthest behind, made substantial progress. By 2009 nearly 90 percent of children in developing countries completed primary school, but completion rates have stalled since, with no appreciable gains in any region (figure 2a). Three regions have attained or are close to attaining complete primary education: East Asia and Pacific, Europe and Central Asia, and Latin America and the Caribbean (figure 2b). Completion rates in the Middle East and North Africa have stayed at 90 percent since 2008. South Asia has reached 88 percent, but progress has been slow. And Sub-Saharan Africa lags behind at 70 percent. Even if the schools in these regions were to now enroll every eligible child in the first grade, they would not be able to achieve a full course of primary education by 2015. But it would help.

Many children enroll in primary school but attend intermittently or drop out entirely. This is particularly true for girls—almost all school systems with low enrollment rates show under-enrollment of girls in primary school, since their work is needed at home (figure 2c). Other obstacles discourage parents from sending their children to school, including the need for boys and girls during planting and harvest, lack of suitable school facilities, absence of teachers, and school fees. The problem is worst in South Asia and Sub-Saharan Africa, where more than 46 million children of primary school age are not in school.

Not all children have the same opportunities to enroll in school or remain in school. Across the world, children in rural areas are less likely to enter school, and when they do, they are likely to drop out sooner. In Ethiopia nearly all urban children complete first grade, but fewer than 80 percent of rural children do (figure 2d). In Senegal, where slightly more than 80 percent of urban children complete first grade, barely half of rural children begin the first grade and only 40 percent remain after nine years. Cambodia follows a similar pattern.

Parents' education makes a big difference in how far children go in school. In Nepal, for example, less than 90 percent of children whose parents lack any education complete first grade and barely 70 percent remain through the ninth (figure 2e). But 95 percent of children from households with some higher education stay through nine grades, and many of those go onto complete secondary school and enter tertiary education.

Income inequality and educational quality are closely linked. Take Senegal (figure 2f). Children from wealthier households (as measured by a household's ownership of certain assets) are more likely to enroll and stay in school than children from poorer households. Thus children from poor households are least likely to acquire the one asset—human capital—that could most help them to escape poverty.

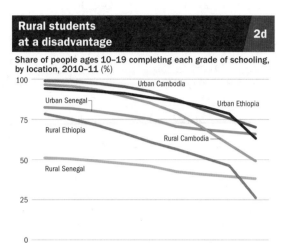

Rural students at a disadvantage — 2d

Share of people ages 10–19 completing each grade of schooling, by location, 2010–11 (%)

Source: Demographic and Health Surveys and World Bank EdStats database.

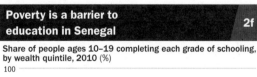

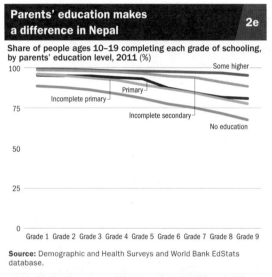

Parents' education makes a difference in Nepal — 2e

Share of people ages 10–19 completing each grade of schooling, by parents' education level, 2011 (%)

Source: Demographic and Health Surveys and World Bank EdStats database.

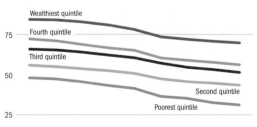

Poverty is a barrier to education in Senegal — 2f

Share of people ages 10–19 completing each grade of schooling, by wealth quintile, 2010 (%)

Source: Demographic and Health Surveys and World Bank EdStats database.

Goal 3 Promote gender equality and empower women

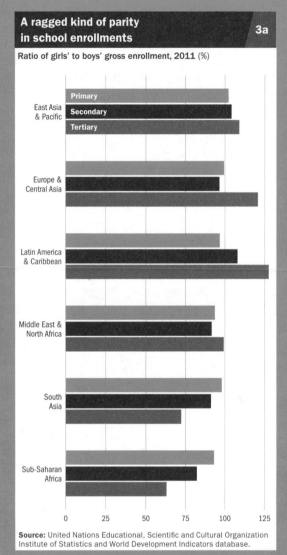

A ragged kind of parity in school enrollments 3a

Ratio of girls' to boys' gross enrollment, 2011 (%)

East Asia & Pacific — Primary, Secondary, Tertiary

Europe & Central Asia

Latin America & Caribbean

Middle East & North Africa

South Asia

Sub-Saharan Africa

0 25 50 75 100 125

Source: United Nations Educational, Scientific and Cultural Organization Institute of Statistics and World Development Indicators database.

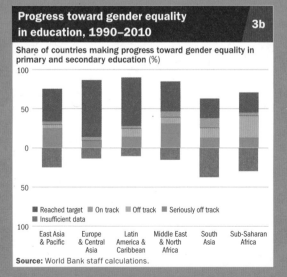

Progress toward gender equality in education, 1990–2010 3b

Share of countries making progress toward gender equality in primary and secondary education (%)

100
50
0
50
100

■ Reached target ■ On track ■ Off track ■ Seriously off track
■ Insufficient data

East Asia & Pacific | Europe & Central Asia | Latin America & Caribbean | Middle East & North Africa | South Asia | Sub-Saharan Africa

Source: World Bank staff calculations.

Women make important contributions to economic and social development. Expanding opportunities for them in the public and private sectors is a core development strategy, and education is the starting point. By enrolling and staying in school, girls gains skills needed to enter the labor market, care for families, and make decisions for themselves. Achieving gender equality in education is an important demonstration that young women are full, contributing members of society.

Girls have made substantial gains in school enrollment. In 1990 girls' primary school enrollment rate in developing countries was only 86 percent of boys'. By 2011 it was 97 percent (figure 3a). Similar improvements have been made in secondary schooling, where girls' enrollments have risen from 78 percent of boys' to 96 percent over the same period. But the averages mask large differences across countries. At the end of 2011, 31 upper middle-income countries had reached or exceeded equal enrollment of girls in primary and secondary education, as had 23 lower middle-income countries but only 9 low-income countries. South Asia and Sub-Saharan Africa are lagging behind (figure 3b).

Patterns of school attendance at the national level mirror those at the regional level: poor households are less likely than wealthy households to keep their children in school, and girls from wealthier households are more likely to enroll in school and stay longer. Ethiopia is just one example of the prevailing pattern documented by household surveys from many developing countries (figure 3c).

More women are participating in public life at the highest levels. The proportion of parliamentary seats held by women continues to increase. In Latin America and the Caribbean women now hold 25 percent of all parliamentary seats (figure 3d). The most impressive gains have been made in the Middle East and North Africa, where the proportion of seats held by women more than tripled between 1990 and 2012. Algeria leads the way with 32 percent. In Nepal a third of parliamentary

 Front | User guide | World view | People | Environment

seats were held by women in 2012. Rwanda continues to lead the world. Since 2008, 56 percent of parliamentary seats have been held by women.

Women work long hours and make important contributions to their families' welfare, but many in the informal sector are unpaid for their labor. The largest proportion of women working in the formal sector is in Europe and Central Asia, where the median proportion of women in wage employment outside the agricultural sector was 46 percent (figure 3e). Latin America and the Caribbean is not far behind, with 42 percent of women in nonagricultural employment. Women's share in paid employment in the nonagricultural sector has risen marginally but remains less than 20 percent in most countries in the Middle East and North Africa and South Asia and less than 35 percent in Sub-Saharan Africa. In these regions full economic empowerment of women remains a distant goal.

Lack of data hampers the ability to understand women's roles in the economy. The Evidence and Data for Gender Equality (EDGE) Initiative is a new partnership, jointly managed by UN Women and the United Nations Statistics Division, in collaboration with member states, the World Bank, the Organisation for Economic Co-operation and Development, and others, that seeks to accelerate the work of gathering indicators on women's education, employment, entrepreneurship, and asset ownership. During its initial phase EDGE will lay the ground work for a database of basic education and employment indicators, developing standards and guidelines for entrepreneurship and assets indicators, and pilot data in several countries. Relevant indicators could include the percentage distribution of the employed population, by sector and sex; the proportion of employed who are employer, by sex; the length of maternity leave; the percentage of firms owned by women; the proportion of the population with access to credit, by sex; and the proportion of the population who own land, by sex.

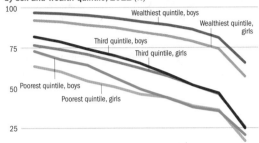

Girls are disadvantaged at every income level in Ethiopia 3c

Share of people ages 10–19 completing each grade of schooling, by sex and wealth quintile, 2011 (%)

Source: Demographic and Health Surveys and World Bank EdStats database.

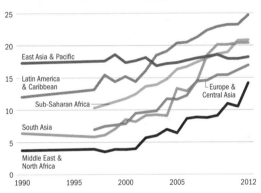

More women in parliaments 3d

Share of seats held by women in national parliaments (%)

Source: Inter-Parliamentary Union and World Development Indicators database.

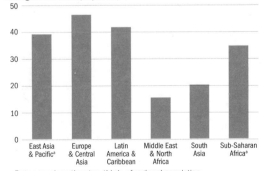

Women still lack opportunities in the labor market 3e

Share of women employed in the nonagricultural sector, median value, most recent year available, 2004–10 (% of total nonagricultural employment)

a. Data cover less than two-thirds of regional population.
Source: International Labour Organization and World Development Indicators database.

Goal 4 Reduce child mortality

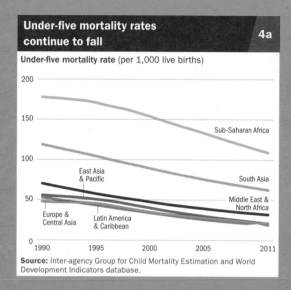

Under-five mortality rates continue to fall **4a**

Under-five mortality rate (per 1,000 live births)

Sub-Saharan Africa
South Asia
East Asia & Pacific
Middle East & North Africa
Europe & Central Asia
Latin America & Caribbean

Source: Inter-agency Group for Child Mortality Estimation and World Development Indicators database.

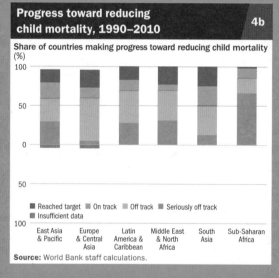

Progress toward reducing child mortality, 1990–2010 **4b**

Share of countries making progress toward reducing child mortality (%)

■ Reached target ■ On track ■ Off track ■ Seriously off track
■ Insufficient data

East Asia & Pacific | Europe & Central Asia | Latin America & Caribbean | Middle East & North Africa | South Asia | Sub-Saharan Africa

Source: World Bank staff calculations.

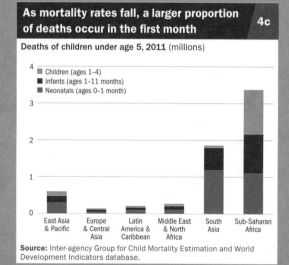

As mortality rates fall, a larger proportion of deaths occur in the first month **4c**

Deaths of children under age 5, 2011 (millions)

■ Children (ages 1–4)
■ Infants (ages 1–11 months)
■ Neonatals (ages 0–1 month)

East Asia & Pacific | Europe & Central Asia | Latin America & Caribbean | Middle East & North Africa | South Asia | Sub-Saharan Africa

Source: Inter-agency Group for Child Mortality Estimation and World Development Indicators database.

In 1990, 12 million children died before their fifth birthday. By 1999 fewer than 10 million did. And in 2012 7 million did. In developing countries the under-five mortality rate fell from an average of 95 per 1,000 live births in 1990 to 56 in 2011, but rates in Sub-Saharan Africa and South Asia remain much higher (figure 4a). Currently, 41 countries are poised to reach the Millennium Development Goal target of a two-thirds reduction in under-five mortality rates by 2015 (figure 4b). Faster improvements over the last decade suggest that many countries are accelerating progress and another 25 could reach the target as soon as 2020. Looking past 2015, still faster progress is possible if high mortality countries give priority to addressing the causes of child mortality. Concomitant reductions in fertility rates, particularly among adolescents, will also help.

Most children die from causes that are readily preventable or curable with existing interventions, such as pneumonia (18 percent), diarrhea (11 percent), and malaria (7 percent). Almost 70 percent of deaths of children under age 5 occur in the first year of life, and 60 percent of those in the first month (figure 4c). Preterm birth complications account for 14 percent of deaths, and complications during birth another 9 percent (UN Inter-Agency Group for Child Mortality Estimation 2012). Therefore reducing child mortality requires addressing the causes of neonatal and infant deaths: inadequate care at birth and afterward, malnutrition, poor sanitation, and exposure to acute and chronic disease. Lower infant and child mortality rates are, in turn, the largest contributors to higher life expectancy in most countries.

Childhood vaccinations are a proven, cost-effective way of reducing childhood illness and death. But despite years of vaccination campaigns, many children in low- and lower middle-income economies remain unprotected. To be successful, vaccination campaigns must reach all children and be sustained over time. Thus it is worrisome that measles vaccination rates in the two highest mortality regions, South Asia and Sub-Saharan Africa, have stagnated in the last three years, at less than 80 percent coverage (figure 4d).

Twenty countries in the developing world accounted for 4.5 million deaths among children under age 5 in 2011, or 65 percent of all such deaths worldwide (figure 4e). These countries are mostly large, often with high birth rates, but many have substantially reduced mortality rates over the past two decades. Of the 20, 11 have reached or are likely to achieve a two-thirds reduction in their under-five mortality rate by 2015: Bangladesh, Brazil, China, the Arab Republic of Egypt, Ethiopia, Indonesia, Madagascar, Malawi, Mexico, Niger, and Turkey. Had the mortality rates of 1990 prevailed in 2011, these 11 countries would have experienced 2 million more deaths. The remaining nine, where progress has been slower, have nevertheless averted 3 million deaths. If India were on track to reach the target, another 440,000 deaths would have been averted.

The data used to monitor child mortality are produced by the Inter-agency Group for Child Mortality Estimation (IGME), which evaluates data from existing sources and then fits a statistical model to data points that are judged to be reliable. The model produces a trend line for under-five mortality rates in each country. Infant mortality and neonatal mortality rates are derived from under-five mortality estimates. The data come from household surveys and, where available, vital registration systems. But surveys are slow and costly. While they remain important tools for investigating certain complex, micro-level problems, vital registration systems are usually better sources of timely statistics. Recent IGME estimates of under-five mortality include new data from vital registration systems for about 70 countries. But many countries lack complete reporting of vital events, and even those that do often misreport cause of death. Vital registration supplemented by surveys and censuses offers the best approach for improving knowledge of morbidity and mortality in all age groups.

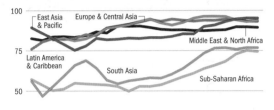

Measles immunization rates are stagnating — 4d

Children ages 12–23 months immunized against measles (%)

Source: World Health Organization, United Nations Children's Fund, and World Development Indicators database.

Five million deaths averted in 20 countries — 4e

Deaths of children under age 5, 2011 (millions)
■ At 2011 mortality rate ■ Averted based on 1990 mortality rate

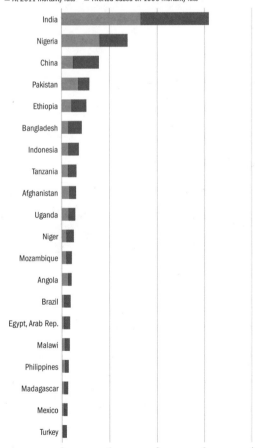

Source: World Bank staff calculations.

Goal 5 Improve maternal health

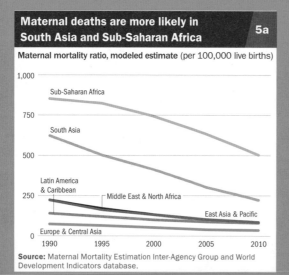

Maternal deaths are more likely in South Asia and Sub-Saharan Africa   5a

Maternal mortality ratio, modeled estimate (per 100,000 live births)

Sub-Saharan Africa
South Asia
Latin America & Caribbean
Middle East & North Africa
East Asia & Pacific
Europe & Central Asia

Source: Maternal Mortality Estimation Inter-Agency Group and World Development Indicators database.

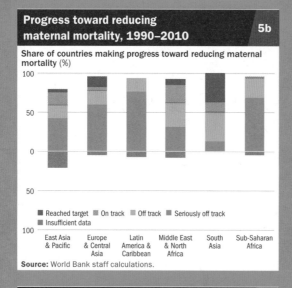

Progress toward reducing maternal mortality, 1990–2010   5b

Share of countries making progress toward reducing maternal mortality (%)

■ Reached target ■ On track ■ Off track ■ Seriously off track
■ Insufficient data

East Asia & Pacific | Europe & Central Asia | Latin America & Caribbean | Middle East & North Africa | South Asia | Sub-Saharan Africa

Source: World Bank staff calculations.

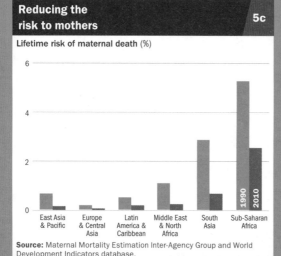

Reducing the risk to mothers   5c

Lifetime risk of maternal death (%)

East Asia & Pacific | Europe & Central Asia | Latin America & Caribbean | Middle East & North Africa | South Asia | Sub-Saharan Africa

1990 | 2010

Source: Maternal Mortality Estimation Inter-Agency Group and World Development Indicators database.

An estimated 287,000 maternal deaths occurred worldwide in 2010, all but 1,700 of them in developing countries. More than half of maternal deaths occur in Sub-Saharan Africa and a quarter in South Asia. And while the number of maternal deaths remains high, South Asia has made great progress in reducing them, reaching a maternal mortality ratio of 220 per 100,000 live births in 2010, down from 620 in 1990, a drop of 65 percent. The Middle East and North Africa and East Asia and Pacific have also reduced their maternal morality ratios more than 60 percent (figure 5a).

These are impressive achievements, but progress in reducing maternal mortality has been slow, far slower than targeted by the Millennium Development Goals, which call for reducing the maternal mortality ratio by 75 percent between 1990 and 2015. But few countries and no developing region on average will achieve this target. Based on progress through 2010, 8 countries have achieved a 75 percent reduction, and 10 more are on track to reach the 2015 target (figure 5b). This is an improvement over the 2008 assessment, suggesting that progress is accelerating. Because of the reductions in Cambodia, China, Lao People's Democratic Republic, and Vietnam, 74 percent of people in East Asia and Pacific live in a country that has reached the target (Vietnam) or is on track to do so by 2015. On average a third of people in low- and middle-income countries live in countries that have reached the target or are on track to do so.

The maternal mortality ratio gives the risk of a maternal death at each birth, a risk compounded with each pregnancy. And because women in poor countries have more children under riskier conditions, their lifetime risk of maternal death may be 100 times greater than for women in high-income countries. Improved health care and lower fertility rates have reduced the lifetime risk in all regions, but women ages 15–49 in Sub-Saharan Africa still face a 2.5 percent chance of dying in childbirth, down from more than 5 percent in 1990 (figure 5c). In Chad and Somalia, both fragile states, lifetime risk is still more than 6 percent, meaning more than 1 woman in 16 will die in childbirth.

Reducing maternal mortality requires a comprehensive approach to women's reproductive health, starting with family planning and access to contraception. In countries with data half of women who are married or in union use some method of birth control. Household surveys of women show that some 200 million women want to delay or cease childbearing, and a substantial proportion say that their last birth was unwanted or mistimed (United Nations 2012). Figure 5d shows the share of women of childbearing age who say they need but are not using contraception. There are large differences within each region. More surveys have been carried out in Sub-Saharan Africa than in any other region, and many show a large unmet need for family planning.

Women who give birth at an early age are likely to bear more children and are at greater risk of death or serious complications from pregnancy. The adolescent birth rate is highest in Sub-Saharan Africa and is declining slowly. A rapid decrease in South Asia has been led by Maldives, Afghanistan, and Pakistan (figure 5e).

Many health problems among pregnant women are preventable or treatable through visits with trained health workers before childbirth. Skilled attendants at delivery and access to hospital treatments are essential for dealing with life-threatening emergencies such as severe bleeding and hypertensive disorders. In South Asia and Sub-Saharan Africa fewer than half of births are attended by doctors, nurses, or trained midwives (figure 5f). Having skilled health workers present for deliveries is key to reducing maternal mortality. In many places women have only untrained caregivers or family members to attend them during childbirth.

A wide range of needs — 5d

Unmet need for contraception, most recent year available, 2006–10 (% of women married or in union ages 15–49)

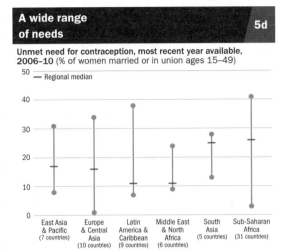

Source: Demographic and Household Surveys, Multiple Indicator Cluster Surveys, and World Development Indicators database.

Fewer young women giving birth — 5e

Adolescent fertility rate (births per 1,000 women ages 15–19)

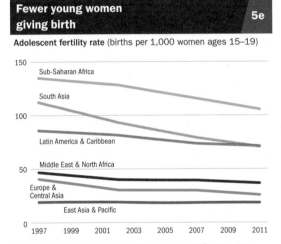

Source: United Nations Population Division and World Development Indicators database.

Every mother needs care — 5f

Births attended by skilled health staff, average of most recent year available for 2007–11 (% of total)

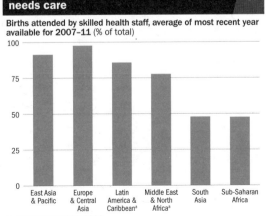

a. Data are for 1998–2002.
Source: United Nations Children's Fund and World Development Indicators database.

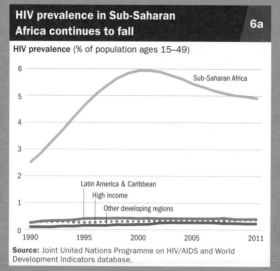

HIV prevalence in Sub-Saharan Africa continues to fall — 6a

HIV prevalence (% of population ages 15–49)

Sub-Saharan Africa

Latin America & Caribbean
High income
Other developing regions

Source: Joint United Nations Programme on HIV/AIDS and World Development Indicators database.

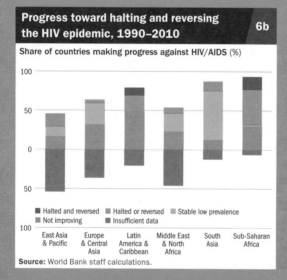

Progress toward halting and reversing the HIV epidemic, 1990–2010 — 6b

Share of countries making progress against HIV/AIDS (%)

■ Halted and reversed ■ Halted or reversed ■ Stable low prevalence
■ Not improving ■ Insufficient data

East Asia & Pacific | Europe & Central Asia | Latin America & Caribbean | Middle East & North Africa | South Asia | Sub-Saharan Africa

Source: World Bank staff calculations.

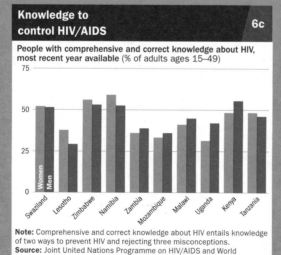

Knowledge to control HIV/AIDS — 6c

People with comprehensive and correct knowledge about HIV, most recent year available (% of adults ages 15–49)

Women
Men

Swaziland, Lesotho, Zimbabwe, Namibia, Zambia, Mozambique, Malawi, Uganda, Kenya, Tanzania

Note: Comprehensive and correct knowledge about HIV entails knowledge of two ways to prevent HIV and rejecting three misconceptions.
Source: Joint United Nations Programme on HIV/AIDS and World Development Indicators database.

Epidemic diseases exact a huge toll in human suffering and lost opportunities for development. Poverty, armed conflict, and natural disasters contribute to the spread of disease and are made worse by it. In Africa the spread of HIV/AIDS has reversed decades of improvement in life expectancy and left millions of children orphaned. Malaria takes a large toll on young children and weakens adults at great cost to their productivity. Tuberculosis killed 1.4 million people in 2010, most of them ages 15–45, and sickened millions more.

There were 34 million people living with HIV/AIDS in 2011, and 2.5 million more people acquired the disease. Sub-Saharan Africa remains the center of the HIV/AIDS epidemic, but the proportion of adults living with AIDS has begun to fall even as the survival rate of those with access to antiretroviral drugs has increased (figures 6a and 6b). By the end of 2010, 6.5 million people worldwide were receiving antiretroviral drugs. This represented the largest one-year increase in coverage but still fell far short of universal access (United Nations 2012).

Altering the course of the HIV epidemic requires changes in behaviors by those already infected by the virus and those at risk of becoming infected. Knowledge of the cause of the disease, its transmission, and what can be done to avoid it is the starting point. The ability to reject false information is another important kind of knowledge. But significant gaps in knowledge remain. In 26 of 31 countries with a generalized epidemic and in which nationally representative surveys were carried out recently, less than half of young women have comprehensive and correct knowledge about HIV (UNAIDS 2012). And less than half of men in 21 of 25 countries had correct knowledge. In only

3 of the 10 countries with the highest HIV prevalence rates in 2011 did more than half the men and women tested demonstrate knowledge of two ways to prevent HIV and reject three misconceptions (figure 6c). In Kenya men scored better than 50 percent, but women fell short. Clearly more work is to be done.

In 2011 there were 8.8 million people newly diagnosed with tuberculosis, but incidence, prevalence, and death rates from tuberculosis are falling (figure 6d). If these trends are sustained, the world could achieve the target of halting and reversing the spread of this disease by 2015. People living with HIV/AIDS, which reduces resistance to tuberculosis, are particularly vulnerable, as are refugees, displaced persons, and prisoners living in close quarters and unsanitary conditions. Well-managed medical intervention using appropriate drug therapy is crucial to stopping the spread of tuberculosis.

There are 300–500 million cases of malaria each year, causing more than 1 million deaths. Malaria is a disease of poverty. But there has been progress against it. In 2011 Armenia was added to the list of countries certified free of the disease. Although malaria occurs in all regions, Sub-Saharan Africa is where the most lethal form of the malaria parasite is most abundant. Insecticide-treated nets have proved to be an effective preventative, and their use in the region is growing: from 2 percent of the population under age 5 in 2000 to 39 percent in 2010 (figure 6e). Better testing and the use of combination therapies with artemisinin-based drugs are improving the treatment of at-risk populations. But malaria is difficult to control. There is evidence of emerging resistance to artemisinins and to pyrethroid insecticides used to treat mosquito nets.

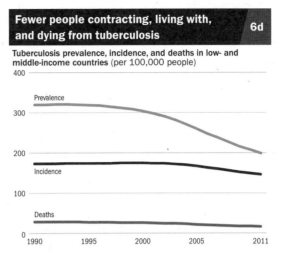

Fewer people contracting, living with, and dying from tuberculosis 6d

Tuberculosis prevalence, incidence, and deaths in low- and middle-income countries (per 100,000 people)

Source: World Health Organization and World Development Indicators database.

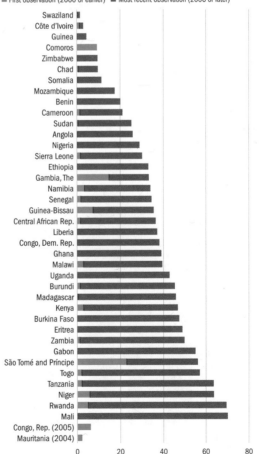

Use of insecticide-treated nets increasing in Sub-Saharan Africa 6e

Use of insecticide-treated nets (% of population under age 5)
■ First observation (2000 or earlier) ■ Most recent observation (2006 or later)

Source: United Nations Children's Fund and World Development Indicators database.

Goal 7 Ensure environmental sustainability

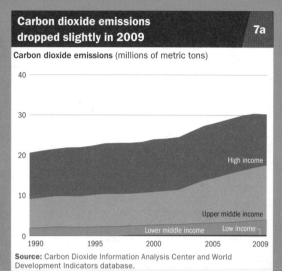

Carbon dioxide emissions dropped slightly in 2009

7a

Carbon dioxide emissions (millions of metric tons)

High income

Upper middle income

Lower middle income   Low income

Source: Carbon Dioxide Information Analysis Center and World Development Indicators database.

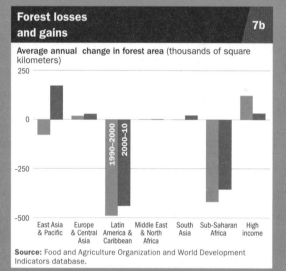

Forest losses and gains

7b

Average annual change in forest area (thousands of square kilometers)

1990–2000   2000–10

East Asia & Pacific   Europe & Central Asia   Latin America & Caribbean   Middle East & North Africa   South Asia   Sub-Saharan Africa   High income

Source: Food and Agriculture Organization and World Development Indicators database.

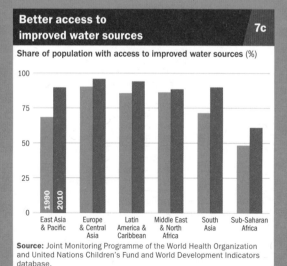

Better access to improved water sources

7c

Share of population with access to improved water sources (%)

1990   2010

East Asia & Pacific   Europe & Central Asia   Latin America & Caribbean   Middle East & North Africa   South Asia   Sub-Saharan Africa

Source: Joint Monitoring Programme of the World Health Organization and United Nations Children's Fund and World Development Indicators database.

The seventh goal of the Millennium Development Goals is the most far-reaching, affecting each person now and in the future. It addresses the condition of the natural and built environments: reversing the loss of natural resources, preserving biodiversity, increasing access to safe water and sanitation, and improving living conditions of people in slums. The overall theme is sustainability, an equilibrium in which people's lives can improve without depleting natural and manmade capital stocks.

The failure to reach a comprehensive agreement on limiting greenhouse gas emissions leaves billions of people vulnerable to climate change. Although the global financial crisis caused a slight decrease in carbon dioxide emissions, such emissions are expected to rise as economic activity resumes in large industrial economies (figure 7a).

The loss of forests threatens the livelihood of poor people, destroys the habitat that harbors biodiversity, and eliminates an important carbon sink that helps moderate the climate. Net losses since 1990 have been substantial, especially in Latin American and the Caribbean and Sub-Saharan Africa, and only partly compensated by net gains elsewhere. The rate of deforestation slowed in the past decade, but on current trends zero net losses will not be reached for another 20 years (figure 7b).

Protecting forests and other terrestrial and marine areas helps protect plant and animal habitats and preserve the diversity of species. By 2010, 13 percent of the world's land area had been protected, but only 1.6 percent of oceans had similar protection. Such measures have slowed the rate of species extinction, but substantial losses continue (United Nations 2012).

The Millennium Development Goals call for halving the proportion of the population without access to improved sanitation facilities and water sources by 2015. In 1990 more than 1 billion people lacked access to drinking water from a convenient, protected source. In developing countries the proportion of people with access to an improved water source rose from 71 percent in 1990 to 86 in 2010 (figure 7c).

In 1990 only 37 percent of the people living in low- and middle-income economies had access to a flush toilet or other form of improved sanitation. By 2010 the access rate had risen to 56 percent. But 2.7 billion people still lack access to improved sanitation, and more than 1 billion practice open defecation, posing enormous health risks. The situation is worse in rural areas, where 43 percent of the population have access to improved sanitation; in urban areas the access rate is 30 percentage points higher (figure 7d). This large disparity, especially in South Asia and Sub-Saharan Africa, is the principal reason the sanitation target of the Millennium Development Goals will not be met.

Achieving sustainable development also requires managing natural resources carefully, since high economic growth can deplete natural capital, such as forests and minerals. Countries that rely heavily on extractive industries have seen large increases in natural resource rents, but their growth will not be sustainable unless they invest in productive assets, including human capital (figure 7e).

The World Bank has constructed a global database to monitor the sustainability of economic progress using wealth accounts, including indicators of adjusted net savings and adjusted net national income. Wealth is defined comprehensively to include stocks of manufactured capital, natural capital, human capital, and social capital. Development is conceived as building wealth and managing a portfolio of assets. The challenge of development is to manage not just the total volume of assets but also the composition of the asset portfolio—that is, how much to invest in different types of capital. Adjusted net savings is a sustainability indicator that measures whether a country is building its wealth sustainably (positive values) or running it down on an unsustainable development path (negative values; figure 7f).

Rural areas lack sanitation facilities   **7d**

Share of population with access to improved sanitation facilities, 2010 (%)

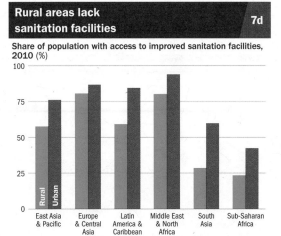

Source: Joint Monitoring Programme of the World Health Organization and United Nations Children's Fund and World Development Indicators database.

Resource rents are a large share of GDP in Africa and the Middle East   **7e**

Resource rents (% of GDP)

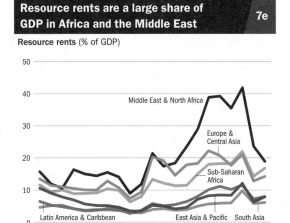

Source: World Bank staff calculations and World Development Indicators database.

A nonsustainable path in Sub-Saharan Africa   **7f**

Share of gross national income, 2008 (%)

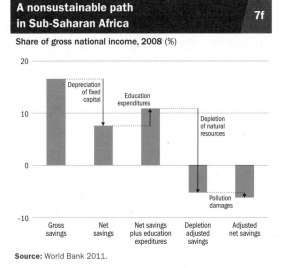

Source: World Bank 2011.

Goal 8 Develop a global partnership for development

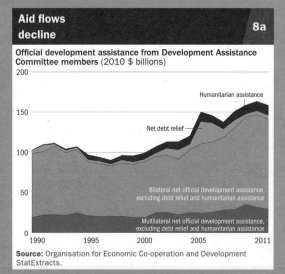

Aid flows decline
8a

Official development assistance from Development Assistance Committee members (2010 $ billions)

Humanitarian assistance

Net debt relief

Bilateral net official development assistance, excluding debt relief and humanitarian assistance

Multilateral net official development assistance, excluding debt relief and humanitarian assistance

1990 1995 2000 2005 2011

Source: Organisation for Economic Co-operation and Development StatExtracts.

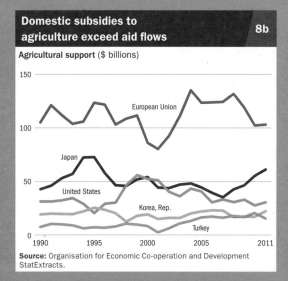

Domestic subsidies to agriculture exceed aid flows
8b

Agricultural support ($ billions)

European Union

Japan

United States

Korea, Rep.

Turkey

1990 1995 2000 2005 2011

Source: Organisation for Economic Co-operation and Development StatExtracts.

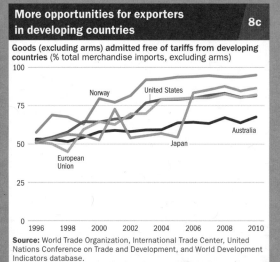

More opportunities for exporters in developing countries
8c

Goods (excluding arms) admitted free of tariffs from developing countries (% total merchandise imports, excluding arms)

Norway

United States

European Union

Japan

Australia

1996 1998 2000 2002 2004 2006 2008 2010

Source: World Trade Organization, International Trade Center, United Nations Conference on Trade and Development, and World Development Indicators database.

The eighth and final goal distinguishes the Millennium Development Goals from previous resolutions and targeted programs. It recognizes the multidimensional nature of development and the need for wealthy countries and developing countries to work together to create an environment in which rapid, sustainable development is possible. Along with increased aid flows and debt relief for the poorest, highly indebted countries, goal 8 recognizes the need to reduce barriers to trade and to share the benefits of new medical and communication technologies. It is also a reminder that development challenges differ for large and small countries and for those that are landlocked or isolated by large expanses of ocean. Building and sustaining a partnership is an ongoing process that does not stop at a specific date or when a target is reached.

After falling through much of the 1990s, official development assistance (ODA) from members of the Organisation for Economic Co-operation and Development's (OECD) Development Assistance Committee (DAC) rose sharply after 2002, but a large part of the increase was in the form of debt relief and humanitarian assistance (figure 8a). The financial crisis that began in 2008 and fiscal austerity in many high-income economies have begun to undermine commitments to increase ODA. Net disbursements of ODA by members of the DAC rose to $134 billion in 2011, but, after accounting for price and exchange rate adjustments, fell 2.3 percent in real terms from 2010. Aid from multilateral organizations remained essentially unchanged at $34.7 billion, a decrease of 6.6 percent in real terms. ODA from DAC members has fallen back to 0.31 percent of their combined gross national income, less than half the UN target of 0.7 percent.

OECD members, mostly high-income economies but also some upper middle-income economies such as Chile, Mexico, and Turkey, continue to spend more on support to domestic agricultural producers than on ODA. In 2011 the OECD

 Front | User guide | World view | People | Environment

estimate of agricultural subsidies was $252 billion, 41 percent of which was to EU producers (figure 8b).

Many rich countries have pledged to open their markets to exports from developing countries, and the share of goods (excluding arms) admitted duty free by OECD economies has been rising. However, arcane rules of origin and phytosanitary standards keep many countries from qualifying for duty-free access. And uncertainty over market access may inhibit development of export industries (figure 8c).

Growing economies, better debt management, and debt relief for the poorest countries have allowed developing countries to substantially reduce their debt burdens. Despite the financial crisis and a 2.3 percent contraction in the global economy in 2009, the debt service to exports ratio in low- and middle-income economies reached a new low of 8.8 percent in 2011. In Europe and Central Asia, where the debt service to exports ratio rose to 26 percent in 2009, higher export earnings have helped return the average to its 2007 level of 17.8 percent (figure 8d).

Telecommunications is an essential tool for development, and new technologies are creating new opportunities everywhere. The growth of fixed-line phone systems has peaked in high-income economies and will never reach the same level of use in developing countries. In high-income economies mobile phone subscriptions have now passed 1 per person, and upper middle-income economies are not far behind (figure 8e).

Mobile phones are one of several ways of accessing the Internet. In 2000 Internet use was spreading rapidly in high-income economies but was barely under way in developing country regions. Now developing countries are beginning to catch up. Since 2000 Internet use per person in developing economies has grown 28 percent a year. Like telephones, Internet use is strongly correlated with income. The low-income economies of South Asia and Sub-Saharan Africa lag behind, but even there Internet access is spreading rapidly (figure 8f).

Debt service burdens continue to fall   8d

Total debt service (% of exports of goods, services, and income)

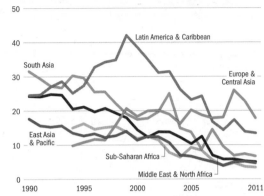

Source: World Development Indicators database.

Telecommunications on the move   8e

Mobile phone subscriptions (per 100 people)

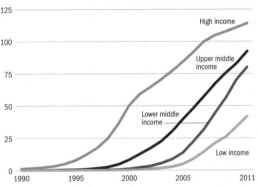

Source: International Telecommunications Union and World Development Indicators database.

More people connecting to the Internet   8f

Internet users (per 100 people)

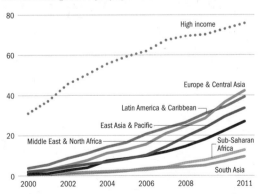

Source: International Telecommunications Union and World Development Indicators database.

Millennium Development Goals

Goals and targets from the Millennium Declaration | Indicators for monitoring progress

Goal 1   Eradicate extreme poverty and hunger

Target 1.A Halve, between 1990 and 2015, the proportion of people whose income is less than $1 a day	1.1 Proportion of population below $1 purchasing power parity (PPP) a day[a] 1.2 Poverty gap ratio [incidence × depth of poverty] 1.3 Share of poorest quintile in national consumption
Target 1.B Achieve full and productive employment and decent work for all, including women and young people	1.4 Growth rate of GDP per person employed 1.5 Employment to population ratio 1.6 Proportion of employed people living below $1 (PPP) a day 1.7 Proportion of own-account and contributing family workers in total employment
Target 1.C Halve, between 1990 and 2015, the proportion of people who suffer from hunger	1.8 Prevalence of underweight children under five years of age 1.9 Proportion of population below minimum level of dietary energy consumption

Goal 2   Achieve universal primary education

Target 2.A Ensure that by 2015 children everywhere, boys and girls alike, will be able to complete a full course of primary schooling	2.1 Net enrollment ratio in primary education 2.2 Proportion of pupils starting grade 1 who reach last grade of primary education 2.3 Literacy rate of 15- to 24-year-olds, women and men

Goal 3   Promote gender equality and empower women

Target 3.A Eliminate gender disparity in primary and secondary education, preferably by 2005, and in all levels of education no later than 2015	3.1 Ratios of girls to boys in primary, secondary, and tertiary education 3.2 Share of women in wage employment in the nonagricultural sector 3.3 Proportion of seats held by women in national parliament

Goal 4   Reduce child mortality

Target 4.A Reduce by two-thirds, between 1990 and 2015, the under-five mortality rate	4.1 Under-five mortality rate 4.2 Infant mortality rate 4.3 Proportion of one-year-old children immunized against measles

Goal 5   Improve maternal health

Target 5.A Reduce by three-quarters, between 1990 and 2015, the maternal mortality ratio	5.1 Maternal mortality ratio 5.2 Proportion of births attended by skilled health personnel
Target 5.B Achieve by 2015 universal access to reproductive health	5.3 Contraceptive prevalence rate 5.4 Adolescent birth rate 5.5 Antenatal care coverage (at least one visit and at least four visits) 5.6 Unmet need for family planning

Goal 6   Combat HIV/AIDS, malaria, and other diseases

Target 6.A Have halted by 2015 and begun to reverse the spread of HIV/AIDS	6.1 HIV prevalence among population ages 15–24 years 6.2 Condom use at last high-risk sex 6.3 Proportion of population ages 15–24 years with comprehensive, correct knowledge of HIV/AIDS 6.4 Ratio of school attendance of orphans to school attendance of nonorphans ages 10–14 years
Target 6.B Achieve by 2010 universal access to treatment for HIV/AIDS for all those who need it	6.5 Proportion of population with advanced HIV infection with access to antiretroviral drugs
Target 6.C Have halted by 2015 and begun to reverse the incidence of malaria and other major diseases	6.6 Incidence and death rates associated with malaria 6.7 Proportion of children under age five sleeping under insecticide-treated bednets 6.8 Proportion of children under age five with fever who are treated with appropriate antimalarial drugs 6.9 Incidence, prevalence, and death rates associated with tuberculosis 6.10 Proportion of tuberculosis cases detected and cured under directly observed treatment short course

Note: The Millennium Development Goals and targets come from the Millennium Declaration, signed by 189 countries, including 147 heads of state and government, in September 2000 (www.un.org/millennium/declaration/ares552e.htm) as updated by the 60th UN General Assembly in September 2005. The revised Millennium Development Goal (MDG) monitoring framework shown here, including new targets and indicators, was presented to the 62nd General Assembly, with new numbering as recommended by the Inter-agency and Expert Group on MDG Indicators at its 12th meeting on November 14, 2007. The goals and targets are interrelated and should be seen as a whole. They represent a partnership between the developed countries and the developing countries "to create an environment—at the national and global levels alike—which is conducive to development and the elimination of poverty." All indicators should be disaggregated by sex and urban-rural location as far as possible.

Goals and targets from the Millennium Declaration | Indicators for monitoring progress

Goal 7   Ensure environmental sustainability

Target 7.A Integrate the principles of sustainable development into country policies and programs and reverse the loss of environmental resources	7.1 Proportion of land area covered by forest 7.2 Carbon dioxide emissions, total, per capita and per $1 GDP (PPP) 7.3 Consumption of ozone-depleting substances
Target 7.B Reduce biodiversity loss, achieving, by 2010, a significant reduction in the rate of loss	7.4 Proportion of fish stocks within safe biological limits 7.5 Proportion of total water resources used 7.6 Proportion of terrestrial and marine areas protected 7.7 Proportion of species threatened with extinction
Target 7.C Halve by 2015 the proportion of people without sustainable access to safe drinking water and basic sanitation	7.8 Proportion of population using an improved drinking water source 7.9 Proportion of population using an improved sanitation facility
Target 7.D Achieve by 2020 a significant improvement in the lives of at least 100 million slum dwellers	7.10 Proportion of urban population living in slums[b]

Goal 8   Develop a global partnership for development

Target 8.A Develop further an open, rule-based, predictable, nondiscriminatory trading and financial system (Includes a commitment to good governance, development, and poverty reduction—both nationally and internationally.)	Some of the indicators listed below are monitored separately for the least developed countries (LDCs), Africa, landlocked developing countries, and small island developing states. **Official development assistance (ODA)** 8.1 Net ODA, total and to the least developed countries, as percentage of OECD/DAC donors' gross national income 8.2 Proportion of total bilateral, sector-allocable ODA of OECD/DAC donors to basic social services (basic education, primary health care, nutrition, safe water, and sanitation)
Target 8.B Address the special needs of the least developed countries (Includes tariff and quota-free access for the least developed countries' exports; enhanced program of debt relief for heavily indebted poor countries (HIPC) and cancellation of official bilateral debt; and more generous ODA for countries committed to poverty reduction.)	8.3 Proportion of bilateral official development assistance of OECD/DAC donors that is untied 8.4 ODA received in landlocked developing countries as a proportion of their gross national incomes 8.5 ODA received in small island developing states as a proportion of their gross national incomes
Target 8.C Address the special needs of landlocked developing countries and small island developing states (through the Programme of Action for the Sustainable Development of Small Island Developing States and the outcome of the 22nd special session of the General Assembly)	**Market access** 8.6 Proportion of total developed country imports (by value and excluding arms) from developing countries and least developed countries, admitted free of duty 8.7 Average tariffs imposed by developed countries on agricultural products and textiles and clothing from developing countries 8.8 Agricultural support estimate for OECD countries as a percentage of their GDP 8.9 Proportion of ODA provided to help build trade capacity
Target 8.D Deal comprehensively with the debt problems of developing countries through national and international measures in order to make debt sustainable in the long term	**Debt sustainability** 8.10 Total number of countries that have reached their HIPC decision points and number that have reached their HIPC completion points (cumulative) 8.11 Debt relief committed under HIPC Initiative and Multilateral Debt Relief Initiative (MDRI) 8.12 Debt service as a percentage of exports of goods and services
Target 8.E In cooperation with pharmaceutical companies, provide access to affordable essential drugs in developing countries	8.13 Proportion of population with access to affordable essential drugs on a sustainable basis
Target 8.F In cooperation with the private sector, make available the benefits of new technologies, especially information and communications	8.14 Fixed-line telephones per 100 population 8.15 Mobile cellular subscribers per 100 population 8.16 Internet users per 100 population

a. Where available, indicators based on national poverty lines should be used for monitoring country poverty trends.

b. The proportion of people living in slums is measured by a proxy, represented by the urban population living in households with at least one of these characteristics: lack of access to improved water supply, lack of access to improved sanitation, overcrowding (three or more people per room), and dwellings made of nondurable material.

1 World view

	Population	Surface area	Population density	Urban population	Gross national income — Atlas method		Gross national income — Purchasing power parity		Gross domestic product	
	millions	thousand sq. km	people per sq. km	% of total population	$ billions	Per capita $	$ billions	Per capita $	% growth	Per capita % growth
	2011	2011	2011	2011	2011	2011	2011	2011	2010–11	2010–11
Afghanistan	35.3	652.2	54	24	16.6	470	40.3ᵃ	1,140ᵃ	5.7	2.9
Albania	3.2	28.8	117	53	12.8	3,980	28.4	8,820	3.0	2.6
Algeria	36.0	2,381.7	15	73	160.8	4,470	299.0ᵃ	8,310ᵃ	2.5	1.0
American Samoa	0.1	0.2	348	93	..	..ᵇ	..	..	..	..
Andorra	0.1	0.5	183	87	..	..ᶜ	..	..	..	..
Angola	19.6	1,246.7	16	59	75.2	3,830ᵈ	102.7	5,230	3.9	1.1
Antigua and Barbuda	0.1	0.4	204	30	1.1	11,940	1.6ᵃ	17,900ᵃ	−5.0	−6.0
Argentina	40.8	2,780.4	15	93	..	..	..	..	..	..
Armenia	3.1	29.7	109	64	10.4	3,360	18.9	6,100	4.6	4.3
Aruba	0.1	0.2	601	47	..	..ᶜ	..	..	..	..
Australia	22.3	7,741.2	3	89	1,111.4	49,790	862.0	38,610	1.9	0.7
Austria	8.4	83.9	102	68	405.7	48,170	354.0	42,030	2.7	2.3
Azerbaijan	9.2	86.6	111	54	48.5	5,290	82.1	8,950	1.0	−0.3
Bahamas, The	0.3	13.9	35	84	7.5	21,970	10.2ᵃ	29,790ᵃ	1.6	0.4
Bahrain	1.3	0.8	1,742	89	20.1	15,920	26.8	21,200	3.0	−3.1
Bangladesh	150.5	144.0	1,156	28	117.8	780	291.7	1,940	6.7	5.4
Barbados	0.3	0.4	637	44	3.5	12,660	5.2ᵃ	18,900ᵃ	1.2	−5.5
Belarus	9.5	207.6	47	75	55.2	5,830	137.0	14,460	5.3	5.5
Belgium	11.0	30.5	364	98	506.2	45,930	431.4	39,150	1.8	0.6
Belize	0.4	23.0	16	45	1.3	3,710	2.2ᵃ	6,090ᵃ	1.9	−1.5
Benin	9.1	112.6	82	45	7.1	780	14.6	1,610	3.5	0.7
Bermuda	0.1	0.1	1,294	100	..	..ᶜ	..	..	−1.9	−1.7
Bhutan	0.7	38.4	19	36	1.6	2,130	4.1	5,570	5.6	3.8
Bolivia	10.1	1,098.6	9	67	20.4	2,020	49.3	4,890	5.2	3.5
Bosnia and Herzegovina	3.8	51.2	74	48	18.0	4,780	34.5	9,190	1.7	1.9
Botswana	2.0	581.7	4	62	15.2	7,470	29.5	14,550	5.7	4.5
Brazil	196.7	8,514.9	23	85	2,107.7	10,720	2,245.8	11,420	2.7	1.8
Brunei Darussalam	0.4	5.8	77	76	12.5	31,800	19.6	49,910	2.2	0.4
Bulgaria	7.3	111.0	68	73	48.8	6,640	105.8	14,400	1.7	4.3
Burkina Faso	17.0	274.2	62	27	9.9	580	22.5	1,330	4.2	1.1
Burundi	8.6	27.8	334	11	2.2	250	5.2	610	4.2	1.9
Cambodia	14.3	181.0	81	20	11.7	820	31.8	2,230	7.1	5.8
Cameroon	20.0	475.4	42	52	24.1	1,210	46.7	2,330	4.2	2.0
Canada	34.5	9,984.7	4	81	1,570.9	45,550	1,367.6	39,660	2.5	1.4
Cape Verde	0.5	4.0	124	63	1.8	3,540	2.0	3,980	5.0	4.1
Cayman Islands	0.1	0.3	236	100	..	..ᶜ	..	..	..	..
Central African Republic	4.5	623.0	7	39	2.1	480	3.6	810	3.3	1.3
Chad	11.5	1,284.0	9	22	8.3	720	17.7	1,540	1.6	−1.0
Channel Islands	0.2	0.2	810	31	..	..ᶜ	..	..	..	..
Chile	17.3	756.1	23	89	212.0	12,280	282.1	16,330	6.0	5.0
China	1,344.1	9,600.0	144	51	6,643.2	4,940	11,270.8	8,390	9.3	8.8
Hong Kong SAR, China	7.1	1.1	6,787	100	254.6	36,010	370.2	52,350	4.9	4.8
Macao SAR, China	0.6	0.0ᵉ	19,848	100	24.7	45,460ᵈ	31.0	56,950	20.7	18.1
Colombia	46.9	1,141.8	42	75	284.9	6,070	448.6	9,560	5.9	4.5
Comoros	0.8	1.9	405	28	0.6	770	0.8	1,110	2.2	−0.4
Congo, Dem. Rep.	67.8	2,344.9	30	34	13.1	190	23.2	340	6.9	4.1
Congo, Rep.	4.1	342.0	12	64	9.3	2,250	13.4	3,240	3.4	1.0

	Population	Surface area	Population density	Urban population	Gross national income				Gross domestic product	
					Atlas method		Purchasing power parity			
	millions	thousand sq. km	people per sq. km	% of total population	$ billions	Per capita $	$ billions	Per capita $	% growth	Per capita % growth
	2011	2011	2011	2011	2011	2011	2011	2011	2010–11	2010–11
Costa Rica	4.7	51.1	93	65	36.1	7,640	56.1[a]	11,860[a]	4.2	2.7
Côte d'Ivoire	20.2	322.5	63	51	22.1	1,090	34.5	1,710	−4.7	−6.7
Croatia	4.4	56.6	79	58	59.6	13,540	82.7	18,780	0.0	0.3
Cuba	11.3	109.9	106	75	..	..[b]	..	..	2.1	2.1
Curaçao	0.1	0.4	328	..	..	..[c]	..	..	..	..
Cyprus	1.1	9.3	121	71	23.7[f]	29,450[f]	24.9[f]	30,970[f]	0.5[f]	0.3[f]
Czech Republic	10.5	78.9	136	73	196.3	18,700	257.0	24,490	1.9	2.1
Denmark	5.6	43.1	131	87	335.1	60,160	233.5	41,920	1.1	0.7
Djibouti	0.9	23.2	39	77	1.1	1,270	2.1	2,450	5.0	3.0
Dominica	0.1	0.8	90	67	0.5	7,030	0.9[a]	13,000[a]	−0.3	−0.2
Dominican Republic	10.1	48.7	208	70	52.6	5,240	94.7[a]	9,420[a]	4.5	3.1
Ecuador	14.7	256.4	59	67	61.7	4,200	124.7	8,510	7.8	6.3
Egypt, Arab Rep.	82.5	1,001.5	83	44	214.7	2,600	504.8	6,120	1.8	0.1
El Salvador	6.2	21.0	301	65	21.7	3,480	41.4[a]	6,640[a]	1.5	0.9
Equatorial Guinea	0.7	28.1	26	40	11.3	15,670	18.4	25,620	7.8	4.8
Eritrea	5.4	117.6	54	21	2.3	430	3.1[a]	580[a]	8.7	5.5
Estonia	1.3	45.2	32	70	20.4	15,260	27.9	20,850	8.3	8.3
Ethiopia	84.7	1,104.3	85	17	31.0	370	93.8	1,110	7.3	5.0
Faeroe Islands	0.0[g]	1.4	35	41	..	..[c]	..	..	..	..
Fiji	0.9	18.3	48	52	3.2	3,720	4.0	4,610	2.0	1.1
Finland	5.4	338.4	18	84	257.3	47,760	202.9	37,660	2.7	2.3
France	65.4	549.2	120	86	2,775.7	42,420	2,349.8	35,910	1.7	1.1
French Polynesia	0.3	4.0	75	51	..	..[c]	..	..	..	..
Gabon	1.5	267.7	6	86	12.4	8,080	21.1	13,740	4.8	2.8
Gambia, The	1.8	11.3	178	57	0.9	500	3.1	1,750	−4.3	−6.9
Georgia	4.5[h]	69.7	79[h]	53[h]	12.8[h]	2,860[h]	24.0[h]	5,350[h]	7.0[h]	6.2[h]
Germany	81.8	357.1	235	74	3,617.7	44,230	3,287.6	40,190	3.0	3.0
Ghana	25.0	238.5	110	52	35.1	1,410	45.2	1,810	14.4	11.8
Greece	11.3	132.0	88	62	276.7	24,490	283.7	25,110	−7.1	−7.0
Greenland	0.1	410.5[i]	0[j]	85	1.5	26,020	..	..	−5.4	−5.4
Grenada	0.1	0.3	309	39	0.8	7,350	1.1[a]	10,350[a]	1.0	0.6
Guam	0.2	0.5	337	93	..	..[c]	..	..	..	..
Guatemala	14.8	108.9	138	50	42.4	2,870	70.3[a]	4,760[a]	3.9	1.3
Guinea	10.2	245.9	42	36	4.4	430	10.5	1,020	3.9	1.5
Guinea-Bissau	1.5	36.1	55	44	0.9	600	1.9	1,230	5.7	3.5
Guyana	0.8	215.0	4	28	2.2	2,900	2.6[a]	3,460[a]	4.2	4.2
Haiti	10.1	27.8	367	53	7.1	700	11.9[a]	1,180[a]	5.6	4.2
Honduras	7.8	112.5	69	52	15.4	1,980	29.7[a]	3,820[a]	3.6	1.6
Hungary	10.0	93.0	110	69	126.9	12,730	202.5	20,310	1.7	2.0
Iceland	0.3	103.0	3	94	11.1	34,820	9.9	31,020	2.6	2.2
India	1,241.5	3,287.3	418	31	1,766.2	1,420	4,524.6	3,640	6.3	4.9
Indonesia	242.3	1,904.6	134	51	712.7	2,940	1,091.4	4,500	6.5	5.4
Iran, Islamic Rep.	74.8	1,745.2	46	69	330.4	4,520	835.5	11,420	..	..
Iraq	33.0	435.2	76	67	87.0	2,640	123.5	3,750	9.9	6.8
Ireland	4.6	70.3	66	62	179.2	39,150	153.4	33,520	0.7	−1.5
Isle of Man	0.1	0.6	146	51	..	..[c]	..	..	..	..
Israel	7.8	22.1	359	92	224.7	28,930	210.5	27,110	4.7	2.8

1 World view

	Population	Surface area	Population density	Urban population	Gross national income				Gross domestic product	
					Atlas method		Purchasing power parity			
	millions	thousand sq. km	people per sq. km	% of total population	$ billions	Per capita $	$ billions	Per capita $	% growth	Per capita % growth
	2011	2011	2011	2011	2011	2011	2011	2011	2010–11	2010–11
Italy	60.7	301.3	206	68	2,144.7	35,320	1,968.9	32,420	0.4	0.0
Jamaica	2.7	11.0	250	52	..	..[b]	..	..	–0.3	..
Japan	127.8	377.9	351	91	5,739.5	44,900	4,516.3	35,330	–0.7	–1.0
Jordan	6.2	89.3	70	83	27.1	4,380	36.6	5,930	2.6	0.4
Kazakhstan	16.6	2,724.9	6	54	136.7	8,260	186.4	11,250	7.5	6.0
Kenya	41.6	580.4	73	24	34.1	820	71.1	1,710	4.4	1.6
Kiribati	0.1	0.8	125	44	0.2	2,030	0.3[a]	3,300[a]	1.8	0.2
Korea, Dem. Rep.	24.5	120.5	203	60	..	..[k]	..	..	..	..
Korea, Rep.	49.8	99.9	513	83	1,039.0	20,870	1,511.7	30,370	3.6	2.9
Kosovo	1.8	10.9	166	..	6.3	3,510	..	..	5.0	3.4
Kuwait	2.8	17.8	158	98	133.8	48,900	147.0	53,720	8.2	5.1
Kyrgyz Republic	5.5	199.9	29	35	5.0	900	12.7	2,290	6.0	4.7
Lao PDR	6.3	236.8	27	34	7.1	1,130	16.2	2,580	8.0	6.5
Latvia	2.1	64.6	33	68	27.4	13,320[d]	39.3	19,090	5.5	14.7
Lebanon	4.3	10.5	416	87	38.9	9,140	61.6	14,470	3.0	2.2
Lesotho	2.2	30.4	72	28	2.7	1,210	4.5	2,050	4.2	3.1
Liberia	4.1	111.4	43	48	1.4	330	2.2	540	9.4	5.9
Libya	6.4	1,759.5	4	78	77.1	12,320	105.2[a]	16,800[a]	2.1	0.3
Liechtenstein	0.0[g]	0.2	227	14	4.9	137,070	..	..	–1.2	–1.9
Lithuania	3.0	65.3	48	67	39.3	12,980[d]	62.9	20,760	5.9	14.8
Luxembourg	0.5	2.6	200	85	40.1	77,390	33.2	64,110	1.7	–0.6
Macedonia, FYR	2.1	25.7	82	59	9.9	4,810	23.5	11,370	2.8	2.7
Madagascar	21.3	587.0	37	33	9.1	430	20.2	950	1.0	–1.9
Malawi	15.4	118.5	163	16	5.6	360	13.4	870	4.3	1.1
Malaysia	28.9	330.8	88	73	253.0	8,770	451.7	15,650	5.1	3.4
Maldives	0.3	0.3	1,067	41	1.8	5,720	2.4	7,430	7.5	6.1
Mali	15.8	1,240.2	13	35	9.7	610	16.8	1,060	2.7	–0.3
Malta	0.4	0.3	1,299	95	7.7	18,620	10.2	24,480	2.1	2.2
Marshall Islands	0.1	0.2	305	72	0.2	3,910	..	..	5.0	3.5
Mauritania	3.5	1,030.7	3	42	3.6	1,030[l]	8.9	2,530	4.0	1.6
Mauritius	1.3	2.0	634	42	10.3	8,040	18.4	14,330	4.1	3.7
Mexico	114.8	1,964.4	59	78	1,081.8	9,420	1,766.4	15,390	3.9	2.7
Micronesia, Fed. Sts.	0.1	0.7	159	23	0.3	2,860	0.4[a]	3,580[a]	2.1	1.6
Moldova	3.6[m]	33.9	124[m]	48[m]	7.1[m]	1,980[m]	13.0[m]	3,640[m]	6.4[m]	6.5[m]
Monaco	0.0[g]	0.0[e]	17,714	100	6.5	183,150	..	..	–2.6	–2.7
Mongolia	2.8	1,564.1	2	69	6.5	2,310	12.0	4,290	17.5	15.7
Montenegro	0.6	13.8	47	63	4.5	7,140	8.7	13,700	3.2	3.1
Morocco	32.3	446.6	72	57	97.6[n]	2,970[n]	160.1[n]	4,880[n]	4.5[n]	3.5[n]
Mozambique	23.9	799.4	30	31	11.1	460	22.9	960	7.1	4.7
Myanmar	48.3	676.6	74	33	..	..[k]	..	..	..	..
Namibia	2.3	824.3	3	38	10.9	4,700	15.4	6,610	4.8	3.0
Nepal	30.5	147.2	213	17	16.6	540	38.4	1,260	3.9	2.1
Netherlands	16.7	41.5	495	83	829.0	49,660	720.3	43,150	1.0	0.5
New Caledonia	0.3	18.6	14	62	..	..[c]	..	..	..	..
New Zealand	4.4	267.7	17	86	127.3	29,140	126.3	28,930	1.0	0.1
Nicaragua	5.9	130.4	49	58	8.9	1,510	21.9[a]	3,730[a]	5.1	3.6
Niger	16.1	1,267.0	13	18	5.8	360	11.6	720	2.3	–1.2

 Front | User guide | World view | People | Environment

	Population	Surface area	Population density	Urban population	Gross national income				Gross domestic product	
					Atlas method		Purchasing power parity			
	millions	thousand sq. km	people per sq. km	% of total population	$ billions	Per capita $	$ billions	Per capita $	% growth	Per capita % growth
	2011	2011	2011	2011	2011	2011	2011	2011	2010–11	2010–11
Nigeria	162.5	923.8	178	50	207.3	1,280	372.8	2,290	7.4	4.7
Northern Mariana Islands	0.1	0.5	133	92	..	..[c]	..	..	..	..
Norway	5.0	323.8	16	79	440.2	88,870	304.4	61,450	1.4	0.1
Oman	2.8	309.5	9	73	53.6	19,260	71.6	25,720	5.5	3.1
Pakistan	176.7	796.1	229	36	198.0	1,120	507.2	2,870	3.0	1.1
Palau	0.0[g]	0.5	45	84	0.1	6,510	0.2[a]	11,080[a]	5.8	5.1
Panama	3.6	75.4	48	75	26.7	7,470	51.8[a]	14,510[a]	10.6	8.9
Papua New Guinea	7.0	462.8	16	13	10.4	1,480	18.0[a]	2,570[a]	9.0	6.6
Paraguay	6.6	406.8	17	62	19.8	3,020	35.4	5,390	6.9	5.0
Peru	29.4	1,285.2	23	77	151.4	5,150	277.6	9,440	6.8	5.6
Philippines	94.9	300.0	318	49	209.7	2,210	393.0	4,140	3.9	2.2
Poland	38.5	312.7	127	61	477.0	12,380[o]	780.8	20,260	4.3	3.4
Portugal	10.6	92.1	115	61	225.6	21,370	259.9	24,620	–1.7	–0.9
Puerto Rico	3.7	8.9	418	99	61.6	16,560	..	..	–2.1	–1.6
Qatar	1.9	11.6	161	99	150.4	80,440	161.6	86,440	18.8	11.7
Romania	21.4	238.4	93	53	174.0	8,140	337.4	15,780	2.5	2.7
Russian Federation	143.0	17,098.2	9	74	1,522.3	10,650	2,917.7	20,410	4.3	3.9
Rwanda	10.9	26.3	444	19	6.2	570	13.9	1,270	8.3	5.1
Samoa	0.2	2.8	65	20	0.6	3,160	0.8[a]	4,270[a]	2.0	1.6
San Marino	0.0[g]	0.1	529	94	..	..[c]	..	..	..	..
São Tomé and Príncipe	0.2	1.0	176	63	0.2	1,350	0.4	2,080	4.9	3.0
Saudi Arabia	28.1	2,149.7[p]	13	82	500.5	17,820	693.7	24,700	6.8	4.4
Senegal	12.8	196.7	66	43	13.7	1,070	24.8	1,940	2.6	–0.1
Serbia	7.3	88.4	83	56	41.3	5,690	83.8	11,550	2.0	2.5
Seychelles	0.1	0.5	187	54	1.0	11,270	2.3[a]	26,280[a]	5.0	5.6
Sierra Leone	6.0	71.7	84	39	2.8	460	6.8	1,140	6.0	3.7
Singapore	5.2	0.7	7,405	100	222.6	42,930	307.8	59,380	4.9	2.7
Sint Maarten	0.0[g]	0.0[e]	1,077	..	..	..[c]	..	..	..	..
Slovak Republic	5.4	49.0	112	55	87.4	16,190	120.4	22,300	3.3	4.0
Slovenia	2.1	20.3	102	50	48.5	23,600	54.4	26,500	–0.2	–0.4
Solomon Islands	0.6	28.9	20	21	0.6	1,110	1.3[a]	2,350[a]	9.0	6.2
Somalia	9.6	637.7	15	38	..	..[k]	..	..	..	..
South Africa	50.6	1,219.1	42	62	352.0	6,960	542.0	10,710	3.1	1.9
South Sudan	10.3[p]	644.3	..	18	..	..[q]	..	..	1.9	–1.7
Spain	46.2	505.4	93	77	1,428.3	30,930	1,451.7	31,440	0.4	0.2
Sri Lanka	20.9	65.6	333	15	53.8	2,580	115.2	5,520	8.3	7.1
St. Kitts and Nevis	0.1	0.3	204	32	0.7	12,610	0.9[a]	16,470[a]	2.1	0.9
St. Lucia	0.2	0.6	289	18	1.2	6,820	2.0[a]	11,220[a]	1.3	0.1
St. Martin	0.0[g]	0.1	563	..	..	..[c]	..	..	..	..
St. Vincent and Grenadines	0.1	0.4	280	49	0.7	6,070	1.1[a]	10,440[a]	0.1	0.1
Sudan	34.3[p,r]	1,861.5[r]	18	33	58.3[u]	1,310[u]	94.7[u]	2,120[u]	4.7[u]	2.2[u]
Suriname	0.5	163.8	3	70	4.1	7,840	4.1[a]	7,730[a]	4.7	3.7
Swaziland	1.1	17.4	62	21	3.7	3,470	6.5	6,110	1.3	0.1
Sweden	9.4	450.3	23	85	502.5	53,170	398.9	42,210	3.9	3.1
Switzerland	7.9	41.3	198	74	604.1	76,350	415.6	52,530	1.9	0.8
Syrian Arab Republic	20.8	185.2	113	56	67.9	2,750	104.0	5,080	..	..
Tajikistan	7.0	142.6	50	27	6.1	870	16.0	2,300	7.4	5.9

	Population	Surface area	Population density	Urban population	Gross national income				Gross domestic product	
					Atlas method		Purchasing power parity			
	millions	thousand sq. km	people per sq. km	% of total population	$ billions	Per capita $	$ billions	Per capita $	% growth	Per capita % growth
	2011	2011	2011	2011	2011	2011	2011	2011	2010–11	2010–11
Tanzania	46.2	947.3	52	27	24.2[v]	540[v]	67.1[v]	1,500[v]	6.4[v]	3.3[v]
Thailand	69.5	513.1	136	34	308.3	4,440	581.4	8,360	0.1	−0.5
Timor-Leste	1.2	14.9	79	28	*3.1*	*2,730*	*5.9*[a]	*5,200*[a]	10.6	7.5
Togo	6.2	56.8	113	38	3.5	570	6.4	1,040	4.9	2.7
Tonga	0.1	0.8	145	24	0.4	3,820	0.5[a]	5,000[a]	4.9	4.5
Trinidad and Tobago	1.3	5.1	262	14	*21.3*	*15,840*	*32.7*[a]	*24,350*[a]	−4.1	−4.4
Tunisia	10.7	163.6	69	66	42.9	4,020[d]	96.0	8,990	−2.0	−3.1
Turkey	73.6	783.6	96	71	766.6	10,410	1,247.3	16,940	8.5	7.2
Turkmenistan	5.1	488.1	11	49	24.5	4,800	44.3[a]	8,690[a]	14.7	13.3
Turks and Caicos Islands	0.0[g]	1.0	41	94	..	..[c]	..	..	..	..
Tuvalu	0.0[g]	0.0[e]	328	51	0.0	4,950	..	..	1.2	1.0
Uganda	34.5	241.6	173	16	17.5	510	45.3	1,310	6.7	3.3
Ukraine	45.7	603.6	79	69	142.9	3,130	321.9	7,040	5.2	5.6
United Arab Emirates	7.9	83.6	94	84	321.7	40,760	377.9	47,890	4.9	−0.1
United Kingdom	62.7	243.6	259	80	2,370.4	37,780	2,255.9	35,950	0.8	0.0
United States	311.6	9,831.5	34	82	15,148.2	48,620	15,211.3	48,820	1.7	1.0
Uruguay	3.4	176.2	19	93	40.0	11,860	49.3	14,640	5.7	5.3
Uzbekistan	29.3	447.4	69	36	44.2	1,510	100.3[a]	3,420[a]	8.3	5.4
Vanuatu	0.2	12.2	20	25	0.7	2,730	1.1[a]	4,330[a]	1.4	−1.0
Venezuela, RB	29.3	912.1	33	94	346.1	11,820	363.9	12,430	4.2	2.6
Vietnam	87.8	331.1	283	31	111.1	1,270	285.5	3,250	5.9	4.8
Virgin Islands (U.S.)	0.1	0.4	313	95	..	..[c]	..	..	..	..
West Bank and Gaza	3.9	6.0	652	74	..	..[q]	..	..	..	..
Yemen, Rep.	24.8	528.0	47	32	26.4	1,070	53.7	2,170	−10.5	−13.2
Zambia	13.5	752.6	18	39	15.7	1,160	20.1	1,490	6.5	2.1
Zimbabwe	12.8	390.8	33	39	8.4	660	..	..	9.4	7.8
World	**6,974.2**[s]	**134,269.2**[s]	**54**[w]	**52**[w]	**66,354.3**[t]	**9,514**[w]	**80,624.2**[t]	**11,560**[w]	**2.7**[w]	**1.6**[w]
Low income	816.8	16,582.1	51	28	466.0	571	1,125.4	1,378	6.0	3.7
Middle income	5,022.4	81,875.7	63	50	20,835.4	4,149	36,311.9	7,230	6.3	5.2
Lower middle income	2,532.7	20,841.9	126	39	4,488.5	1,772	9,719.0	3,837	5.5	3.9
Upper middle income	2,489.7	61,033.8	42	61	16,340.5	6,563	26,646.2	10,703	6.6	5.9
Low & middle income	5,839.2	98,457.7	61	47	21,324.4	3,652	37,436.4	6,411	6.3	5.0
East Asia & Pacific	1,974.2	16,301.7	125	49	8,387.3	4,248	14,344.6	7,266	8.3	7.6
Europe & Central Asia	408.1	23,613.7	18	65	3,156.6	7,734	5,845.7	14,323	5.9	5.4
Latin America & Carib.	589.0	20,393.6	29	79	5,050.3	8,574	6,822.0	11,582	4.7	3.6
Middle East & N. Africa	336.5	8,775.4	39	59	*1,279.5*	*3,866*	*2,619.2*	*8,052*	*0.2*	*2.4*
South Asia	1,656.5	5,131.1	347	31	2,174.5	1,313	5,523.5	3,335	6.1	4.6
Sub-Saharan Africa	874.8	24,242.3	37	37	1,100.8	1,258	1,946.2	2,225	4.7	2.1
High income	1,135.0	35,811.5	33	81	45,242.5	39,861	43,724.5	38,523	1.5	0.9
Euro area	332.9	2,628.4	131	76	12,871.5	38,661	11,735.7	35,250	1.5	1.2

a. Based on regression; others are extrapolated from the 2005 International Comparison Program benchmark estimates. b. Estimated to be upper middle income ($4,036–$12,475). c. Estimated to be high income ($12,476 or more). d. Included in the aggregates for upper middle-income economies based on earlier data. e. Greater than 0 but less than 50. f. Data are for the area controlled by the government of Cyprus. g. Greater than 0 but less than 50,000. h. Excludes Abkhazia and South Ossetia. i. Refers to area free from ice. j. Greater than 0 but less than 0.5. k. Estimated to be low income ($1,025 or less). l. Included in the aggregates for low-income economies based on earlier data. m. Excludes Transnistria. n. Includes Former Spanish Sahara. o. Included in the aggregates for high-income economies based on earlier data. p. Provisional estimate. q. Estimated to be lower middle income ($1,026–$4,035). r. Excludes South Sudan. s. Sum of available data (see *Statistical methods*). t. Missing data are imputed (see *Statistical methods*). u. Excludes South Sudan after July 9, 2011. v. Covers mainland Tanzania only. w. Weighted average (see *Statistical methods*).

About the data

Population, land area, income (as measured by gross national income, GNI), and output (as measured by gross domestic product, GDP) are basic measures of the size of an economy. They also provide a broad indication of actual and potential resources and are therefore used throughout *World Development Indicators* to normalize other indicators.

Population

Population estimates are usually based on national population censuses. Estimates for the years before and after the census are interpolations or extrapolations based on demographic models. Errors and undercounting occur even in high-income countries; in developing countries errors may be substantial because of limits in the transport, communications, and other resources required to conduct and analyze a full census.

The quality and reliability of official demographic data are also affected by public trust in the government, government commitment to full and accurate enumeration, confidentiality and protection against misuse of census data, and census agencies' independence from political influence. Moreover, comparability of population indicators is limited by differences in the concepts, definitions, collection procedures, and estimation methods used by national statistical agencies and other organizations that collect the data.

Of the 214 economies in the table, 180 (about 86 percent) conducted a census during the 2000 census round (1995–2004). As of January 2012, 141 countries have completed a census for the 2010 census round (2005–14). The currentness of a census and the availability of complementary data from surveys or registration systems are important indicators of demographic data quality. See *Primary data documentation* for the most recent census or survey year and for the completeness of registration. Some European countries' registration systems offer complete information on population in the absence of a census.

Current population estimates for developing countries that lack recent census data and pre- and post-census estimates for countries with census data are provided by the United Nations Population Division and other agencies. The cohort component method—a standard method for estimating and projecting population—requires fertility, mortality, and net migration data, often collected from sample surveys, which can be small or limited in coverage. Population estimates are from demographic modeling and so are susceptible to biases and errors from shortcomings in the model and in the data. Because the five-year age group is the cohort unit and five-year period data are used, interpolations to obtain annual data or single age structure may not reflect actual events or age composition.

Surface area

The surface area of an economy includes inland bodies of water and some coastal waterways. Surface area thus differs from land area, which excludes bodies of water, and from gross area, which may include offshore territorial waters. Land area is particularly important for understanding an economy's agricultural capacity and the environmental effects of human activity. Innovations in satellite mapping and computer databases have resulted in more precise measurements of land and water areas.

Urban population

There is no consistent and universally accepted standard for distinguishing urban from rural areas, in part because of the wide variety of situations across countries. Most countries use an urban classification related to the size or characteristics of settlements. Some define urban areas based on the presence of certain infrastructure and services. And other countries designate urban areas based on administrative arrangements. Because the estimates in the table are based on national definitions of what constitutes a city or metropolitan area, cross-country comparisons should be made with caution. To estimate urban populations, ratios of urban to total population obtained from the United Nations were applied to the World Bank's estimates of total population.

Size of the economy

GNI measures total domestic and foreign value added claimed by residents. GNI comprises GDP plus net receipts of primary income (compensation of employees and property income) from nonresident sources. GDP is the sum of gross value added by all resident producers in the economy plus any product taxes (less subsidies) not included in the valuation of output. GNI is calculated without deducting for depreciation of fabricated assets or for depletion and degradation of natural resources. Value added is the net output of an industry after adding up all outputs and subtracting intermediate inputs. The industrial origin of value added is determined by the International Standard Industrial Classification revision 3. The World Bank uses GNI per capita in U.S. dollars to classify countries for analytical purposes and to determine borrowing eligibility. For definitions of the income groups in *World Development Indicators*, see *User guide.*

When calculating GNI in U.S. dollars from GNI reported in national currencies, the World Bank follows the *World Bank Atlas* conversion method, using a three-year average of exchange rates to smooth the effects of transitory fluctuations in exchange rates. (For further discussion of the *World Bank Atlas* method, see *Statistical methods*.)

Because exchange rates do not always reflect differences in price levels between countries, the table also converts GNI and GNI per capita estimates into international dollars using purchasing power parity (PPP) rates. PPP rates provide a standard measure allowing comparison of real levels of expenditure between countries, just as conventional price indexes allow comparison of real values over time.

PPP rates are calculated by simultaneously comparing the prices of similar goods and services among a large number of countries. In the most recent round of price surveys conducted by the International Comparison Program (ICP) in 2005, 146 countries and territories participated, including China for the first time, India for the first time since 1985, and almost all African countries. The PPP conversion factors presented in the table come from three sources. For 47 high- and upper middle-income countries conversion factors are provided by Eurostat and the Organisation for Economic Co-operation and Development (OECD); PPP estimates for these countries incorporate new price data collected since 2005. For the remaining 2005 ICP countries the PPP estimates are extrapolated from the 2005 ICP benchmark results, which account for relative price changes between each economy and the United States. For countries that did not participate in the 2005 ICP round, the PPP estimates are imputed using a statistical model. More information on the results of the 2005 ICP is available at www.worldbank.org/data/icp.

Growth rates of GDP and GDP per capita are calculated using the least squares method and constant price data in local currency. Constant price U.S. dollar series are used to calculate regional and income group growth rates. The growth rates in the table are annual averages. Methods of computing growth rates are described in *Statistical methods.*

Definitions

• **Population** is based on the de facto definition of population, which counts all residents regardless of legal status or citizenship—except for refugees not permanently settled in the country of asylum, who are generally considered part of the population of their country of origin. The values shown are midyear estimates. • **Surface area** is a country's total area, including areas under inland bodies of water and some coastal waterways. • **Population density** is midyear population divided by land area. • **Urban population** is the midyear population of areas defined as urban in each country and reported to the United Nations. • **Gross national income,** *Atlas* **method,** is the sum of value added by all resident producers plus any product taxes (less subsidies) not included in the valuation of output plus net receipts of primary income (compensation of employees and property income) from abroad. Data are in current U.S. dollars converted using the *World Bank Atlas* method (see *Statistical methods*). • **Gross national income, purchasing power parity,** is GNI converted to international dollars using PPP rates. An international dollar has the same purchasing power over GNI that a U.S. dollar has in the United States. • **Gross national income per capita** is GNI divided by midyear population. • **Gross domestic product** is the sum of value added by all resident producers plus any product taxes (less subsidies) not included in the valuation of output. Growth is calculated from constant price GDP data in local currency. • **Gross domestic product per capita** is GDP divided by midyear population.

Data sources

The World Bank's population estimates are compiled and produced by its Development Data Group in consultation with its Human Development Network, operational staff, and country offices. The United Nations Population Division (2011) is a source of the demographic data for more than half the countries, most of them developing countries. Other important sources are census reports and other statistical publications from national statistical offices; household surveys by national agencies, ICF International (for MEASURE DHS), and the U.S. Centers for Disease Control and Prevention; Eurostat's *Demographic Statistics;* the Secretariat of the Pacific Community's Statistics and Demography Programme; and the U.S. Bureau of the Census's International Data Base.

Data on surface and land area are from the Food and Agriculture Organization, which gathers these data from national agencies through annual questionnaires and by analyzing the results of national agricultural censuses.

Data on urban population shares are from United Nations Population Division (2010).

GNI, GNI per capita, GDP growth, and GDP per capita growth are estimated by World Bank staff based on national accounts data collected by World Bank staff during economic missions or reported by national statistical offices to other international organizations such as the OECD. PPP conversion factors are estimates by Eurostat/OECD and by World Bank staff based on data collected by the ICP.

References

Eurostat (Statistical Office of the European Communities). n.d. *Demographic Statistics.* http://epp.eurostat.ec.europa.eu/portal/page/portal/eurostat/home/. Luxembourg.

ICF International. Various years. *Demographic and Health Surveys.* http://www.measuredhs.com. Calverton, MD.

OECD (Organisation for Economic Co-operation and Development). n.d. OECD.StatExtracts database. http://stats.oecd.org/. Paris.

UNAIDS (Joint United Nations Programme on HIV/AIDS). 2012. *Global Report: UNAIDS Report on the Global AIDS Epidemic 2012.* www.unaids.org/en/resources/publications/2012/. Geneva.

United Nations Inter-Agency Group for Child Mortality Estimation. 2012. *Levels and Trends in Child Mortality: Report 2012.* www.childinfo.org/files/Child_Mortality_Report_2012.pdf. New York.

United Nations. 2012. *The Millennium Development Goals Report 2012.* New York.

United Nations Population Division. 2010. *World Urbanization Prospects: The 2009 Revision.* New York: United Nations, Department of Economic and Social Affairs.

———. 2011. *World Population Prospects: The 2010 Revision.* New York: United Nations, Department of Economic and Social Affairs.

World Bank. 2011. *The Changing Wealth of Nations: Measuring Sustainable Development for the New Millennium.* Washington, DC.

———. n.d. PovcalNet online database. http://iresearch.worldbank.org/PovcalNet/index.htm

To access the World Development Indicators online tables, use the URL http://wdi.worldbank.org/table/ and the table number (for example, http://wdi.worldbank.org/table/1.1). To view a specific indicator online, use the URL http://data.worldbank.org/indicator/ and the indicator code (for example, http://data.worldbank.org/indicator/SP.POP.TOTL).

1.1 Size of the economy

Population ♀♂	SP.POP.TOTL
Surface area	AG.SRF.TOTL.K2
Population density	EN.POP.DNST
Gross national income, *Atlas* method	NY.GNP.ATLS.CD
Gross national income per capita, *Atlas* method	NY.GNP.PCAP.CD
Purchasing power parity gross national income	NY.GNP.MKTP.PP.CD
Purchasing power parity gross national income, Per capita	NY.GNP.PCAP.PP.CD
Gross domestic product	NY.GDP.MKTP.KD.ZG
Gross domestic product, Per capita	NY.GDP.PCAP.KD.ZG

1.2 Millennium Development Goals: eradicating poverty and saving lives

Share of poorest quintile in national consumption or income	SI.DST.FRST.20
Vulnerable employment ♀♂	SL.EMP.VULN.ZS
Prevalence of malnutrition, Underweight ♀♂	SH.STA.MALN.ZS
Primary completion rate ♀♂	SE.PRM.CMPT.ZS
Ratio of girls to boys enrollments in primary and secondary education ♀♂	SE.ENR.PRSC.FM.ZS
Under-five mortality rate ♀♂	SH.DYN.MORT

1.3 Millennium Development Goals: protecting our common environment

Maternal mortality ratio, Modeled estimate	SH.STA.MMRT
Contraceptive prevalence rate	SP.DYN.CONU.ZS
HIV prevalence	SH.DYN.AIDS.ZS
Incidence of tuberculosis	SH.TBS.INCD

Carbon dioxide emissions per capita	EN.ATM.CO2E.PC
Nationally protected terrestrial and marine areas	ER.PTD.TOTL.ZS
Access to improved sanitation facilities	SH.STA.ACSN
Individuals using the Internet	..[a]

1.4 Millennium Development Goals: overcoming obstacles

This table provides data on net official development assistance by donor, least developed countries' access to high-income markets, and the Debt Initiative for Heavily Indebted Poor Countries. ..[a]

1.5 Women in development

Female population ♀♂	SP.POP.TOTL.FE.ZS
Life expectancy at birth, Male ♀♂	SP.DYN.LE00.MA.IN
Life expectancy at birth, Female ♀♂	SP.DYN.LE00.FE.IN
Pregnant women receiving prenatal care	SH.STA.ANVC.ZS
Teenage mothers	SP.MTR.1519.ZS
Women in wage employment in nonagricultural sector	SL.EMP.INSV.FE.ZS
Unpaid family workers, Male ♀♂	SL.FAM.WORK.MA.ZS
Unpaid family workers, Female ♀♂	SL.FAM.WORK.FE.ZS
Female part-time employment ♀♂	SL.TLF.PART.TL.FE.ZS
Female legislators, senior officials, and managers	SG.GEN.LSOM.ZS
Women in parliaments	SG.GEN.PARL.ZS
Female-headed households	SP.HOU.FEMA.ZS

♀♂ Data disaggregated by sex are available in the World Development Indicators database.
a. Available online only as part of the table, not as an individual indicator.

Poverty rates

	International poverty line in local currency		Population below international poverty lines[a]									
	$1.25 a day 2005	$2 a day 2005	Survey year[b]	Population below $1.25 a day %	Poverty gap at $1.25 a day %	Population below $2 a day %	Poverty gap at $2 a day %	Survey year[b]	Population below $1.25 a day %	Poverty gap at $1.25 a day %	Population below $2 a day %	Poverty gap at $2 a day %
Albania	75.5	120.8	2005	<2	<0.5	7.9	1.5	2008	<2	<0.5	4.3	0.9
Algeria	48.4[c]	77.5[c]	1988	7.6	1.2	24.6	6.7	1995	6.8	1.4	23.6	6.5
Angola	88.1	141.0		..	..	..	..	2000	54.3	29.9	70.2	42.4
Argentina	1.7	2.7	2009[d,e]	2.0	1.2	3.4	1.7	2010[d,e]	<2	0.7	<2	0.9
Armenia	245.2	392.4	2008	<2	<0.5	12.4	2.3	2010	2.5	<0.5	19.9	4.0
Azerbaijan	2,170.9	3,473.5	2001	6.3	1.1	27.1	6.8	2008	<2	<0.5	2.8	0.6
Bangladesh	31.9	51.0	2005	50.5	14.2	80.3	34.3	2010	43.3	11.2	76.5	30.4
Belarus	949.5	1,519.2	2008	<2	<0.5	<2	<0.5	2010	<2	<0.5	<2	<0.5
Belize	1.8[c]	2.9[c]	1998[f]	11.3	4.7	26.3	10.0	1999[f]	12.2	5.5	22.0	9.9
Benin	344.0	550.4		..	..	..	..	2003	47.3	15.7	75.3	33.5
Bhutan	23.1	36.9	2003	26.2	7.0	49.5	18.8	2007	10.2	1.8	29.8	8.5
Bolivia	3.2	5.1	2007[e]	13.1	6.6	24.7	10.9	2008[e]	15.6	8.6	24.9	13.1
Bosnia and Herzegovina	1.1	1.7	2004	<2	<0.5	<2	<0.5	2007	<2	<0.5	<2	<0.5
Botswana	4.2	6.8	1986	35.6	13.8	54.7	25.8	1994	31.2	11.0	49.4	22.3
Brazil	2.0	3.1	2008[f]	6.0	3.4	11.3	5.3	2009[f]	6.1	3.6	10.8	5.4
Bulgaria	0.9	1.5	2003	<2	<0.5	<2	<0.5	2007	<2	<0.5	<2	<0.5
Burkina Faso	303.0	484.8	2003	56.5	20.3	81.2	39.3	2009	44.6	14.7	72.6	31.7
Burundi	558.8	894.1	1998	86.4	47.3	95.4	64.1	2006	81.3	36.4	93.5	56.1
Cambodia	2,019.1	3,230.6	2008	22.8	4.9	53.3	17.4	2009	18.6	3.6	49.5	15.1
Cameroon	368.1	589.0	2001	10.8	2.3	32.5	9.5	2007	9.6	1.2	30.4	8.2
Cape Verde	97.7	156.3		..	..	..	..	2002	21.0	6.1	40.9	15.2
Central African Republic	384.3	614.9	2003	62.4	28.3	81.9	45.3	2008	62.8	31.3	80.1	46.8
Chad	409.5	655.1		..	..	..	..	2003	61.9	25.6	83.3	43.9
Chile	484.2	774.7	2006[f]	<2	0.5	3.2	1.1	2009[f]	<2	0.7	2.7	1.2
China	5.1[g]	8.2[g]	2008[h]	13.1	3.2	29.8	10.1	2009[h]	11.8	2.8	27.2	9.1
Colombia	1,489.7	2,383.5	2009[f]	9.7	4.7	18.5	8.2	2010[f]	8.2	3.8	15.8	6.8
Comoros	368.0	588.8		..	..	..	..	2004	46.1	20.8	65.0	34.2
Congo, Dem. Rep.	395.3	632.5		..	..	..	..	2006	87.7	52.8	95.2	67.6
Congo, Rep.	469.5	751.1		..	..	..	..	2005	54.1	22.8	74.4	38.8
Costa Rica	348.7[c]	557.9[c]	2008[f]	2.4	1.5	5.0	2.3	2009[f]	3.1	1.8	6.0	2.7
Côte d'Ivoire	407.3	651.6	2002	23.3	6.8	46.8	17.6	2008	23.8	7.5	46.3	17.8
Croatia	5.6	8.9[c]	2004	<2	<0.5	<2	<0.5	2008	<2	<0.5	<2	<0.5
Czech Republic	19.0	30.4	1993[e]	<2	<0.5	<2	<0.5	1996[e]	<2	<0.5	<2	<0.5
Djibouti	134.8	215.6		..	..	..	..	2002	18.8	5.3	41.2	14.6
Dominican Republic	25.5[c]	40.8[c]	2009[f]	3.0	0.7	10.0	2.7	2010[f]	2.2	<0.5	9.9	2.4
Ecuador	0.6	1.0	2009[f]	6.4	2.9	13.5	5.5	2010[f]	4.6	2.1	10.6	4.1
Egypt, Arab Rep.	2.5	4.0	2005	2.0	<0.5	18.5	3.5	2008	<2	<0.5	15.4	2.8
El Salvador	6.0[c]	9.6[c]	2008[f]	5.4	1.9	14.0	4.8	2009[f]	9.0	4.4	16.9	7.6
Estonia	11.0	17.7	2003	<2	<0.5	2.6	<0.5	2004	<2	<0.5	<2	0.5
Ethiopia	3.4	5.5	2005	39.0	9.6	77.6	28.9	2011	30.7	8.2	66.0	23.6
Fiji	1.9	3.1	2003	29.2	11.3	48.7	21.8	2009	5.9	1.1	22.9	6.0
Gabon	554.7	887.5		..	..	..	..	2005	4.8	0.9	19.6	5.0
Gambia, The	12.9	20.7	1998	65.6	33.8	81.2	49.1	2003	29.8	9.8	55.9	24.4
Georgia	1.0	1.6	2008	15.3	4.6	32.2	11.7	2010	18.0	5.8	35.6	13.7
Ghana	5,594.8	8,951.6	1998	39.1	14.4	63.3	28.5	2006	28.6	9.9	51.8	21.3
Guatemala	5.7[c]	9.1[c]	2004[f]	24.4	13.2	39.2	20.2	2006[f]	13.5	4.7	26.3	10.5
Guinea	1,849.5	2,959.1	2003	56.3	21.3	80.8	39.7	2007	43.3	15.0	69.6	31.0

	International poverty line in local currency		Population below international poverty lines[a]									
	$1.25 a day 2005	$2 a day 2005	Survey year[b]	Population below $1.25 a day %	Poverty gap at $1.25 a day %	Population below $2 a day %	Poverty gap at $2 a day %	Survey year[b]	Population below $1.25 a day %	Poverty gap at $1.25 a day %	Population below $2 a day %	Poverty gap at $2 a day %
Guinea-Bissau	355.3	568.6	1993	52.1	20.6	75.7	37.4	2002	48.9	16.6	78.0	34.9
Guyana	131.5[c]	210.3[c]	1993[e]	6.9	1.5	17.1	5.4	1998[e]	8.7	2.8	18.0	6.7
Haiti	24.2[c]	38.7[c]		..	..	..	..	2001	61.7	32.3	77.5	46.7
Honduras	12.1[c]	19.3[c]	2008[f]	21.4	11.8	32.6	17.5	2009[f]	17.9	9.4	29.8	14.9
Hungary	171.9	275.0	2004	<2	<0.5	<2	<0.5	2007	<2	<0.5	<2	<0.5
India	19.5[i]	31.2[i]	2005[h]	41.6	10.5	75.6	29.5	2010[h]	32.7	7.5	68.7	24.5
Indonesia	5,241.0[i]	8,385.7[i]	2009[h]	20.4	4.1	52.7	16.5	2010[h]	18.1	3.3	46.1	14.3
Iran, Islamic Rep.	3,393.5	5,429.6	1998	<2	<0.5	8.3	1.8	2005	<2	<0.5	8.0	1.8
Iraq	799.8	1,279.7		..	..	..	..	2007	2.8	<0.5	21.4	4.4
Jamaica	54.2[c]	86.7[c]	2002	<2	<0.5	8.5	1.5	2004	<2	<0.5	5.4	0.8
Jordan	0.6	1.0	2008	<2	<0.5	2.1	<0.5	2010	<2	<0.5	<2	<0.5
Kazakhstan	81.2	129.9	2008	<2	<0.5	<2	<0.5	2009	<2	<0.5	<2	<0.5
Kenya	40.9	65.4	1997	19.6	4.6	42.7	14.7	2005	43.4	16.9	67.2	31.8
Kyrgyz Republic	16.2	26.0	2009	6.2	1.4	21.7	6.0	2010	6.7	1.5	22.9	6.4
Lao PDR	4,677.0	7,483.2	2002	44.0	12.1	76.9	31.1	2008	33.9	9.0	66.0	24.8
Latvia	0.4	0.7	2008	<2	<0.5	<2	<0.5	2009	<2	<0.5	<2	<0.5
Lesotho	4.3	6.9	1994	46.2	25.6	59.7	36.1	2003	43.4	20.8	62.3	33.1
Liberia	0.6	1.0		..	..	..	..	2007	83.8	40.9	94.9	59.6
Lithuania	2.1	3.3	2004	<2	<0.5	<2	0.5	2008	<2	<0.5	<2	<0.5
Macedonia, FYR	29.5	47.2	2009	<2	<0.5	5.9	0.9	2010	<2	<0.5	6.9	1.2
Madagascar	945.5	1,512.8	2005	67.8	26.5	89.6	46.9	2010	81.3	43.3	92.6	60.1
Malawi	71.2	113.8	1998	83.1	46.0	93.5	62.3	2004	73.9	32.3	90.5	51.8
Malaysia	2.6	4.2	2007[e]	<2	<0.5	2.9	<0.5	2009[e]	<2	<0.5	2.3	<0.5
Maldives	358.3	573.5		..	..	..	..	2004	<2	<0.5	12.2	2.5
Mali	362.1	579.4	2006	51.4	18.8	77.1	36.5	2010	50.4	16.4	78.7	35.2
Mauritania	157.1	251.3	2004	25.4	7.0	52.6	19.2	2008	23.4	6.8	47.7	17.7
Mexico	9.6	15.3	2008	<2	<0.5	5.2	1.3	2010	<2	<0.5	4.5	1.0
Micronesia, Fed. Sts.	0.8[c]	1.3[c]		..	..	..	..	2000[d]	31.2	16.3	44.7	24.5
Moldova	6.0	9.7	2009	<2	<0.5	7.1	1.2	2010	<2	<0.5	4.4	0.7
Montenegro	0.6	1.0	2008	<2	<0.5	<2	<0.5	2010	<2	<0.5	<2	<0.5
Morocco	6.9	11.0	2001	6.3	0.9	24.3	6.3	2007	2.5	0.5	14.0	3.2
Mozambique	14,532.1	23,251.4	2003	74.7	35.4	90.0	53.6	2008	59.6	25.1	81.8	42.9
Namibia	6.3	10.1	1993[e]	49.1	24.6	62.2	36.5	2004[e]	31.9	9.5	51.1	21.8
Nepal	33.1	52.9	2003	53.1	18.4	77.3	36.6	2010	24.8	5.6	57.3	19.0
Nicaragua	9.1[c]	14.6[c]	2001[e]	14.4	3.7	34.4	11.5	2005[e]	11.9	2.4	31.7	9.6
Niger	334.2	534.7	2005	50.2	18.3	75.3	35.6	2008	43.6	12.4	75.2	30.8
Nigeria	98.2	157.2	2004	63.1	28.7	83.1	45.9	2010	68.0	33.7	84.5	50.2
Pakistan	25.9	41.4	2006	22.6	4.1	61.0	18.8	2008	21.0	3.5	60.2	17.9
Panama	0.8[c]	1.2[c]	2009[f]	5.9	1.8	14.6	4.9	2010[f]	6.6	2.1	13.8	5.1
Papua New Guinea	2.1[c]	3.4[c]		..	..	..	..	1996	35.8	12.3	57.4	25.5
Paraguay	2,659.7	4,255.6	2009[f]	7.6	3.2	14.2	6.0	2010[f]	7.2	3.0	13.2	5.7
Peru	2.1	3.3	2009[f]	5.5	1.6	14.0	4.6	2010[f]	4.9	1.3	12.7	4.1
Philippines	30.2	48.4	2006	22.6	5.5	45.0	16.4	2009	18.4	3.7	41.5	13.8
Poland	2.7	4.3	2009	<2	<0.5	<2	<0.5	2010	<2	<0.5	<2	<0.5
Romania	2.1	3.4	2009	<2	<0.5	<2	0.5	2010	<2	<0.5	<2	<0.5
Russian Federation	16.7	26.8	2008	<2	<0.5	<2	<0.5	2009	<2	<0.5	<2	<0.5
Rwanda	295.9	473.5	2006	72.1	34.8	87.4	52.2	2011	63.2	26.6	82.4	44.6

Poverty rates

	International poverty line in local currency		Population below international poverty lines[a]									
	$1.25 a day 2005	$2 a day 2005	Survey year[b]	Population below $1.25 a day %	Poverty gap at $1.25 a day %	Population below $2 a day %	Poverty gap at $2 a day %	Survey year[b]	Population below $1.25 a day %	Poverty gap at $1.25 a day %	Population below $2 a day %	Poverty gap at $2 a day %
São Tomé and Príncipe	7,953.9	12,726.3		..	..	..	..	2001	28.2	7.9	54.2	20.6
Senegal	372.8	596.5	2005	33.5	10.8	60.4	24.7	2011	29.6	9.1	55.2	21.9
Serbia	42.9	68.6	2009	<2	<0.5	<2	<0.5	2010	<2	<0.5	<2	<0.5
Seychelles	5.6[c]	9.0[c]	2000	<2	<0.5	<2	<0.5	2007	<2	<0.5	<2	<0.5
Sierra Leone	1,745.3	2,792.4	1990	62.8	44.8	75.0	54.0	2003	53.4	20.3	76.1	37.5
Slovak Republic	23.5	37.7	2008[e]	<2	<0.5	<2	<0.5	2009[e]	<2	<0.5	<2	<0.5
Slovenia	198.2	317.2	2003	<2	<0.5	<2	<0.5	2004	<2	<0.5	<2	<0.5
South Africa	5.7	9.1	2006	17.4	3.3	35.7	12.3	2009	13.8	2.3	31.3	10.2
Sri Lanka	50.0	80.1	2007	7.0	1.0	29.1	7.4	2010	4.1	0.7	23.9	5.4
St. Lucia	2.4[c]	3.8[c]		..	..	..	..	1995	20.9	7.2	40.6	15.5
Sudan	154.4	247.0		..	..	..	..	2009	19.8	5.5	44.1	15.4
Suriname	2.3[c]	3.7[c]		..	..	..	..	1999	15.5	5.9	27.2	11.7
Swaziland	4.7	7.5	2001	62.9	29.4	81.0	45.8	2010	40.6	16.0	60.4	29.3
Syrian Arab Republic	30.8	49.3		..	..	..	..	2004	<2	<0.5	16.9	3.3
Tajikistan	1.2	1.9	2007	14.7	4.4	37.0	12.2	2009	6.6	1.2	27.7	7.0
Tanzania	603.1	964.9	2000	84.6	41.6	95.3	60.3	2007	67.9	28.1	87.9	47.5
Thailand	21.8	34.9	2009[j]	<2	<0.5	4.6	0.8	2010[j]	<2	<0.5	4.1	0.7
Togo	352.8	564.5	2006	38.7	11.4	69.3	27.9	2011	28.2	8.8	52.7	20.9
Trinidad and Tobago	5.8[c]	9.2[c]	1988[e]	<2	<0.5	8.6	1.9	1992[e]	4.2	1.1	13.5	3.9
Tunisia	0.9	1.4	2005	<2	<0.5	8.1	1.8	2010	<2	<0.5	4.3	1.1
Turkey	1.3	2.0	2008	<2	<0.5	4.2	0.7	2010	<2	<0.5	4.7	1.4
Turkmenistan	5,961.1[c]	9,537.7[c]	1993[e]	63.5	25.8	85.7	44.9	1998[e]	24.8	7.0	49.7	18.4
Uganda	930.8	1,489.2	2006	51.5	19.1	75.6	36.4	2009	38.0	12.2	64.7	27.4
Ukraine	2.1	3.4	2009	<2	<0.5	<2	<0.5	2010	<2	<0.5	<2	<0.5
Uruguay	19.1	30.6	2009[f]	<2	<0.5	<2	<0.5	2010[f]	<2	<0.5	<2	<0.5
Venezuela, RB	1,563.9	2,502.2	2005[f]	13.4	8.2	21.9	11.6	2006[f]	6.6	3.7	12.9	5.9
Vietnam	7,399.9	11,839.8	2006	21.4	5.3	48.1	16.3	2008	16.9	3.8	43.4	13.5
West Bank and Gaza	2.7[c]	4.3[c]	2007	<2	<0.5	2.5	0.5	2009	<2	<0.5	<2	<0.5
Yemen, Rep.	113.8	182.1	1998	12.9	3.0	36.4	11.1	2005	17.5	4.2	46.6	14.8
Zambia	3,537.9	5,660.7	2004	64.3	32.8	81.5	48.3	2006	68.5	37.0	82.6	51.8

a. Based on nominal per capita consumption averages and distributions estimated parametrically from grouped household survey data, unless otherwise noted. b. Refers to the year in which the underlying household survey data were collected or, when the data collection period bridged two calendar years, the year in which most of the data were collected. c. Based on purchasing power parity (PPP) dollars imputed using regression. d. Covers urban areas only. e. Based on per capita income averages and distribution data estimated parametrically from grouped household survey data. f. Estimated nonparametrically from nominal income per capita distributions based on unit-record household survey data. g. PPP conversion factor based on urban prices. h. Population-weighted average of urban and rural estimates. i. Based on benchmark national PPP estimate rescaled to account for cost-of-living differences in urban and rural areas. j. Estimated nonparametrically from nominal consumption per capita distributions based on unit-record household survey data.

Trends in poverty indicators by region, 1990–2015

Region	1990	1993	1996	1999	2002	2005	2008	2010 provisional	2015 projection	Trend, 1990–2010
Share of population living on less than 2005 PPP $1.25 a day (%)										
East Asia & Pacific	56.2	50.7	35.9	35.6	27.6	17.1	14.3	12.5	5.5	
Europe & Central Asia	1.9	2.9	3.9	3.8	2.3	1.3	0.5	0.7	0.4	
Latin America & Caribbean	12.2	11.4	11.1	11.9	11.9	8.7	6.5	5.5	4.9	
Middle East & North Africa	5.8	4.8	4.8	5.0	4.2	3.5	2.7	2.4	2.6	
South Asia	53.8	51.7	48.6	45.1	44.3	39.4	36.0	31.0	23.2	
Sub-Saharan Africa	56.5	59.4	58.1	57.9	55.7	52.3	49.2	48.5	42.3	
Total	43.1	41.0	34.8	34.1	30.8	25.1	22.7	20.6	15.5	
People living on less than 2005 PPP $1.25 a day (millions)										
East Asia & Pacific	926	871	640	656	523	332	284	251	115	
Europe & Central Asia	9	14	18	18	11	6	2	3	2	
Latin America & Caribbean	53	53	54	60	63	48	37	32	30	
Middle East & North Africa	13	12	12	14	12	10	9	8	9	
South Asia	617	632	631	619	640	598	571	507	406	
Sub-Saharan Africa	290	330	349	376	390	395	399	414	408	
Total	1,908	1,910	1,704	1,743	1,639	1,389	1,302	1,215	970	
Regional distribution of people living on less than $1.25 a day (% of total population living on less than $1.25 a day)										
East Asia & Pacific	48.5	45.6	37.6	37.6	31.9	23.9	21.8	20.7	11.8	
Europe & Central Asia	0.5	0.7	1.1	1.0	0.6	0.5	0.2	0.3	0.2	
Latin America & Caribbean	2.8	2.7	3.1	3.4	3.8	3.4	2.9	2.7	3.1	
Middle East & North Africa	0.7	0.6	0.7	0.8	0.7	0.8	0.7	0.7	1.0	
South Asia	32.3	33.1	37.0	35.5	39.1	43.1	43.8	41.7	41.9	
Sub-Saharan Africa	15.2	17.3	20.5	21.6	23.8	28.4	30.7	34.1	42.1	
Average daily consumption or income of people living on less than 2005 PPP $1.25 a day (2005 PPP $)										
East Asia & Pacific	0.83	0.85	0.89	0.87	0.89	0.95	0.95	0.97	..	
Europe & Central Asia	0.90	0.90	0.91	0.92	0.93	0.88	0.88	0.85	..	
Latin America & Caribbean	0.71	0.69	0.68	0.67	0.65	0.63	0.62	0.60	..	
Middle East & North Africa	1.02	1.02	1.01	1.01	1.01	0.99	0.97	0.96	..	
South Asia	0.88	0.89	0.91	0.91	0.92	0.94	0.95	0.96	..	
Sub-Saharan Africa	0.69	0.68	0.69	0.69	0.70	0.71	0.71	0.71	..	
Total	0.82	0.83	0.85	0.84	0.85	0.87	0.87	0.87	..	
Survey coverage (% of total population represented by underlying survey data)										
East Asia & Pacific	92.4	93.3	93.7	93.4	93.5	93.2	93.6	93.5	..	
Europe & Central Asia	81.5	87.3	97.1	93.9	96.3	94.7	89.9	85.3	..	
Latin America & Caribbean	94.9	91.8	95.9	97.7	97.5	95.9	94.5	86.9	..	
Middle East & North Africa	76.8	65.3	81.7	70.0	21.5	85.7	46.7	30.8	..	
South Asia	96.5	98.2	98.1	20.1	98.0	98.0	97.9	94.5	..	
Sub-Saharan Africa	46.0	68.8	68.0	53.1	65.7	82.7	81.7	64.1	..	
Total	86.4	89.4	91.6	68.2	87.8	93.0	90.2	84.7	..	

Source: World Bank PovcalNet.

Poverty rates

The World Bank produced its first global poverty estimates for developing countries for *World Development Report 1990: Poverty* (World Bank 1990) using household survey data for 22 countries (Ravallion, Datt, and van de Walle 1991). Since then there has been considerable expansion in the number of countries that field household income and expenditure surveys. The World Bank's Development Research Group maintains a database that is updated regularly as new survey data become available (and thus may contain more recent data or revisions that are not incorporated into the table) and conducts a major reassessment of progress against poverty about every three years.

This year the database has been updated with global and regional extreme poverty estimates for 2010, which are provisional due to low coverage in household survey data availability for recent years (2008–12). The projections to 2015 of poverty rates use the 2010 provisional estimates as a baseline and assume that average household income or consumption will grow in line with the aggregate economic projections reported in this year's *Global Monitoring Report* (World Bank 2013) but that inequality within countries will remain unchanged. This methodology was first used and described in the *Global Economic Prospects* report (World Bank 2000). Estimates of the number of people living in extreme poverty are based on population projections in the World Bank's HealthStats database (http://datatopics.worldbank.org/hnp).

PovcalNet (http://iresearch.worldbank.org/PovcalNet) is an interactive computational tool that allows users to replicate these internationally comparable $1.25 and $2 a day global, regional and country-level poverty estimates and to compute poverty measures for custom country groupings and for different poverty lines. The Poverty and Equity Data portal (http://povertydata.worldbank.org/poverty/home) provides access to the database and user-friendly dashboards with graphs and interactive maps that visualize trends in key poverty and inequality indicators for different regions and countries. The country dashboards display trends in poverty measures based on the national poverty lines (see online table 2.7) alongside the internationally comparable estimates in the table, produced from and consistent with PovcalNet.

Data availability

The World Bank's internationally comparable poverty monitoring database now draws on income or detailed consumption data collected from interviews with 1.23 million randomly sampled households through more than 850 household surveys collected by national statistical offices in nearly 130 countries. Despite progress in the last decade, the challenges of measuring poverty remain. The timeliness, frequency, quality, and comparability of household surveys need to increase substantially, particularly in the poorest countries. The availability and quality of poverty monitoring data remain low in small states, fragile situations, and low-income countries and even some middle-income countries.

The low frequency and lack of comparability of the data available in some countries create uncertainty over the magnitude of poverty reduction. The table on trends in poverty indicators reports the percentage of the regional and global population represented by household survey samples collected during the reference year or during the two preceding or two subsequent years (in other words, within a five-year window centered on the reference year). Data coverage in Sub-Saharan Africa and the Middle East and North Africa remains low and variable. The need to improve household survey programs for monitoring poverty is clearly urgent. But institutional, political, and financial obstacles continue to limit data collection, analysis, and public access.

Data quality

Besides the frequency and timeliness of survey data, other data quality issues arise in measuring household living standards. The surveys ask detailed questions on sources of income and how it was spent, which must be carefully recorded by trained personnel. Income is generally more difficult to measure accurately, and consumption comes closer to the notion of living standards. And income can vary over time even if living standards do not. But consumption data are not always available: the latest estimates reported here use consumption for about two-thirds of countries.

However, even similar surveys may not be strictly comparable because of differences in timing, sampling frames, or the quality and training of enumerators. Comparisons of countries at different levels of development also pose a potential problem because of differences in the relative importance of the consumption of nonmarket goods. The local market value of all consumption in kind (including own production, particularly important in underdeveloped rural economies) should be included in total consumption expenditure, but may not be. Most survey data now include valuations for consumption or income from own production, but valuation methods vary.

The statistics reported here are based on consumption data or, when unavailable, on income data. Analysis of some 20 countries for which both were available from the same surveys found income to yield a higher mean than consumption but also higher inequality. When poverty measures based on consumption and income were compared, the two effects roughly cancelled each other out: there was no significant statistical difference.

Invariably some sampled households do not participate in surveys because they refuse to do so or because nobody is at home during the interview visit. This is referred to as "unit nonresponse" and is distinct from "item nonresponse," which occurs when some of the sampled respondents participate but refuse to answer certain questions, such as those pertaining to income or consumption. To the extent that survey nonresponse is random, there is no concern regarding biases in survey-based inferences; the sample will still be representative of the population. However, households with different income might not be equally likely to respond. Richer households may be less likely to participate because of the high opportunity cost of their time or concerns about intrusion in their affairs. It is conceivable that the poorest can likewise be underrepresented; some are homeless or nomadic and hard to reach in standard household survey designs, and some may be physically or socially isolated and thus less likely to be interviewed. This can bias both poverty and inequality measurement if not corrected for (Korinek, Mistiaen, and Ravallion 2007).

International poverty lines

International comparisons of poverty estimates entail both conceptual and practical problems. Countries have different definitions of poverty, and consistent comparisons across countries can be difficult. Local poverty lines tend to have higher purchasing power in rich countries, where more generous standards are used, than in poor countries. Poverty measures based on an international poverty line attempt to hold the real value of the poverty line constant across countries, as is done when making comparisons over time. Since *World Development Report 1990* the World Bank has aimed to apply a common standard in measuring extreme poverty, anchored to what *poverty* means in the world's poorest countries. The welfare of people living in different countries can be measured on a common scale by adjusting for differences in the purchasing power of currencies. The commonly used $1 a day standard, measured in 1985 international prices and adjusted to local currency using purchasing power parities (PPPs), was chosen for *World Development Report 1990* because it was typical of the poverty lines in low-income countries at the time. Early editions of *World Development Indicators* used PPPs from the Penn World Tables to convert values in local currency to equivalent purchasing power measured in U.S dollars. Later editions used 1993 consumption PPP estimates produced by the World Bank.

International poverty lines were recently revised using the new data on PPPs compiled in the 2005 round of the International Comparison Program, along with data from an expanded set of household income and expenditure surveys. The new extreme poverty line is set at $1.25 a day in 2005 PPP terms, which represents the mean of the poverty lines found in the poorest 15 countries ranked by per capita consumption. The new poverty line maintains the same standard for extreme poverty—the poverty line typical of the poorest countries in the world—but updates it using the latest information on the cost of living in developing countries. PPP exchange rates are used to estimate global poverty because they take into account the local prices of goods and services not traded internationally. But PPP rates were designed for comparing aggregates from national accounts, not for making international poverty comparisons. As a result, there is no certainty that an international poverty line measures the same degree of need or deprivation across countries. So-called poverty PPPs, designed to compare the consumption of the poorest people in the world, might provide a better basis for comparison of poverty across countries. Work on these measures is ongoing.

Definitions

• **International poverty line in local currency** is the international poverty lines of $1.25 and $2.00 a day in 2005 prices, converted to local currency using the PPP conversion factors estimated by the International Comparison Program. • **Survey year** is the year in which the underlying data were collected or, when the data collection period bridged two calendar years, the year in which most of the data were collected. • **Population below $1.25 a day** and **population below $2 a day** are the percentages of the population living on less than $1.25 a day and $2 a day at 2005 international prices. As a result of revisions in PPP exchange rates, consumer price indexes, or welfare aggregates, poverty rates for individual countries cannot be compared with poverty rates reported in earlier editions. The PovcalNet online database and tool always contain the most recent full time series of comparable country data. • **Poverty gap** is the mean shortfall from the poverty line (counting the nonpoor as having zero shortfall), expressed as a percentage of the poverty line. This measure reflects the depth of poverty as well as its incidence.

Data sources

The poverty measures are prepared by the World Bank's Development Research Group. The international poverty lines are based on nationally representative primary household surveys conducted by national statistical offices or by private agencies under the supervision of government or international agencies and obtained from government statistical offices and World Bank Group country departments. For details on data sources and methods used in deriving the World Bank's latest estimates, see http://iresearch.worldbank.org/PovcalNet/index.htm.

References

Chen, Shaohua, and Martin Ravallion. 2011. "The Developing World Is Poorer Than We Thought, But No Less Successful in the Fight Against Poverty." *Quarterly Journal of Economics* 125(4): 1577–1625.

Korinek, Anton, Johan A. Mistiaen, and Martin Ravallion. 2007. "An Econometric Method of Correcting for Unit Nonresponse Bias in Surveys." *Journal of Econometrics* 136: 213–35.

Ravallion, Martin, Guarav Datt, and Dominique van de Walle. 1991. "Quantifying Absolute Poverty in the Developing World." *Review of Income and Wealth* 37(4): 345–61.

Ravallion, Martin, Shaohua Chen, and Prem Sangraula. 2009. "Dollar a Day Revisited." *World Bank Economic Review* 23(2): 163–84.

World Bank. 1990. *World Development Report 1990: Poverty.* Washington, DC.

———. 2000. *Global Economic Prospects and the Developing Countries.* Washington, DC.

———. 2008. *Poverty Data: A Supplement to World Development Indicators 2008.* Washington, DC.

———. 2013. *Global Monitoring Report: Rural-Urban Dynamics and the Millennium Development Goals.* Washington, DC.

PEOPLE

Front   User guide   World view   People   Environment

The indicators in the *People* section present demographic trends and forecasts alongside indicators of education, health, jobs, social protection, poverty, and the distribution of income. Together they provide a multidimensional portrait of human development.

Data updates in this edition include provisional estimates of global and regional extreme poverty rates for 2010—measured as the proportion of the population living on less than $1.25 a day. The availability, frequency, and quality of poverty monitoring data remain low, especially in small states and in countries and territories with fragile situations. While estimates may change marginally as additional country data become available, it is now clear that the first Millennium Development Goal target—cutting the global extreme poverty rate to half its 1990 level—was achieved before the 2015 target date. In 1990, the benchmark year for the Millennium Development Goals, the extreme poverty rate was 43.1 percent. Estimates for 2010 show that the extreme poverty rate had fallen to 20.6 percent.

In addition to extreme poverty rates, the *People* section includes many other indicators used to monitor the Millennium Development Goals. Following the adoption of the Millennium Declaration by the United Nations General Assembly in 2000, various international agencies including the World Bank resolved to invest in using high-quality harmonized data to monitor the Millennium Development Goals. These efforts range from providing technical and financial assistance to strengthen country statistical systems to fostering international collaboration through participation in the United Nations Inter-Agency and Expert Group on the Millennium Development Goal Indicators and several thematic inter-agency groups. These forums bring together agency subject matter specialists with leading academic and local experts. Successful thematic inter-agency efforts have improved estimates on child mortality, child malnutrition, as well as maternal mortality, one of the most challenging indicators to measure.

For 2013 the *People* section includes improved child malnutrition indicators produced by the United Nations Children's Fund, the World Health Organization, and the World Bank using a harmonized dataset and the same statistical methodology to estimate global, regional, and income group aggregates.

Another result is the improvement in monitoring HIV prevalence. Initial efforts relied solely on country surveillance systems that collected data from pregnant women who attended sentinel antenatal clinics. Now the methodology measuring this indicator uses all available information—including blood test data collected through nationally representative sample surveys—and the models account for the effects of antiretroviral therapy and urbanization (see *About the data* for online table 2.20).

In addition to providing insights into differences between countries and between groups of countries, the *People* section includes indicators disaggregated by location and by socioeconomic and demographic strata within countries, such as gender, age, and wealth quintile. These data provide a deeper perspective on the disparities within countries. New indicators for 2013 include sex-disaggregated data on the under-five mortality rate, sex-disaggregated youth labor force participation rates, and numerous indicators from the World Bank's Atlas of Social Protection Indicators of Resilience and Equity database.

Highlights

East Asia & Pacific: Narrowing gaps in access to improved sanitation facilities and water sources

Share of population with access (%)
■ To improved sanitation facilities ■ To improved water sources

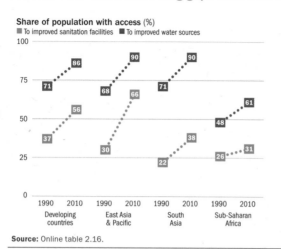

Source: Online table 2.16.

During the past 20 years the share of the developing world's population with access to improved sanitation facilities and water sources has risen substantially. East Asia and Pacific has made above-average progress on improving both and narrowing the gap between them, driven by a rapid expansion in access to improved sanitation from 30 percent in 1990 to 66 percent in 2010. In South Asia progress on access to an improved water source was almost on par with East Asia and Pacific, but access to improved sanitation facilities remains very low. Indeed, the region fares only marginally better than Sub-Saharan Africa, which progressed substantially slower over the past two decades. But both regions made progress on expanding the share of the population with access to an improved water source.

Europe & Central Asia: Variation in prevalence of underweight children

Prevalence of child malnutrition, underweight, most recent year, 2005–11 (% of children under age 5)

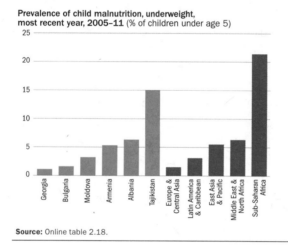

Source: Online table 2.18.

Malnourishment in children has been linked to poverty, low levels of education, and poor access to health services. It increases the risk of death, inhibits cognitive development, and can adversely affect health status during adulthood. Adequate nutrition is a cornerstone for development, health, and the survival of current and future generations. Europe and Central Asia has the lowest prevalence (1.5 percent) of underweight children among developing regions, but there is substantial variation across countries. At 3.2 percent, prevalence in Moldova is more like that in Latin America and the Caribbean countries; at 5.3 percent, prevalence in Armenia is more like that in East Asia and Pacific countries; and at 6.3 percent, prevalence in Albania is more like that in Middle East and North African countries. Tajikistan, a low-income country, at 15 percent has the highest proportion of underweight children in the region.

Latin America & Caribbean: Income inequality falling but remains among the world's highest

Gini coefficient, most recent value, 2000–11

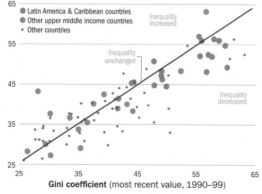

Gini coefficient (most recent value, 1990–99)

Source: Online table 2.9 and World Bank PovcalNet.

The Gini coefficient, a common indicator of income inequality, measures how much the per capita income distribution within a country deviates from perfect equality. (A Gini coefficient of 0 represents perfect equality, and a value of 100 perfect inequality.) Trends in developing countries over the past two decades suggest that many countries have become less unequal, but trends differ by region and by income. Inequality in Latin America and the Caribbean fell notably in almost all upper middle-income countries but remains among the highest worldwide. The Gini coefficient is higher than the Latin America and the Caribbean average in only two other upper middle-income countries and in only a few low- and lower middle-income countries.

Front | User guide | World view | People | Environment

Middle East & North Africa: Many educated women are not participating in the labor force

More than 70 percent of girls in the Middle East and North Africa attend secondary school (higher than most developing countries), but labor force participation rates have stagnated at around 20 percent since 1990 (lower than most developing countries). Eight of the ten countries with the largest gap between their labor force participation rate and secondary enrollment ratio are in the Middle East and North Africa. (Costa Rica and Sri Lanka are the only countries in the top 10 not from the region.) Morocco and the Republic of Yemen have the smallest gap, but they also have the lowest secondary enrollment ratio. In addition to whether women participate in economic activities, where and in what condition women work are also important. The region also has the largest gender gap in the share of vulnerable employment (see online table 2.4).

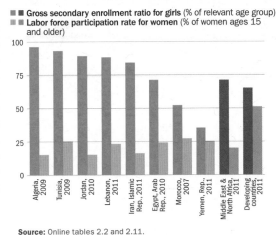

■ ■ **Gross secondary enrollment ratio for girls** (% of relevant age group)
■ ■ **Labor force participation rate for women** (% of women ages 15 and older)

Source: Online tables 2.2 and 2.11.

South Asia: In India more girls than boys die before their fifth birthday

The ratio of girls' to boys' under-five mortality rate varies across developing countries, but on average it is 0.96. East Asia and Pacific has the largest variation among developing regions. At one extreme is Palau, where mortality rates for boys are two-thirds higher than that for girls. Biologically, boys are more vulnerable than girls, so under-five mortality rates are usually higher for boys than girls. This biological advantage can be reversed, however, by socioeconomic factors such as gender inequalities in nutrition and medical care or discrimination against girls. India and the Solomon Islands are the only developing countries where more girls than boys die before their fifth birthday. In India under-five mortality rates for girls and boys have improved, but the ratio of girls' to boys' under-five deaths has stayed at around 1.1 since 1990.

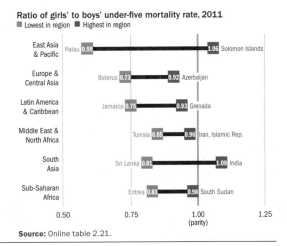

Ratio of girls' to boys' under-five mortality rate, 2011
■ Lowest in region ■ Highest in region

Source: Online table 2.21.

Sub-Saharan Africa: Different demographic transition paths at varying speeds

Today, one of every nine children in Sub-Saharan Africa dies before their fifth birthday, and fertility rates there remain higher than any-where else in the developing world. Sub-Saharan countries pro-gressed over the past four decades, but they are moving along dif-ferent paths at varying speeds. Gabon, ahead of the curve, had the under-five mortality and total fertility rates in 1980 that the region has today. Niger made little progress between 1970 and 1990 but has since seen rapid improvements in its under-five mortality rate and a marginal decline in its fertility rate. In 1970 Côte d'Ivoire had an average mortality rate but a high fertility rate. Its mortality rate declined quickly until 1980, thereafter its fertility rate declined rap-idly and overtook the region by 2010. Mali, which had the highest under-five mortality rate in 1970, took until 2010 to reach the rate the region passed in 1990.

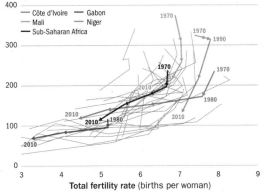

Under-five mortality rate (per 1,000 live births)

Source: Online table 2.21.

2 People

	Prevalence of child malnutrition, underweight	Under-five mortality rate	Maternal mortality ratio	Adolescent fertility rate	Prevalence of HIV	Primary completion rate	Youth literacy rate	Labor force participation rate	Vulnerable employment	Unemployment	Female legislators, senior officials, and managers
			Modeled estimate	births per 1,000 women ages 15–19	% of population ages 15–49	% of relevant age group	% ages 15–24	% ages 15 and older	Unpaid family workers and own-account workers % of total employment	% of total labor force	% of total
	% of children under age 5	per 1,000 live births	per 100,000 live births								
	2005–11ª	2011	2010	2011	2011	2011	2005–11ª	2011	2007–11ª	2007–11ª	2007–11ª
Afghanistan	..	101	460	103	<0.1	..	..	49	..	..	..
Albania	6.3	14	27	16	..	..	99	60	..	13.8	..
Algeria	3.7	30	97	6	..	94	92	44	..	10.0	..
American Samoa	..	..	..	..	..	..	..	..	..	..	..
Andorra	..	3	..	..	..	63	..	..	..	..	..
Angola	15.6	158	450	153	2.1	..	73	70	..	..	..
Antigua and Barbuda	..	8	..	..	..	98	..	..	..	..	..
Argentina	2.3	14	77	55	0.4	..	99	61	19	7.2	..
Armenia	5.3	18	30	34	0.2	83	100	59	38	28.6	22
Aruba	..	..	..	28	..	..	99	..	4	5.7	40
Australia	..	5	7	13	0.2	..	..	66	9	5.1	37
Austria	..	4	4	10	0.4	..	..	61	9	4.1	27
Azerbaijan	8.4	45	43	32	<0.1	93	100	65	55	5.4	7
Bahamas, The	..	16	47	29	2.8	..	..	74	..	13.7	52
Bahrain	..	10	20	15	..	..	100	71	2	..	..
Bangladesh	41.3	46	240	70	<0.1	..	77	71	..	5.0	..
Barbados	..	20	51	41	0.9	111	..	70	..	11.2	47
Belarus	1.3	6	4	21	0.4	104	100	56	..	..	..
Belgium	..	4	8	12	0.3	..	..	54	10	7.1	30
Belize	4.9	17	53	72	2.3	110	..	65	..	8.2	..
Benin	20.2	106	350	100	1.2	75	55	73	..	..	..
Bermuda	..	..	..	..	..	..	..	..	..	..	..
Bhutan	12.7	54	180	46	0.3	103ᵇ	74	72	71	3.1	27
Bolivia	4.5	51	190	75	0.3	..	99	72	55	3.4	29
Bosnia and Herzegovina	1.6	8	8	14	..	76	100	46	25	27.6	..
Botswana	11.2	26	160	45	23.4	..	95	77	..	..	..
Brazil	2.2	16	56	76	0.3	..	98	70	25	8.3	36
Brunei Darussalam	..	7	24	23	..	120	100	66	..	..	..
Bulgaria	..	12	11	38	<0.1	..	98	54	9	11.2	37
Burkina Faso	26.0	146	300	119	1.1	..	39	84	..	3.3	..
Burundi	35.2	139	800	20	1.3	62	78	83	..	..	..
Cambodia	29.0	43	250	35	0.6	90	87	83	69	0.2	21
Cameroon	16.6	127	690	118	4.6	78	83	71	76	3.8	..
Canada	..	6	12	12	0.3	..	..	67	..	7.4	36
Cape Verde	..	21	79	72	1.0	95	98	67	..	..	..
Cayman Islands	..	..	..	..	..	..	..	99	..	4.0	44
Central African Republic	28.0	164	890	100	4.6	43	65	79	..	..	..
Chad	..	169	1,100	143	3.1	38	47	72	..	..	..
Channel Islands	..	..	..	9	..	..	..	..	..	..	..
Chile	0.5	9	25	56	0.5	..	99	60	24	7.1	..
China	3.4	15	37	9	<0.1	..	99	74	..	4.1	..
Hong Kong SAR, China	..	..	..	4	..	91	..	59	7	3.4	32
Macao SAR, China	..	..	..	4	..	..	100	72	4	2.6	31
Colombia	3.4	18	92	69	0.5	112	98	67	49	11.6	..
Comoros	..	79	280	52	<0.1	..	86	58	..	..	..
Congo, Dem. Rep.	28.2	168	540	177	..	65	..	71	..	..	..
Congo, Rep.	11.8	99	560	114	3.3	..	80	71	..	..	..

	Prevalence of child malnutrition, underweight	Under-five mortality rate	Maternal mortality ratio	Adolescent fertility rate	Prevalence of HIV	Primary completion rate	Youth literacy rate	Labor force participation rate	Vulnerable employment Unpaid family workers and own-account workers	Unemployment	Female legislators, senior officials, and managers
	% of children under age 5	per 1,000 live births	Modeled estimate per 100,000 live births	births per 1,000 women ages 15–19	% of population ages 15–49	% of relevant age group	% ages 15–24	% ages 15 and older	% of total employment	% of total labor force	% of total
	2005–11[a]	2011	2010	2011	2011	2011	2005–11[a]	2011	2007–11[a]	2007–11[a]	2007–11[a]
Costa Rica	1.1	10	40	63	0.3	99	98	63	20	7.7	35
Côte d'Ivoire	29.4	115	400	110	3.0	59	67	67	..	..	..
Croatia	..	5	17	13	<0.1	..	100	53	18	13.4	25
Cuba	1.3	6	73	44	0.2	99	100	57	..	2.5	..
Curaçao	..	..	..	..	..	..	..	..	..	..	..
Cyprus	..	3	10	6	..	..	100	65	14	7.7	14
Czech Republic	..	4	5	10	<0.1	..	..	59	14	6.7	26
Denmark	..	4	12	5	0.2	..	..	64	6	7.6	28
Djibouti	29.6	90	200	20	1.4	57[b]	..	52	..	..	..
Dominica	..	12	..	..	..	94	..	..	..	..	..
Dominican Republic	3.4	25	150	105	0.7	92	97	65	37	12.4	31
Ecuador	..	23	110	81	0.4	112	99	68	42	4.2	..
Egypt, Arab Rep.	6.8	21	66	42	<0.1	..	88	49	27	9.0	11
El Salvador	6.6	15	81	77	0.6	101	96	62	38	7.0	29
Equatorial Guinea	..	118	240	116	4.7	52	98	87	..	..	..
Eritrea	..	68	240	56	0.6	..	89	85	..	..	..
Estonia	..	4	2	18	1.3	..	100	62	5	12.5	36
Ethiopia	29.2	77	350	53	1.4	58	55	84	..	..	..
Faeroe Islands	..	..	..	..	..	..	..	..	..	..	..
Fiji	..	16	26	43	<0.1	103	..	60	..	8.6	..
Finland	..	3	5	9	<0.1	..	..	60	9	7.7	32
France	..	4	8	6	0.4	..	..	56	7	9.3	39
French Polynesia	..	..	..	49	..	..	..	58	..	11.7	..
Gabon	..	66	230	83	5.0	..	98	61	..	..	..
Gambia, The	15.8	101	360	69	1.5	66	67	78	..	..	..
Georgia	1.1	21	67	41	0.2	..	100	64	63	15.1	34
Germany	1.1	4	7	7	0.2	..	..	60	7	5.9	30
Ghana	14.3	78	350	64	1.5	99[b]	81	69	..	..	..
Greece	1.1	4	3	10	0.2	..	99	55	29	17.7	23
Greenland	..	..	..	..	..	..	..	..	..	..	..
Grenada	..	13	24	37	..	..	..	..	..	..	..
Guam	..	..	..	50	..	..	..	61	..	..	..
Guatemala	13.0	30	120	103	0.8	87	68	..	..	4.1	..
Guinea	20.8	126	610	138	1.4	..	63	72	..	..	..
Guinea-Bissau	17.2	161	790	99	2.5	..	72	73	..	..	..
Guyana	11.1	36	280	57	1.1	85	..	60	..	21.0	..
Haiti	18.9	70	350	42	1.8	..	72	65	..	..	..
Honduras	8.6	21	100	87	..	101	95	62	53	4.8	..
Hungary	..	6	21	14	<0.1	..	99	51	7	10.9	40
Iceland	..	3	5	12	0.3	..	..	75	8	7.1	40
India	43.5	61	200	77	..	..	81	56	81	3.5	14
Indonesia	18.6	32	220	43	0.3	..	99	68	57	6.6	22
Iran, Islamic Rep.	..	25	21	26	0.2	106	99	45	42	10.5	13
Iraq	7.1	38	63	88	..	..	83	42	..	..	..
Ireland	..	4	6	11	0.3	..	..	61	12	14.4	33
Isle of Man	..	..	..	..	..	..	..	..	..	..	..
Israel	..	4	7	14	0.2	..	..	57	7	5.6	32

2 People

	Prevalence of child malnutrition, underweight % of children under age 5 2005–11[a]	Under-five mortality rate per 1,000 live births 2011	Maternal mortality ratio Modeled estimate per 100,000 live births 2010	Adolescent fertility rate births per 1,000 women ages 15–19 2011	Prevalence of HIV % of population ages 15–49 2011	Primary completion rate % of relevant age group 2011	Youth literacy rate % ages 15–24 2005–11[a]	Labor force participation rate % ages 15 and older 2011	Vulnerable employment Unpaid family workers and own-account workers % of total employment 2007–11[a]	Unemployment % of total labor force 2007–11[a]	Female legislators, senior officials, and managers % of total 2007–11[a]
Italy	..	4	4	5	0.4	..	100	48	18	8.4	25
Jamaica	1.9	18	110	71	1.8	..	95	64	37	12.7	..
Japan	..	3	5	6	<0.1	..	..	60	11	4.5	..
Jordan	1.9	21	63	24	..	..	99	42	9	12.9	..
Kazakhstan	4.9	28	51	26	0.2	108[b]	100	72	30	5.4	38
Kenya	16.4	73	360	99	6.2	..	93	67	..	..	..
Kiribati	..	47	..	..	..	..	..	..	..	..	..
Korea, Dem. Rep.	18.8	33	81	1	..	..	100	78	..	..	..
Korea, Rep.	..	5	16	5	<0.1	..	..	60	25	3.4	10
Kosovo	..	..	..	..	..	..	..	..	..	45.4	..
Kuwait	1.7	11	14	14	..	..	99	68	..	..	..
Kyrgyz Republic	2.7	31	71	33	0.4	96	100	67	..	8.2	..
Lao PDR	31.6	42	470	32	0.3	93	84	78	..	..	..
Latvia	..	8	34	14	0.7	93	100	61	8	15.4	45
Lebanon	5.2	9	25	16	<0.1	87	99	46	28	9.0	8
Lesotho	13.5	86	620	63	23.3	68	92	66	..	25.3	..
Liberia	20.4	78	770	127	1.0	66	77	61	79	3.7	..
Libya	5.6	16	58	3	..	..	100	53	..	..	..
Liechtenstein	..	2	..	..	..	101	..	..	..	..	..
Lithuania	..	6	8	17	<0.1	95	100	59	8	15.4	38
Luxembourg	..	3	20	9	0.3	..	..	57	6	4.9	24
Macedonia, FYR	1.8	10	10	19	..	..	99	56	23	31.4	28
Madagascar	..	62	240	125	0.3	73	65	86	..	..	..
Malawi	13.8	83	460	108	10.0	71	87	83	..	..	..
Malaysia	12.9	7	29	11	0.4	..	98	60	22	3.4	25
Maldives	17.8	11	60	11	<0.1	107	99	66	..	..	..
Mali	27.9	176	540	172	1.1	55	44	53	83	..	..
Malta	..	6	8	13	<0.1	..	98	51	9	6.4	23
Marshall Islands	..	26	..	..	..	97	..	..	..	..	..
Mauritania	15.9	112	510	73	1.1	..	68	54	..	31.2	..
Mauritius	..	15	60	33	1.0	..	97	60	15	7.9	23
Mexico	3.4	16	50	67	0.3	104	98	62	29	5.3	31
Micronesia, Fed. Sts.	..	42	100	20	..	..	..	..	..	..	..
Moldova	3.2	16	41	30	0.5	91	99	42	29	6.7	38
Monaco	..	4	..	..	..	..	..	..	..	..	..
Mongolia	5.3	31	63	19	<0.1	115	96	60	58	..	47
Montenegro	2.2	7	8	15	..	99[b]	99	..	..	19.7	31
Morocco	3.1	33	100	12	0.2	99[b]	79	50	52	8.9	13
Mozambique	18.3	103	490	129	11.3	56	72	85	..	..	..
Myanmar	22.6	62	200	13	0.6	..	96	79	..	..	..
Namibia	17.5	42	200	58	13.4	..	93	64	14	37.6	..
Nepal	29.1	48	170	90	0.3	..	83	84	..	2.7	..
Netherlands	..	4	6	4	0.2	..	..	65	11	4.4	30
New Caledonia	..	..	..	20	..	100	..	58	..	..	..
New Zealand	..	6	15	21	<0.1	..	..	68	12	6.5	40
Nicaragua	5.7	26	95	106	0.2	..	87	63	47	8.0	..
Niger	39.9	125	590	196	0.8	46	37	65	..	..	..

	Prevalence of child malnutrition, underweight % of children under age 5 2005–11a	Under-five mortality rate per 1,000 live births 2011	Maternal mortality ratio Modeled estimate per 100,000 live births 2010	Adolescent fertility rate births per 1,000 women ages 15–19 2011	Prevalence of HIV % of population ages 15–49 2011	Primary completion rate % of relevant age group 2011	Youth literacy rate % ages 15–24 2005–11a	Labor force participation rate % ages 15 and older 2011	Vulnerable employment Unpaid family workers and own-account workers % of total employment 2007–11a	Unemployment % of total labor force 2007–11a	Female legislators, senior officials, and managers % of total 2007–11a
Nigeria	26.7	124	630	113	3.7	..	72	56	..	..	..
Northern Mariana Islands	..	..	..	..	..	..	..	..	..	..	..
Norway	..	3	7	8	0.2	..	..	66	5	3.3	31
Oman	8.6	9	32	9	..	107	98	61	..	..	..
Pakistan	30.9	72	260	29	<0.1	67	71	53	63	5.0	3
Palau	..	19	..	..	..	..	..	..	..	..	..
Panama	3.9	20	92	77	0.8	101	98	66	29	4.5	46
Papua New Guinea	18.1	58	230	63	0.7	..	68	72	..	4.0	..
Paraguay	3.4	22	99	68	0.3	..	99	72	42	5.6	34
Peru	4.5	18	67	50	0.4	97	97	76	40	7.8	19
Philippines	20.7	25	99	48	<0.1	..	98	64	41	7.0	55
Poland	..	6	5	13	<0.1	..	100	56	18	9.6	38
Portugal	..	3	8	13	0.7	..	100	62	16	12.7	33
Puerto Rico	..	..	20	51	..	..	87	45	..	15.7	43
Qatar	..	8	7	16	..	96	97	86	0	0.6	10
Romania	..	13	27	29	<0.1	..	97	56	32	7.4	31
Russian Federation	..	12	34	25	..	..	100	63	6	6.6	37
Rwanda	11.7	54	340	36	2.9	..	77	86	..	2.4	..
Samoa	..	19	100	26	..	98	99	61	..	..	..
San Marino	..	2	..	..	..	93	..	..	..	2.6	18
São Tomé and Príncipe	14.4	89	70	58	1.0	115	95	60	..	..	..
Saudi Arabia	5.3	9	24	20	..	106	98	50	..	5.4	8
Senegal	19.2	65	370	93	0.7	63	65	77	..	..	..
Serbia	1.8	7	12	20	<0.1	99	99	..	27	19.2	33
Seychelles	..	14	..	..	..	125	99	..	..	..	..
Sierra Leone	21.3	185	890	112	1.6	74	59	68	..	..	..
Singapore	..	3	3	6	<0.1	..	100	67	10	2.9	34
Sint Maarten	..	..	..	..	..	..	..	..	..	..	..
Slovak Republic	..	8	6	17	<0.1	..	..	59	12	13.5	31
Slovenia	..	3	12	5	<0.1	..	100	59	13	8.2	38
Solomon Islands	11.5	22	93	66	..	..	..	67	..	..	..
Somalia	32.8	180	1,000	68	0.7	..	..	57	..	..	..
South Africa	8.7	47	300	52	17.3	..	98	52	10	24.7	31
South Sudan	..	121	..	..	3.1	..	..	..	..	..	..
Spain	..	4	6	11	0.4	..	100	59	11	21.6	30
Sri Lanka	21.6	12	35	22	<0.1	..	98	55	42	4.9	24
St. Kitts and Nevis	..	7	..	..	..	93	..	..	..	..	..
St. Lucia	..	16	35	57	..	93	..	71	..	14.0	..
St. Martin	..	..	..	..	..	..	..	..	..	..	..
St. Vincent and Grenadines	..	21	48	55	..	..	..	67	..	..	..
Sudan	31.7	86d	730	55	0.4d	..	87	54	..	..	..
Suriname	7.5	30	130	36	1.0	88	98	55	..	..	..
Swaziland	7.3	104	320	71	26.0	77	94	57	..	..	..
Sweden	..	3	4	6	0.2	..	..	64	7	7.5	35
Switzerland	..	4	8	4	0.4	..	..	68	9	4.1	33
Syrian Arab Republic	10.1	15	70	38	..	106	95	43	33	8.4	9
Tajikistan	15.0	63	65	26	0.3	104	100	66	..	..	..

	Prevalence of child malnutrition, underweight	Under-five mortality rate	Maternal mortality ratio	Adolescent fertility rate	Prevalence of HIV	Primary completion rate	Youth literacy rate	Labor force participation rate	Vulnerable employment	Unemployment	Female legislators, senior officials, and managers
	% of children under age 5	per 1,000 live births	Modeled estimate per 100,000 live births	births per 1,000 women ages 15–19	% of population ages 15–49	% of relevant age group	% ages 15–24	% ages 15 and older	Unpaid family workers and own-account workers % of total employment	% of total labor force	% of total
	2005–11a	2011	2010	2011	2011	2011	2005–11a	2011	2007–11a	2007–11a	2007–11a
Tanzania	16.2	68	460	129	5.8	81b	77	89	..	..	..
Thailand	7.0	12	48	38	1.2	..	98	72	54	0.7	25
Timor-Leste	45.3	54	300	55	..	72	80	57	70	3.6	..
Togo	20.5	110	300	57	3.4	77	82	81	..	..	..
Tonga	..	15	110	19	..	..	99	64	..	..	..
Trinidad and Tobago	..	28	46	32	1.5	..	100	66	..	4.6	..
Tunisia	3.3	16	56	5	<0.1	..	97	48	..	13.0	..
Turkey	..	15	20	32	<0.1	..	98	50	33	9.8	10
Turkmenistan	..	53	67	17	..	..	100	61	..	..	..
Turks and Caicos Islands	..	..	..	..	..	..	..	..	..	5.4	..
Tuvalu	1.6	30	..	..	..	..	..	..	..	..	..
Uganda	16.4	90	310	131	7.2	55	87	78	..	4.2	..
Ukraine	..	10	32	27	0.8	97	100	59	..	7.9	39
United Arab Emirates	..	7	12	24	..	..	95	79	1	4.0	10
United Kingdom	..	5	12	30	0.3	..	..	62	12	7.8	34
United States	..	8	21	30	0.7	..	..	64	..	8.9	43
Uruguay	..	10	29	59	0.6	..	99	66	22	6.0	40
Uzbekistan	4.4	49	28	13	..	93	100	61	..	..	..
Vanuatu	11.7	13	110	51	..	..	94	71	70	4.6	29
Venezuela, RB	3.7	15	92	88	0.6	95	99	66	33	8.3	..
Vietnam	20.2	22	59	24	0.5	104	97	77	63	2.0	..
Virgin Islands (U.S.)	..	..	..	23	..	..	..	62	..	..	..
West Bank and Gaza	2.2	22	..	49	..	91	99	41	26	23.7	10
Yemen, Rep.	..	77	200	69	0.2	63	85	49	..	14.6	..
Zambia	14.9	83	440	140	12.5	..	74	79	..	..	..
Zimbabwe	10.1	67	570	56	14.9	..	99	86	..	..	..
World	**15.7 w**	**51 w**	**210 w**	**53 w**	**0.8 w**	**90 w**	**90 w**	**64 w**	**.. w**	**5.9 w**	
Low income	22.6c	95	410	92	2.4	68	74	75	..	..	
Middle income	16.0c	46	190	50	..	..	91	64	..	5.2	
Lower middle income	24.3c	62	260	66	..	..	84	58	71	4.9	
Upper middle income	2.9c	20	62	30	0.6	..	99	69	..	5.0	
Low & middle income	17.4c	56	230	57	1.0	89	88	65	..	5.2	
East Asia & Pacific	5.5c	21	83	19	0.2	..	99	73	..	4.2	
Europe & Central Asia	1.5c	21	32	26	..	98	99	59	18	8.0	
Latin America & Carib.	3.1c	19	81	71	0.4	102	97	66	31	7.7	
Middle East & N. Africa	6.3c	32	81	37	..	90	91	46	..	10.6	
South Asia	33.2c	62	220	71	..	..	79	57	78	3.5	
Sub-Saharan Africa	21.4c	109	500	106	4.9	70	72	70	..	..	
High income	1.7c	6	14	17	0.4	100	100	60	..	8.1	
Euro area	..	4	6	8	0.3	99	100	57	11	10.1	

a. Data are for the most recent year available. b. Data are for 2012. c. Calculated by World Bank staff using the United Nations Children's Fund, World Health Organization, and World Bank harmonized database and aggregation method. d. Excludes South Sudan.

 Front  User guide | World view | People | Environment

About the data

Though not included in the table due to space limitations, many indicators in this section are available disaggregated by sex, place of residence, wealth, and age in the World Development Indicators database.

Child malnutrition

Good nutrition is the cornerstone for survival, health, and development. Well-nourished children perform better in school, grow into healthy adults, and in turn give their children a better start in life. Well-nourished women face fewer risks during pregnancy and childbirth, and their children set off on firmer developmental paths, both physically and mentally. Undernourished children have lower resistance to infection and are more likely to die from common childhood ailments such as diarrheal diseases and respiratory infections. Frequent illness saps the nutritional status of those who survive, locking them into a vicious cycle of recurring sickness and faltering growth.

The proportion of underweight children is the most common child malnutrition indicator. Being even mildly underweight increases the risk of death and inhibits cognitive development in children. And it perpetuates the problem across generations, as malnourished women are more likely to have low-birthweight babies. Estimates of prevalence of underweight children are from the World Health Organization's (WHO) Global Database on Child Growth and Malnutrition, a standardized compilation of child growth and malnutrition data from national nutritional surveys. To better monitor global child malnutrition, the United Nations Children's Fund (UNICEF), the WHO, and the World Bank have jointly produced estimates for 2011 and trends since 1990 for regions, income groups, and the world, using a harmonized database and aggregation method.

Under-five mortality

Mortality rates for children and others are important indicators of health status. When data on the incidence and prevalence of diseases are unavailable, mortality rates may be used to identify vulnerable populations. And they are among the indicators most frequently used to compare socioeconomic development across countries.

The main sources of mortality data are vital registration systems and direct or indirect estimates based on sample surveys or censuses. A complete vital registration system—covering at least 90 percent of vital events in the population—is the best source of age-specific mortality data. But complete vital registration systems are fairly uncommon in developing countries. Thus estimates must be obtained from sample surveys or derived by applying indirect estimation techniques to registration, census, or survey data (see *Primary data documentation*). Survey data are subject to recall error.

To make estimates comparable and to ensure consistency across estimates by different agencies, the United Nations Inter-agency Group for Child Mortality Estimation, which comprises UNICEF, WHO, the United Nations Population Division, the World Bank, and other universities and research institutes, has developed and adopted a statistical method that uses all available information to reconcile differences. Trend lines are obtained by fitting a country-specific regression model of mortality rates against their reference dates. (For further discussion of childhood mortality estimates, see UN Inter-agency Group for Child Mortality Estimation 2012; for detailed background data and for a graphic presentation, see www .childmortality.org).

Maternal mortality

Measurements of maternal mortality are subject to many types of errors. In countries with incomplete vital registration systems, deaths of women of reproductive age or their pregnancy status may not be reported, or the cause of death may not be known. Even in high-income countries with reliable vital registration systems, misclassification of maternal deaths has been found to lead to serious underestimation. Surveys and censuses can be used to measure maternal mortality by asking respondents about survivorship of sisters. But these estimates are retrospective, referring to a period approximately five years before the survey, and may be affected by recall error. Further, they reflect pregnancy-related deaths (deaths while pregnant or within 42 days of pregnancy termination, irrespective of the cause of death) and need to be adjusted to conform to the strict definition of maternal death.

Maternal mortality ratios in the table are modeled estimates based on work by the WHO, UNICEF, United Nations Population Fund (UNFPA), and World Bank and include country-level time series data. For countries without complete registration data but with other types of data and for countries with no data, maternal mortality is estimated with a multilevel regression model using available national maternal mortality data and socioeconomic information, including fertility, birth attendants, and gross domestic product. The methodology differs from that used for previous estimates, so data presented here should not be compared across editions.

Adolescent fertility

Reproductive health is a state of physical and mental well-being in relation to the reproductive system and its functions and processes. Means of achieving reproductive health include education and services during pregnancy and childbirth, safe and effective contraception, and prevention and treatment of sexually transmitted diseases. Complications of pregnancy and childbirth are the leading cause of death and disability among women of reproductive age in developing countries.

Adolescent pregnancies are high risk for both mother and child. They are more likely to result in premature delivery, low birthweight, delivery complications, and death. Many adolescent pregnancies are unintended, but young girls may continue their pregnancies, giving up opportunities for education and employment, or seek unsafe abortions. Estimates of adolescent fertility rates are based on vital registration systems or, in their absence, censuses or sample surveys and are generally considered reliable measures of fertility in the recent past. Where no empirical information on age-specific fertility rates is available, a model is used to estimate the share of births to adolescents. For countries without vital registration systems fertility rates are generally based on extrapolations from trends observed in censuses or surveys from earlier years.

Prevalence of HIV

HIV prevalence rates reflect the rate of HIV infection in each country's population. Low national prevalence rates can be misleading, however. They often disguise epidemics that are initially concentrated in certain localities or population groups and threaten to spill over into the wider population. In many developing countries most new infections occur in young adults, with young women especially vulnerable.

Data on HIV prevalence are from the Joint United Nations Programme on HIV/AIDS. Changes in procedures and assumptions for estimating the data and better coordination with countries have resulted in improved estimates. New models track the course of HIV epidemics and their impacts, making full use of information on HIV prevalence trends from surveillance data as well as survey data. The models include the effect of antiretroviral therapy, take into account reduced infectivity among people receiving antiretroviral therapy (which is having a larger impact on HIV prevalence and allowing HIV-positive people to live longer), and allow for changes in urbanization over time (important because prevalence is higher in urban areas and because many countries have seen rapid urbanization over the past two decades). The estimates include plausible bounds, available at http://data.worldbank.org, which reflect the certainty associated with each of the estimates.

Primary completion

Many governments publish statistics that indicate how their education systems are working and developing—statistics on enrollment and efficiency indicators such as repetition rates, pupil–teacher ratios, and cohort progression. The primary completion rate, also called the gross intake ratio to last grade of primary education, is a core indicator of an education system's performance. It reflects an education system's coverage and the educational attainment of students. It is a key measure of progress toward the Millennium Development Goals and the Education for All initiative. However, a high primary completion rate does not necessarily mean high levels of student learning.

The indicator reflects the primary cycle as defined by the International Standard Classification of Education (ISCED97), ranging from three or four years of primary education (in a very small number of countries) to five or six years (in most countries) and seven (in a small number of countries). It is a proxy that should be taken as an upper estimate of the actual primary completion rate, since data limitations preclude adjusting for students who drop out during the final year of primary education. There are many reasons why the primary completion rate may exceed 100 percent. The numerator may include late entrants and overage children who have repeated one or more grades of primary education as well as children who entered school early, while the denominator is the number of children at the entrance age for the last grade of primary education.

Youth literacy

The youth literacy rate for ages 15–24 is a standard measure of recent progress in student achievement. It reflects the accumulated outcomes of primary education by indicating the proportion of the population that has acquired basic literacy and numeracy skills over the previous 10 years or so. In practice, however, literacy is difficult to measure. Estimating literacy rates requires census or survey measurements under controlled conditions. Many countries estimate the number of literate people from self-reported data. Some use educational attainment data as a proxy but apply different lengths of school attendance or levels of completion. Because definitions and methods of data collection differ across countries, data should be used cautiously. Generally, literacy encompasses numeracy, the ability to make simple arithmetic calculations.

Data on youth literacy are compiled by the United Nations Educational, Scientific and Cultural Organization (UNESCO) Institute for Statistics based on national censuses and household surveys during 1985–2011 and, for countries without recent literacy data, using the Global Age-Specific Literacy Projection Model.

Labor force participation

The labor force is the supply of labor available for producing goods and services in an economy. It includes people who are currently employed, people who are unemployed but seeking work, and first-time job-seekers. Not everyone who works is included, however. Unpaid workers, family workers, and students are often omitted, and some countries do not count members of the armed forces. Labor force size tends to vary during the year as seasonal workers enter and leave.

Data on the labor force are compiled by the International Labour Organization (ILO) from labor force surveys, censuses, and establishment censuses and surveys and from administrative records such as employment exchange registers and unemployment insurance schemes. Labor force surveys are the most comprehensive source for internationally comparable labor force data. Labor force data from population censuses are often based on a limited number of questions on the economic characteristics of individuals, with little scope to probe. Establishment censuses and surveys provide data on the employed population only, not unemployed workers, workers in small establishments, or workers in the informal sector (ILO, *Key Indicators of the Labour Market 2001-2002*).

Besides the data sources, there are other important factors that affect data comparability, such as census or survey reference period, definition of working age, and geographic coverage. For country-level information on source, reference period, or definition, consult the footnotes in the World Development Indicators database or the ILO's Key Indicators of the Labour Market, 7th edition, database.

The labor force participation rates in the table are estimates from the ILO's Key Indicators of the Labour Market, 7th edition, database. These harmonized estimates use strict data selection criteria and enhanced methods to ensure comparability across countries and over time to avoid the inconsistencies mentioned above. Estimates are based mainly on labor force surveys, with other sources (population censuses and nationally reported estimates) used only when no survey data are available. Because other employment data are mostly national estimates, caution should be used when comparing labor force participation rate and other employment data.

Vulnerable employment

The proportion of unpaid family workers and own-account workers in total employment is derived from information on status in employment. Each group faces different economic risks, and unpaid family workers and own-account workers are the most vulnerable—and therefore the most likely to fall into poverty. They are the least likely to have formal work arrangements, are the least likely to have social protection and safety nets to guard against economic shocks, and are often incapable of generating enough savings to offset these shocks. A high proportion of unpaid family workers in a country indicates weak development, little job growth, and often a large rural economy.

Data on vulnerable employment are drawn from labor force and general household sample surveys, censuses, and official estimates. Besides the limitation mentioned for calculating labor force participation rates, there are other reasons to limit comparability. For example, information provided by the Organisation for Economic Co-operation and Development relates only to civilian employment, which can result in an underestimation of "employees" and "workers not classified by status," especially in countries with large armed forces. While the categories of unpaid family workers and own-account workers would not be affected, their relative shares would be.

Unemployment

The ILO defines the unemployed as members of the economically active population who are without work but available for and seeking work, including people who have lost their jobs or who have voluntarily left work. Some unemployment is unavoidable. At any time some workers are temporarily unemployed—between jobs as employers look for the right workers and workers search for better jobs. Such unemployment, often called frictional unemployment, results from the normal operation of labor markets.

Changes in unemployment over time may reflect changes in the demand for and supply of labor, but they may also reflect changes in reporting practices. In countries without unemployment or welfare benefits people eke out a living in vulnerable employment. In countries with well-developed safety nets workers can afford to wait for suitable or desirable jobs. But high and sustained unemployment indicates serious inefficiencies in resource allocation.

The criteria for people considered to be seeking work, and the treatment of people temporarily laid off or seeking work for the first time, vary across countries. In many developing countries it is especially difficult to measure employment and unemployment in agriculture. The timing of a survey can maximize the effects of seasonal unemployment in agriculture. And informal sector employment is difficult to quantify where informal activities are not tracked.

Data on unemployment are drawn from labor force sample surveys and general household sample surveys, censuses, and official estimates. Administrative records, such as social insurance statistics and employment office statistics, are not included because of their limitations in coverage.

Women tend to be excluded from the unemployment count for various reasons. Women suffer more from discrimination and from structural, social, and cultural barriers that impede them from seeking work. Also, women are often responsible for the care of children and the elderly and for household affairs. They may not be available for work during the short reference period, as they need to make arrangements before starting work. Further, women are considered to be employed when they are working part-time or in temporary jobs, despite the instability of these jobs or their active search for more secure employment.

Female legislators, senior officials, and managers

Despite much progress in recent decades, gender inequalities remain pervasive in many dimensions of life. But while gender inequalities exist throughout the world, they are most prevalent in developing countries. Inequalities in the allocation of education, health care, nutrition, and political voice matter because of their strong association with well-being, productivity, and economic growth. These patterns of inequality begin at an early age, with boys routinely receiving a larger share of education and health spending than girls, for example. The share of women in high-skilled occupations such as legislators, senior officials, and managers indicates women's status and role in the labor force and society at large. Women are vastly underrepresented in decisionmaking positions in government, although there is some evidence of recent improvement.

Definitions

• **Prevalence of child malnutrition, underweight,** is the percentage of children under age 5 whose weight for age is more than two standard deviations below the median for the international reference population ages 0–59 months. Data are based on the WHO child growth standards released in 2006. • **Under-five mortality rate** is the probability of a child born in a specific year dying before reaching age 5, if subject to the age-specific mortality rates of that year. The probability is derived from life tables and is expressed as a rate per 1,000 live births. • **Maternal mortality ratio, modeled estimate,** is the number of women who die from pregnancy-related causes while pregnant or within 42 days of pregnancy termination, per 100,000 live births. • **Adolescent fertility rate** is the number of births per 1,000 women ages 15–19. • **Prevalence of HIV** is the percentage of people who are infected with HIV in the relevant age group. • **Primary completion rate** is the number of new entrants (enrollments minus repeaters) in the last grade of primary education, regardless of age, divided by the population at the entrance age for the last grade of primary education. Data limitations preclude adjusting for students who drop out during the final year of primary education. • **Youth literacy rate** is the percentage of the population ages 15–24 that can, with understanding, both read and write a short simple statement about their everyday life. • **Labor force participation rate** is the proportion of the population ages 15 and older that engages actively in the labor market, by either working or looking for work during a reference period. • **Vulnerable employment** is unpaid family workers and own-account workers as a percentage of total employment. • **Unemployment** is the share of the labor force without work but available for and seeking employment. Definitions of labor force and unemployment may differ by country. • **Female legislators, senior officials, and managers** are the percentage of legislators, senior officials, and managers (International Standard Classification of Occupations–88 category 1) who are female.

Data sources

Data on child malnutrition prevalence are from the WHO's Global Database on Child Growth and Malnutrition (www.who.int/nutgrowthdb/en/). Data on under-five mortality rates are from UN Inter-agency Group for Child Mortality Estimation (2012) and are based mainly on household surveys, censuses, and vital registration data. Modeled estimates of maternal mortality ratios are from WHO and others (2012). Data on adolescent fertility rates are from United Nations Population Division (2011), with annual data linearly interpolated by the World Bank's Development Data Group. Data on HIV prevalence are from UNAIDS (2012). Data on primary completion rates and literacy rates are from the UNESCO Institute for Statistics (www.uis.unesco.org). Data on labor force participation rates, vulnerable employment, unemployment, and female legislators, senior officials, and managers are from the ILO's Key Indicators of the Labour Market, 7th edition, database.

References

De Onis, Mercedes, Monika Blössner, Elaine Borghi, Richard Morris, and Edward A. Frongillo. 2004. "Methodology for Estimating Regional and Global Trends of Child Malnutrition." *International Journal of Epidemiology* 33: 1260–70.

ILO (International Labour Organization).Various years. *Key Indicators of the Labour Market.* Geneva: International Labour Office.

UNAIDS (Joint United Nations Programme on HIV/AIDS). 2012. *Global Report: UNAIDS Report on the Global AIDS Epidemic 2012.* Geneva.

UNICEF (United Nations Children's Fund), WHO (World Health Organization), and World Bank. 2012. *Joint Child Malnutrition Estimates—Levels and Trends.* www.who.int/nutgrowthdb/jme_unicef_who_wb.pdf. New York: UNICEF.

UN Inter-agency Group for Child Mortality Estimation. 2012. *Levels and Trends in Child Mortality: Report 2012.* New York.

United Nations Population Division. 2011. *World Population Prospects: The 2010 Revision.* New York: United Nations, Department of Economic and Social Affairs.

WHO (World Health Organization), UNICEF (United Nations Children's Fund), UNFPA (United Nations Population Fund), and World Bank. 2012. *Trends in Maternal Mortality: 1990 to 2010.* Geneva: WHO.

World Bank. n.d. PovcalNet online database. http://iresearch.worldbank.org/PovcalNet. Washington, DC.

To access the World Development Indicators online tables, use the URL http://wdi.worldbank.org/table/ and the table number (for example, http://wdi.worldbank.org/table/2.1). To view a specific indicator online, use the URL http://data.worldbank.org/indicator/ and the indicator code (for example, http://data.worldbank.org/indicator/SP.POP.TOTL).

2.1 Population dynamics

Population ♀♂	SP.POP.TOTL
Population growth	SP.POP.GROW
Population ages 0–14 ♀♂	SP.POP.0014.TO.ZS
Population ages 15–64 ♀♂	SP.POP.1564.TO.ZS
Population ages 65+ ♀♂	SP.POP.65UP.TO.ZS
Dependency ratio, Young	SP.POP.DPND.YG
Dependency ratio, Old	SP.POP.DPND.OL
Crude death rate	SP.DYN.CDRT.IN
Crude birth rate	SP.DYN.CBRT.IN

2.2 Labor force structure

Labor force participation rate, Male ♀♂	SL.TLF.CACT.MA.ZS
Labor force participation rate, Female ♀♂	SL.TLF.CACT.FE.ZS
Labor force, Total ♀♂	SL.TLF.TOTL.IN
Labor force, Average annual growth	..[a,b]
Labor force, Female ♀♂	SL.TLF.TOTL.FE.ZS

2.3 Employment by sector

Agriculture, Male ♀♂	SL.AGR.EMPL.MA.ZS
Agriculture, Female ♀♂	SL.AGR.EMPL.FE.ZS
Industry, Male ♀♂	SL.IND.EMPL.MA.ZS
Industry, Female ♀♂	SL.IND.EMPL.FE.ZS
Services, Male ♀♂	SL.SRV.EMPL.MA.ZS
Services, Female ♀♂	SL.SRV.EMPL.FE.ZS

2.4 Decent work and productive employment

Employment to population ratio, Total ♀♂	SL.EMP.TOTL.SP.ZS
Employment to population ratio, Youth ♀♂	SL.EMP.1524.SP.ZS
Vulnerable employment, Male ♀♂	SL.EMP.VULN.MA.ZS
Vulnerable employment, Female ♀♂	SL.EMP.VULN.FE.ZS
GDP per person employed	SL.GDP.PCAP.EM.KD

2.5 Unemployment

Unemployment, Male ♀♂	SL.UEM.TOTL.MA.ZS
Unemployment, Female ♀♂	SL.UEM.TOTL.FE.ZS
Youth unemployment, Male ♀♂	SL.UEM.1524.MA.ZS
Youth unemployment, Female ♀♂	SL.UEM.1524.FE.ZS
Long-term unemployment, Total ♀♂	SL.UEM.LTRM.ZS
Long-term unemployment, Male ♀♂	SL.UEM.LTRM.MA.ZS
Long-term unemployment, Female ♀♂	SL.UEM.LTRM.FE.ZS
Unemployment by educational attainment, Primary ♀♂	SL.UEM.PRIM.ZS
Unemployment by educational attainment, Secondary ♀♂	SL.UEM.SECO.ZS
Unemployment by educational attainment, Tertiary ♀♂	SL.UEM.TERT.ZS

2.6 Children at work

Children in employment, Total ♀♂	SL.TLF.0714.ZS
Children in employment, Male ♀♂	SL.TLF.0714.MA.ZS
Children in employment, Female ♀♂	SL.TLF.0714.FE.ZS
Work only ♀♂	SL.TLF.0714.WK.ZS
Study and work ♀♂	SL.TLF.0714.SW.ZS
Employment in agriculture ♀♂	SL.AGR.0714.ZS
Employment in manufacturing ♀♂	SL.MNF.0714.ZS
Employment in services ♀♂	SL.SRV.0714.ZS
Self-employed ♀♂	SL.SLF.0714.ZS
Wage workers ♀♂	SL.WAG0714.ZS
Unpaid family workers ♀♂	SL.FAM.0714.ZS

2.7 Poverty rates at national poverty lines

Poverty headcount ratio, Rural	SI.POV.RUHC
Poverty headcount ratio, Urban	SI.POV.URHC
Poverty headcount ratio, National	SI.POV.NAHC
Poverty gap, Rural	SI.POV.RUGP
Poverty gap, Urban	SI.POV.URGP
Poverty gap, National	SI.POV.NAGP

2.8 Poverty rates at international poverty lines

Population living below 2005 PPP $1.25 a day	SI.POV.DDAY
Poverty gap at 2005 PPP $1.25 a day	SI.POV.2DAY
Population living below 2005 PPP $2 a day	SI.POV.GAPS
Poverty gap at 2005 PPP $2 a day	SI.POV.GAP2

2.9 Distribution of income or consumption

Gini index	SI.POV.GINI
Share of consumption or income, Lowest 10% of population	SI.DST.FRST.10
Share of consumption or income, Lowest 20% of population	SI.DST.FRST.20
Share of consumption or income, Second 20% of population	SI.DST.02ND.20
Share of consumption or income, Third 20% of population	SI.DST.03RD.20
Share of consumption or income, Fourth 20% of population	SI.DST.04TH.20

Share of consumption or income, Highest 20% of population	SI.DST.05TH.20
Share of consumption or income, Highest 10% of population	SI.DST.10TH.10

2.10 Education inputs

Public expenditure per student, Primary	SE.XPD.PRIM.PC.ZS
Public expenditure per student, Secondary	SE.XPD.SECO.PC.ZS
Public expenditure per student, Tertiary	SE.XPD.TERT.PC.ZS
Public expenditure on education, % of GDP	SE.XPD.TOTL.GD.ZS
Public expenditure on education, % of total government expenditure	SE.XPD.TOTL.GB.ZS
Trained teachers in primary education ♀♂	SE.PRM.TCAQ.ZS
Primary school pupil-teacher ratio	SE.PRM.ENRL.TC.ZS

2.11 Participation in education

Preprimary gross enrollment ratio ♀♂	SE.PRE.ENRR
Primary gross enrollment ratio ♀♂	SE.PRM.ENRR
Secondary gross enrollment ratio ♀♂	SE.SEC.ENRR
Tertiary gross enrollment ratio ♀♂	SE.TER.ENRR
Primary net enrollment rate ♀♂	SE.PRM.NENR
Secondary net enrollment rate ♀♂	SE.SEC.NENR
Primary adjusted net enrollment rate, Male ♀♂	SE.PRM.TENR.MA
Primary adjusted net enrollment rate, Female ♀♂	SE.PRM.TENR.FE
Primary school-age children out of school, Male ♀♂	SE.PRM.UNER.MA
Primary school-age children out of school, Female ♀♂	SE.PRM.UNER.FE

2.12 Education efficiency

Gross intake ratio in first grade of primary education, Male ♀♂	SE.PRM.GINT.MA.ZS
Gross intake ratio in first grade of primary education, Female ♀♂	SE.PRM.GINT.FE.ZS
Reaching grade 5, Male ♀♂	SE.PRM.PRS5.MA.ZS
Reaching grade 5, Female ♀♂	SE.PRM.PRS5.FE.ZS
Reaching last grade of primary education, Male ♀♂	SE.PRM.PRSL.MA.ZS
Reaching last grade of primary education, Female ♀♂	SE.PRM.PRSL.FE.ZS
Repeaters in primary education, Male ♀♂	SE.PRM.REPT.MA.ZS
Repeaters in primary education, Female ♀♂	SE.PRM.REPT.FE.ZS
Transition rate to secondary education, Male ♀♂	SE.SEC.PROG.MA.ZS
Transition rate to secondary education, Female ♀♂	SE.SEC.PROG.FE.ZS

2.13 Education completion and outcomes

Primary completion rate, Total ♀♂	SE.PRM.CMPT.ZS
Primary completion rate, Male ♀♂	SE.PRM.CMPT.MA.ZS
Primary completion rate, Female ♀♂	SE.PRM.CMPT.FE.ZS
Youth literacy rate, Male ♀♂	SE.ADT.1524.LT.MA.ZS
Youth literacy rate, Female ♀♂	SE.ADT.1524.LT.FE.ZS
Adult literacy rate, Male ♀♂	SE.ADT.LITR.MA.ZS
Adult literacy rate, Female ♀♂	SE.ADT.LITR.FE.ZS

2.14 Education gaps by income and gender

This table provides education survey data for the poorest and richest quintiles.   ..[b]

2.15 Health systems

Total health expenditure	SH.XPD.TOTL.ZS
Public health expenditure	SH.XPD.PUBL
Out-of-pocket health expenditure	SH.XPD.OOPC.ZS
External resources for health	SH.XPD.EXTR.ZS
Health expenditure per capita, $	SH.XPD.PCAP
Health expenditure per capita, PPP $	SH.XPD.PCAP.PP.KD
Physicians	SH.MED.PHYS.ZS
Nurses and midwives	SH.MED.NUMW.P3
Community health workers	SH.MED.CMHW.P3
Hospital beds	SH.MED.BEDS.ZS
Completeness of birth registration	SP.REG.BRTH.ZS

2.16 Disease prevention coverage and quality

Access to an improved water source	SH.H2O.SAFE.ZS
Access to improved sanitation facilities	SH.STA.ACSN
Child immunization rate, Measles	SH.IMM.MEAS
Child immunization rate, DTP3	SH.IMM.IDPT
Children with acute respiratory infection taken to health provider	SH.STA.ARIC.ZS
Children with diarrhea who received oral rehydration and continuous feeding	SH.STA.ORCF.ZS
Children sleeping under treated bed nets	SH.MLR.NETS.ZS
Children with fever receiving antimalarial drugs	SH.MLR.TRET.ZS
Tuberculosis treatment success rate	SH.TBS.CURE.ZS
Tuberculosis case detection rate	SH.TBS.DTEC.ZS

2.17 Reproductive health

Total fertility rate	SP.DYN.TFRT.IN
Adolescent fertility rate	SP.ADO.TFRT
Unmet need for contraception	SP.UWT.TFRT
Contraceptive prevalence rate	SP.DYN.CONU.ZS
Pregnant women receiving prenatal care	SH.STA.ANVC.ZS
Births attended by skilled health staff	SH.STA.BRTC.ZS
Maternal mortality ratio, National estimate	SH.STA.MMRT.NE
Maternal mortality ratio, Modeled estimate	SH.STA.MMRT
Lifetime risk of maternal mortality	SH.MMR.RISK

2.18 Nutrition and growth

Prevalence of undernourishment	SN.ITK.DEFC.ZS
Prevalence of underweight, Male ♀♂	SH.STA.MALN.MA.ZS
Prevalence of underweight, Female ♀♂	SH.STA.MALN.FE.ZS
Prevalence of stunting, Male ♀♂	SH.STA.STNT.MA.ZS
Prevalence of stunting, Female ♀♂	SH.STA.STNT.FE.ZS
Prevalence of wasting, Male ♀♂	SH.STA.WAST.MA.ZS
Prevalence of wasting, Female ♀♂	SH.STA.WAST.FE.ZS
Prevalence of overweight children, Male ♀♂	SH.STA.OWGH.MA.ZS
Prevalence of overweight children, Female ♀♂	SH.STA.OWGH.FE.ZS

2.19 Nutrition intake and supplements

Low-birthweight babies	SH.STA.BRTW.ZS
Exclusive breastfeeding	SH.STA.BFED.ZS
Consumption of iodized salt	SN.ITK.SALT.ZS
Vitamin A supplementation	SN.ITK.VITA.ZS
Prevalence of anemia among children under age 5	SH.ANM.CHLD.ZS
Prevalence of anemia among pregnant women	SH.PRG.ANEM

2.20 Health risk factors and future challenges

Prevalence of smoking, Male ♀♂	SH.PRV.SMOK.MA
Prevalence of smoking, Female ♀♂	SH.PRV.SMOK.FE
Incidence of tuberculosis	SH.TBS.INCD
Prevalence of diabetes	SH.STA.DIAB.ZS
Prevalence of HIV, Total	SH.DYN.AIDS.ZS

Women's share of population ages 15+ living with HIV ♀♂	SH.DYN.AIDS.FE.ZS
Prevalence of HIV, Youth male ♀♂	SH.HIV.1524.MA.ZS
Prevalence of HIV, Youth female ♀♂	SH.HIV.1524.FE.ZS
Antiretroviral therapy coverage	SH.HIV.ARTC.ZS
Death from communicable diseases and maternal, prenatal, and nutrition conditions	SH.DTH.COMM.ZS
Death from non-communicable diseases	SH.DTH.NCOM.ZS
Death from injuries	SH.DTH.INJR.ZS

2.21 Mortality

Life expectancy at birth ♀♂	SP.DYN.LE00.IN
Neonatal mortality rate	SH.DYN.NMRT
Infant mortality rate	SP.DYN.IMRT.IN
Under-five mortality rate, Total ♀♂	SH.DYN.MORT
Under-five mortality rate, Male ♀♂	SH.DYN.MORT.MA
Under-five mortality rate, Female ♀♂	SH.DYN.MORT.FE
Adult mortality rate, Male ♀♂	SP.DYN.AMRT.MA
Adult mortality rate, Female ♀♂	SP.DYN.AMRT.FE

2.22 Health gaps by income

This table provides health survey data for the poorest and richest quintiles.	..[b]

♀♂ Data disaggregated by sex are available in the World Development Indicators database.

a. Derived from data elsewhere in the World Development Indicators database.

b. Available online only as part of the table, not as an individual indicator.

ENVIRONMENT

Front | ? User guide | World view | People | Environment

The Millennium Development Goals call for integrating principles of environmental sustainability into country policies and programs and reversing environmental losses. Whether the world continues to sustain itself depends largely on properly managing its natural resources. The indicators in the *Environment* section measure resource use and the way human activities affect the natural and built environment. They include measures of environmental goods (forest, water, cultivatable land) and of degradation (pollution, deforestation, loss of habitat, and loss of biodiversity). These indicators show that growing populations and expanding economies have placed greater demands on land, water, forests, minerals, and energy sources. But new technologies, increasing productivity, and better policies can ensure that future development is environmentally and socially sustainable.

Nowhere are these risks and opportunities more intertwined than in the global effort to mitigate the effects of climate change. A continuing rise in temperature, accompanied by changes in precipitation patterns, is projected for this century, as are more frequent, severe, and prolonged climate-related events such as floods and droughts—posing risks for agriculture, food production, and water supplies. Poor countries and the poorest people in all countries are most vulnerable to the changing climate.

The 2012 edition of *World Development Indicators* included two new tables on climate change. The first presents data on carbon dioxide emissions by economic sector from the International Energy Agency's annual time series statistics. And the second contains country indicators on climate variability, exposure to impact, and resilience.

Other indicators in this section describe land use, agriculture and food production, forests and biodiversity, threatened species, water resources, energy use and efficiency, electricity production and use, greenhouse gas emissions, urbanization, traffic and congestion, air pollution, government commitments, and natural resource rents.

Where possible, the indicators come from international sources and are standardized to facilitate comparison across countries. But ecosystems span national boundaries, and access to natural resources may vary within countries. For example, water may be abundant in some parts of a country but scarce in others, and countries often share water resources. Land productivity and optimal land use may be location specific, but widely separated regions can have common characteristics. Greenhouse gas emissions and climate change are measured globally, but their effects are experienced locally, shaping people's lives and opportunities. Measuring environmental phenomena and their effects at the subnational, national, and supranational levels remains a major challenge for achieving long-term, sustainable development.

East Asia & Pacific: More access to improved sanitation facilities

Share of population with access to improved sanitation facilities (%)

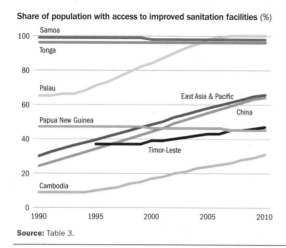

Source: Table 3.

East Asia and Pacific has more than doubled the proportion of people with access to improved sanitation facilities. This is an impressive achievement, bringing access to basic sanitation facilities to more than 700 million additional people, mostly in China. Because of its size, China dominates the regional average of East Asia and Pacific. But some countries progressed even faster than China, such as Palau, with 100 percent access in 2010. At the other end of the spectrum is Cambodia, where only 31 percent of the population has access.

Europe & Central Asia: Emissions fall but per capita carbon dioxide emissions remain high

Carbon dioxide emissions (metric tons per capita)

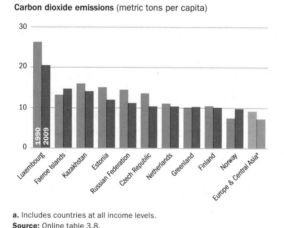

a. Includes countries at all income levels.
Source: Online table 3.8.

Carbon dioxide emissions, largely a byproduct of energy production and use, account for the largest portion of greenhouse gases released each year. Greenhouse gases—including carbon dioxide, methane, nitrous oxide, and other industrial gases (hydrofluorocarbons, perfluorocarbons, and sulfur hexafluoride)—are associated with global warming and environmental damage. In 2009 the world released an estimated 32 billion metric tons of carbon dioxide, up 44 percent from 1990. In Europe and Central Asia carbon dioxide emissions fell 25 percent over the same period, but emissions per capita remain the highest among developing regions. Emissions of other greenhouse gases have also risen over the last two decades. In 2010 global emissions were estimated at 7.5 billion metric tons of carbon dioxide equivalent for methane, 2.9 billion for nitrous dioxide, and 1.0 billion for other industrial gases.

Latin America & Caribbean: The leader in clean and efficient energy

Energy use, 2010 (%)

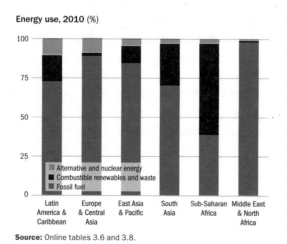

Source: Online tables 3.6 and 3.8.

Latin America and the Caribbean remains one of the world's most efficient energy-using regions, measured by the ratio of gross domestic product to energy use. Latin American countries averaged $7.70 of output per kilogram of oil-equivalent energy used in 2010 (in 2005 purchasing power parity dollars), up 12 percent from 1990. Peru, Colombia, Panama, Costa Rica, and Uruguay were the region's most efficient energy users. Clean energy from noncarbon energy sources, which consists of alternative energy (geothermal, solar, and hydropower) and nuclear energy, is also on the rise, accounting for 9.2 percent of world energy use in 2010, but 10.4 percent in Latin America and the Caribbean, highest among developing regions. The increase in carbon dioxide emissions slowed, but the region's emissions still rose more than 57 percent between 1990 and 2009. Mexico, Brazil, República Bolivariana de Venezuela, Argentina, and Colombia were the largest emitters.

Middle East & North Africa: The most water-stressed region

The world has about 42 trillion cubic meters of available freshwater, but distribution is drastically uneven. The Middle East and North Africa is the most water-stressed region, with less than 1 percent of global renewable freshwater resources. At 226 billion cubic meters, the region has only 673 cubic meters of water per person, the lowest among developing regions. By contrast, Latin America and the Caribbean, with 32 percent of world resources, has 22,810 cubic meters per person; Europe and Central Asia, with 12 percent, has 12,516 cubic meters per person; and East Asia and Pacific, with 21 percent, has 4,446 cubic meters per person.

Renewable internal freshwater resources, 2011 (%)

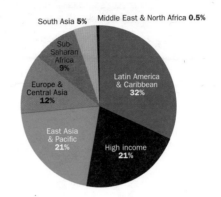

Source: Online table 3.5.

South Asia: Some of the world's most polluted cities

South Asia has some of the most polluted air in the world, as measured by the concentration of fine suspended particulates of fewer than 10 microns in diameter (PM10), capable of penetrating deep into the respiratory tract and causing severe health damage. The PM10 estimates measure the annual exposure of the average urban resident to outdoor particulate matter. Globally, air pollution has fallen from 78 micrograms per cubic meter to 41 over the last two decades. Among developing regions the highest concentrations are in South Asia (62) and the Middle East and North Africa (59). City-level PM10 concentration data, however, indicate that Sub-Saharan Africa has the most cities with high levels of pollution among developing regions. Even so, the PM10 concentration has dropped significantly in Sub-Saharan Africa, falling 65 percent over 1990–2010.

Particulates of less than 10 microns in diameter, 2010
(micrograms per cubic meter)

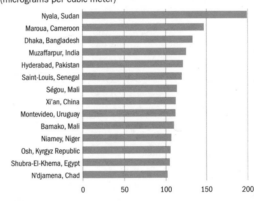

Source: Online tables 3.13 and 3.14.

Sub-Saharan Africa: Use of biomass energy for cooking and heating increases health risks

Combustible renewables and waste, 2010 (% of energy use)

Many poor people depend on biomass energy from plant materials or animal waste for cooking and heating. Millions of deaths are caused by indoor air pollution each year, due largely to indoor particulate pollution. Many are children, who die of acute respiratory infections from burning fuel wood, crop residues, or animal dung (WHO 2004). These sources of energy account for 66 percent of total energy used by more than 800 million low-income inhabitants of the world. In Sub-Saharan Africa use of combustible renewables and waste, which account for more than half of total energy use, has risen almost 3 percent over the last two decades. For this region, where an estimated 67 percent of the population lacks access to any form of electrical services, use of biomass and coal—the primary cooking and heating fuel—is still on the rise.

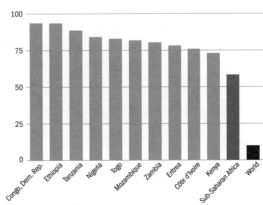

Source: Online tables 1.1 and 3.6.

	Deforestation[a] average annual % 2000–10	Nationally protected areas Terrestrial and marine areas % of total territorial area 2010	Internal renewable freshwater resources[b] Per capita cubic meters 2011	Access to improved water source % of total population 2010	Access to improved sanitation facilities % of total population 2010	Urban population average annual % growth 1990–2011	Particulate matter concentration urban-population-weighted PM10 micrograms per cubic meter 2010	Carbon dioxide emissions million metric tons 2009	Energy use Per capita kilograms of oil equivalent 2010	Electricity production billion kilowatt hours 2010
Afghanistan	0.00	0.4	1,335	50	37	4.0	30	6.3	..	..
Albania	−0.10	8.4	8,364	95	94	2.4	38	3.0	648	7.6
Algeria	0.57	6.2	313	83	95	2.6	69	121.3	1,138	45.6
American Samoa	0.19	16.7	..	..	..	1.9	..	..	..	..
Andorra	0.00	6.1	3,663	100	100	0.9	18	0.5	..	..
Angola	0.21	12.1	7,544	51	58	4.1	58	26.7	716	5.3
Antigua and Barbuda	0.20	1.0	580	..	..	1.0	13	0.5	..	..
Argentina	0.81	5.3	6,771	..	..	1.0	57	174.7	1,847	125.3
Armenia	1.48	8.0	2,212	98	90	0.3	45	4.5	791	6.5
Aruba	0.00	0.0	..	100	..	0.8	..	2.3	..	..
Australia	0.37	12.5	22,039	100	100	1.3	13	400.2	5,653	241.5
Austria	−0.13	22.9	6,529	100	100	0.7	27	62.3	4,034	67.9
Azerbaijan	0.00	7.1	885	80	82	1.8	27	49.1	1,307	18.7
Bahamas, The	0.00	1.0	58	..	100	1.5	..	2.6	..	..
Bahrain	−3.55	0.7	3	..	..	4.9	44	24.2	7,754	13.2
Bangladesh	0.18	1.6	698	81	56	3.0	115	51.0	209	42.3
Barbados	0.00	0.1	292	100	100	1.4	35	1.6	..	..
Belarus	−0.43	7.2	3,927	100	93	0.4	6	60.3	2,922	34.9
Belgium	−0.16	13.2	1,089	100	100	1.2	21	103.6	5,586	93.8
Belize	0.67	20.6	44,868	98	90	3.0	12	0.4	..	..
Benin	1.04	23.3	1,132	75	13	4.2	48	4.9	413	0.2
Bermuda	0.00	5.1	..	..	..	0.7	..	0.5	..	..
Bhutan	−0.34	28.3	105,653	96	44	3.9	20	0.4	..	..
Bolivia	0.50	18.5	30,085	88	27	2.2	57	14.5	737	6.9
Bosnia and Herzegovina	0.00	0.6	9,461	99	95	0.9	21	30.1	1,703	17.1
Botswana	0.99	30.9	1,182	96	62	2.2	64	4.4	1,128	0.5
Brazil	0.50	26.0	27,551	98	79	1.2	18	367.1	1,363	515.7
Brunei Darussalam	0.44	29.6	20,939	..	..	2.2	44	9.3	8,308	3.9
Bulgaria	−1.53	8.9	2,858	100	100	−1.7	40	42.8	2,370	46.0
Burkina Faso	1.01	14.2	737	79	17	6.2	65	1.7	..	..
Burundi	1.40	4.8	1,173	72	46	4.9	24	0.2	..	..
Cambodia	1.34	23.4	8,431	64	31	2.1	42	4.6	355	1.0
Cameroon	1.05	9.0	13,629	77	49	3.3	59	6.7	363	5.9
Canada	0.00	6.2	82,647	100	100	1.2	15	513.9	7,380	607.8
Cape Verde	−0.36	0.2	599	88	61	2.1	..	0.3	..	..
Cayman Islands	0.00	1.5	..	96	96	0.9	..	0.5	..	..
Central African Republic	0.13	17.7	31,425	67	34	2.6	35	0.2	..	..
Chad	0.66	9.4	1,301	51	13	3.0	83	0.4	..	..
Channel Islands	..	0.5	..	..	..	0.8	..	..	..	..
Chile	−0.25	13.3	51,188	96	96	1.1	46	66.7	1,807	60.4
China	−1.57	16.0	2,093	91	64	3.0	59	7,687.1	1,807	4,208.3
Hong Kong SAR, China	..	41.8	..	..	..	0.1	..	37.0	1,951	38.3
Macao SAR, China	..	..	..	..	..	2.2	..	1.5	..	..
Colombia	0.17	20.5	45,006	92	77	1.7	19	71.2	696	56.8
Comoros	9.34	..	1,592	95	36	2.9	30	0.1	..	..
Congo, Dem. Rep.	0.20	10.0	13,283	45	24	4.3	35	2.7	360	7.9
Congo, Rep.	0.07	9.7	53,626	71	18	3.0	57	1.9	363	0.6

	Deforestation[a]	Nationally protected areas	Internal renewable freshwater resources[b]	Access to improved water source	Access to improved sanitation facilities	Urban population	Particulate matter concentration	Carbon dioxide emissions	Energy use	Electricity production
	average annual % 2000–10	Terrestrial and marine areas % of total territorial area 2010	Per capita cubic meters 2011	% of total population 2010	% of total population 2010	average annual % growth 1990–2011	urban-population-weighted PM10 micrograms per cubic meter 2010	million metric tons 2009	Per capita kilograms of oil equivalent 2010	billion kilowatt hours 2010
Costa Rica	−0.93	17.6	23,780	97	95	2.2	27	8.3	998	9.6
Côte d'Ivoire	−0.15	21.8	3,813	80	24	3.5	30	6.6	485	6.0
Croatia	−0.19	9.5	8,562	99	99	0.2	22	21.5	1,932	14.0
Cuba	−1.66	5.3	3,387	94	91	−0.1	15	31.6	975	17.4
Curaçao	..	..	..	..	..	..	..	..	..	..
Cyprus	−0.09	4.5	699	100	100	1.4	27	8.2	2,215	5.4
Czech Republic	−0.08	15.1	1,253	100	98	−0.3	16	108.1	4,193	85.3
Denmark	−1.14	4.1	1,077	100	100	0.6	15	45.7	3,470	38.8
Djibouti	0.00	0.0	331	88	50	2.0	28	0.5	..	..
Dominica	0.58	3.7	..	..	..	0.1	20	0.1	..	..
Dominican Republic	0.00	24.1	2,088	86	83	2.1	14	20.3	840	15.9
Ecuador	1.81	38.0	29,456	94	92	2.2	19	30.1	836	17.7
Egypt, Arab Rep.	−1.73	6.1	22	99	95	2.1	78	216.1	903	146.8
El Salvador	1.45	1.4	2,850	88	87	1.3	28	6.3	677	6.0
Equatorial Guinea	0.69	14.0	36,100	..	..	3.2	6	4.8	..	..
Eritrea	0.28	3.8	517	61	14	5.2	61	0.5	142	0.3
Estonia	0.12	22.6	9,486	98	95	0.1	9	16.0	4,155	13.0
Ethiopia	1.08	18.4	1,440	44	21	3.7	47	7.9	400	5.0
Faeroe Islands	0.00	..	..	..	..	0.8	11	0.7	..	..
Fiji	−0.34	0.2	32,876	98	83	1.7	20	0.8	..	..
Finland	0.14	8.5	19,858	100	100	0.6	15	53.6	6,787	80.7
France	−0.39	17.1	3,057	100	100	1.2	12	363.4	4,031	564.3
French Polynesia	−3.97	0.1	..	100	98	1.1	..	0.9	..	..
Gabon	0.00	14.6	106,892	87	33	2.3	7	1.6	1,418	1.8
Gambia, The	−0.41	1.3	1,689	89	68	3.7	60	0.4	..	..
Georgia	0.09	3.4	12,958	98	95	1.0	49	5.8	700	10.1
Germany	0.00	42.3	1,308	100	100	0.2	16	734.6	4,003	622.1
Ghana	2.08	14.0	1,214	86	14	3.6	22	7.4	382	8.4
Greece	−0.81	9.9	5,133	100	98	0.3	27	94.9	2,440	57.4
Greenland	0.00	40.1	..	100	100	0.2	..	0.6	..	..
Grenada	0.00	0.1	..	..	97	1.3	19	0.2	..	..
Guam	0.00	3.6	..	100	99	1.3	..	..	..	..
Guatemala	1.40	29.5	7,400	92	78	3.4	51	15.2	713	8.8
Guinea	0.54	6.4	22,110	74	18	3.8	55	1.2	..	..
Guinea-Bissau	0.48	26.9	10,342	64	20	3.6	48	0.3	..	..
Guyana	0.00	4.8	318,766	94	84	0.5	20	1.6	..	..
Haiti	0.76	0.1	1,285	69	17	3.8	35	2.3	229	0.6
Honduras	2.06	13.9	12,371	87	77	3.1	34	7.7	601	6.7
Hungary	−0.62	5.1	602	100	100	0.4	15	48.7	2,567	37.4
Iceland	−4.99	13.2	532,892	100	100	0.4	18	2.0	16,882	17.1
India	−0.46	4.8	1,165	92	34	2.5	52	1,979.4	566	959.9
Indonesia	0.51	6.4	8,332	82	54	2.5	60	451.8	867	169.8
Iran, Islamic Rep.	0.00	6.9	1,718	96	100	1.3	56	602.1	2,817	233.0
Iraq	−0.09	0.1	1,068	79	73	2.8	88	109.0	1,180	50.2
Ireland	−1.53	1.2	10,707	100	99	2.7	13	41.6	3,218	28.4
Isle of Man	0.00	..	..	..	..	0.5	..	..	..	..
Israel	−0.07	15.1	97	100	100	1.9	21	67.2	3,005	58.6

	Deforestation[a]	Nationally protected areas	Internal renewable freshwater resources[b]	Access to improved water source	Access to improved sanitation facilities	Urban population	Particulate matter concentration	Carbon dioxide emissions	Energy use	Electricity production
		Terrestrial and marine areas % of total territorial area	Per capita cubic meters	% of total population	% of total population	average annual % growth	urban-population-weighted PM10 micrograms per cubic meter	million metric tons	Per capita kilograms of oil equivalent	billion kilowatt hours
	average annual % 2000–10	2010	2011	2010	2010	1990–2011	2010	2009	2010	2010
Italy	−0.90	15.9	3,005	100	..	0.7	21	400.8	2,815	298.8
Jamaica	0.11	7.3	3,475	93	80	0.4	27	8.6	1,131	4.2
Japan	−0.05	10.9	3,364	100	100	0.9	24	1,101.1	3,898	1,110.8
Jordan	0.00	1.9	110	97	98	2.5	30	22.5	1,191	14.8
Kazakhstan	0.17	2.5	3,886	95	97	1.3	18	225.8	4,595	82.6
Kenya	0.33	11.7	497	59	32	4.4	30	12.4	483	7.5
Kiribati	0.00	22.6	..	..	..	1.8	..	0.1	..	..
Korea, Dem. Rep.	2.00	3.9	2,740	98	80	0.6	52	75.1	761	21.7
Korea, Rep.	0.11	3.0	1,303	98	100	1.1	30	509.4	5,060	496.7
Kosovo	..	..	..	..	..	..	..	..	1,372	5.2
Kuwait	−2.57	1.1	0	99	100	2.9	91	80.2	12,204	57.0
Kyrgyz Republic	−1.07	6.9	8,873	90	93	1.5	35	6.7	536	11.4
Lao PDR	0.49	16.6	30,280	67	63	4.7	45	1.8	..	..
Latvia	−0.34	16.4	8,133	99	78	−8.4	12	6.7	1,971	6.6
Lebanon	−0.45	0.4	1,127	100	..	0.9	25	21.0	1,526	15.7
Lesotho	−0.47	0.5	2,384	78	26	3.7	38	..	..	..
Liberia	0.67	1.6	48,443	73	18	4.1	31	0.5	..	..
Libya	0.00	0.1	109	..	97	1.3	65	62.9	3,013	31.6
Liechtenstein	0.00	42.4	..	..	..	0.5	24	..	..	..
Lithuania	−0.68	14.4	5,135	92	86	−8.0	16	12.8	2,107	5.0
Luxembourg	0.00	20.0	1,930	100	100	2.5	12	10.1	8,343	3.2
Macedonia, FYR	−0.41	4.9	2,616	100	88	0.4	17	11.3	1,402	7.3
Madagascar	0.45	2.5	15,810	46	15	4.8	28	1.8	..	..
Malawi	0.97	15.0	1,049	83	51	4.1	29	1.1	..	..
Malaysia	0.54	13.7	20,098	100	96	2.5	18	198.3	2,558	125.3
Maldives	0.00	..	94	98	97	4.1	28	1.0	..	..
Mali	0.61	2.4	3,788	64	22	4.9	111	0.6	..	..
Malta	0.00	1.7	121	100	100	0.1	..	2.5	2,013	2.1
Marshall Islands	0.00	0.6	..	94	75	1.9	..	0.1	..	..
Mauritania	2.66	1.1	113	50	26	3.0	68	2.1	..	..
Mauritius	1.00	0.7	2,139	99	89	0.4	16	3.8	..	..
Mexico	0.30	11.9	3,563	96	85	1.6	30	446.2	1,570	271.0
Micronesia, Fed. Sts.	−0.04	0.1	..	..	..	0.9	..	0.1	..	..
Moldova	−1.77	1.4	281	96	85	1.4	36	4.5	731	3.6
Monaco	0.00	98.1	..	100	100	0.1	..	..	..	..
Mongolia	0.73	13.4	12,428	82	51	2.9	96	14.5	1,189	4.5
Montenegro	0.00	11.5	..	98	90	0.4	..	3.1	1,303	4.2
Morocco	−0.23	1.5	899	83	70	1.6	23	48.8	517	22.3
Mozambique	0.54	14.8	4,191	47	18	3.1	22	2.6	436	16.7
Myanmar	0.93	5.2	20,750	83	76	2.5	40	11.1	292	7.5
Namibia	0.97	14.7	2,651	93	32	3.3	42	3.6	702	1.5
Nepal	0.70	17.0	6,501	89	31	3.8	27	3.5	341	3.2
Netherlands	−0.14	15.2	659	100	100	0.9	30	169.7	5,021	118.1
New Caledonia	0.00	23.9	..	..	..	1.4	48	3.0	..	..
New Zealand	−0.01	20.0	74,230	100	..	0.9	11	32.1	4,166	44.8
Nicaragua	2.01	36.8	32,318	85	52	1.9	21	4.5	542	3.7
Niger	0.98	7.1	218	49	9	5.0	96	1.2	..	..

	Deforestation[a] average annual % 2000–10	Nationally protected areas Terrestrial and marine areas % of total territorial area 2010	Internal renewable freshwater resources[b] Per capita cubic meters 2011	Access to improved water source % of total population 2010	Access to improved sanitation facilities % of total population 2010	Urban population average annual % growth 1990–2011	Particulate matter concentration urban-population- weighted PM10 micrograms per cubic meter 2010	Carbon dioxide emissions million metric tons 2009	Energy use Per capita kilograms of oil equivalent 2010	Electricity production billion kilowatt hours 2010
Nigeria	3.67	12.6	1,360	58	31	3.8	38	70.2	714	26.1
Northern Mariana Islands	0.53	28.4	..	98	..	0.5	..	..	..	..
Norway	−0.80	10.9	77,124	100	100	1.6	16	47.1	6,637	124.1
Oman	0.00	9.3	492	89	99	2.6	95	41.1	7,188	19.8
Pakistan	2.24	9.8	311	92	48	2.7	91	161.2	487	94.5
Palau	−0.18	4.8	..	85	100	1.6	..	0.2	..	..
Panama	0.36	11.5	41,275	93	69	2.3	45	7.8	1,073	7.5
Papua New Guinea	0.48	1.4	114,203	40	45	2.8	16	3.5	..	..
Paraguay	0.97	5.4	14,311	86	71	2.6	64	4.5	742	54.1
Peru	0.18	13.1	54,966	85	71	1.5	42	47.4	667	35.9
Philippines	−0.75	5.0	5,050	92	74	2.2	17	68.6	434	67.7
Poland	−0.31	21.8	1,391	..	90	0.8	33	298.9	2,657	157.1
Portugal	−0.11	6.1	3,600	99	100	0.1	18	57.4	2,213	53.7
Puerto Rico	−1.76	4.4	1,915	..	..	−0.3	15	..	..	..
Qatar	0.00	1.4	30	100	100	6.3	20	70.3	12,799	28.1
Romania	−0.32	7.8	1,978	89	73	−0.2	11	79.5	1,632	60.3
Russian Federation	0.00	9.2	30,169	97	70	0.6	15	1,574.4	4,927	1,036.1
Rwanda	−2.38	10.0	868	65	55	4.6	21	0.7	..	..
Samoa	0.00	1.2	..	96	98	−0.5	..	0.2	..	..
San Marino	0.00	..	..	..	..	0.7	8	..	..	..
São Tomé and Príncipe	0.00	..	12,936	89	26	2.9	28	0.1	..	..
Saudi Arabia	0.00	29.9	85	..	..	2.5	96	432.8	6,168	240.1
Senegal	0.49	23.5	2,021	72	52	3.4	77	4.6	272	3.0
Serbia	−0.99	6.0	1,158	99	92	0.2	..	46.3	2,141	37.4
Seychelles	0.00	0.9	..	..	..	0.1	..	0.7	..	..
Sierra Leone	0.69	4.3	26,678	55	13	3.2	39	1.4	..	..
Singapore	0.00	3.4	116	100	100	2.1	23	31.9	6,456	45.4
Sint Maarten	..	..	..	..	..	..	..	..	..	..
Slovak Republic	−0.06	23.2	2,334	100	100	−0.7	13	33.9	3,280	27.5
Slovenia	−0.16	13.1	9,095	99	100	0.1	26	15.3	3,520	16.2
Solomon Islands	0.25	0.1	80,939	..	..	4.8	31	0.2	..	..
Somalia	1.07	0.5	628	29	23	3.6	26	0.6	..	..
South Africa	0.00	6.9	886	91	79	1.9	18	499.0	2,738	256.6
South Sudan	..	..	..	..	..	4.7	..	..	..	..
Spain	−0.68	7.6	2,408	100	100	0.4	24	288.2	2,773	299.9
Sri Lanka	1.12	15.0	2,530	91	92	1.6	65	12.7	478	10.8
St. Kitts and Nevis	0.00	0.8	452	99	96	1.5	15	0.3	..	..
St. Lucia	−0.07	2.0	..	96	65	−2.6	31	0.4	..	..
St. Martin	0.00	..	..	..	..	..	..	..	..	..
St. Vincent and Grenadines	−0.27	1.2	..	..	..	0.8	22	0.2	..	..
Sudan	0.08	4.2	672	58	26	2.6[c]	137	14.3	371	7.8
Suriname	0.01	12.2	166,220	92	83	1.5	20	2.5	..	..
Swaziland	−0.84	3.0	2,472	71	57	1.0	30	1.0	..	..
Sweden	−0.30	10.0	18,097	100	100	0.9	10	43.7	5,468	148.5
Switzerland	−0.38	24.9	5,106	100	100	1.2	20	41.6	3,349	66.1
Syrian Arab Republic	−1.29	0.6	343	90	95	2.5	54	65.3	1,063	46.4
Tajikistan	0.00	4.1	9,096	64	94	1.6	29	2.8	336	16.4

	Deforestation[a] average annual % 2000–10	Nationally protected areas Terrestrial and marine areas % of total territorial area 2010	Internal renewable freshwater resources[b] Per capita cubic meters 2011	Access to improved water source % of total population 2010	Access to improved sanitation facilities % of total population 2010	Urban population average annual % growth 1990–2011	Particulate matter concentration urban-population-weighted PM10 micrograms per cubic meter 2010	Carbon dioxide emissions million metric tons 2009	Energy use Per capita kilograms of oil equivalent 2010	Electricity production billion kilowatt hours 2010
Tanzania	1.13	26.9	1,817	53	10	4.8	19	7.0	448	4.4
Thailand	0.02	17.3	3,229	96	96	1.7	53	271.7	1,699	159.5
Timor-Leste	1.40	6.4	6,986	69	47	4.2	..	0.2	..	..
Togo	5.13	11.0	1,868	61	13	3.4	27	1.5	446	0.1
Tonga	0.00	9.4	..	100	96	0.9	..	0.2	..	..
Trinidad and Tobago	0.32	9.6	2,852	94	92	2.3	97	47.8	15,913	8.5
Tunisia	−1.86	1.3	393	94	85	1.5	23	25.2	913	16.1
Turkey	−1.11	1.9	3,083	100	90	2.5	35	277.8	1,445	211.2
Turkmenistan	0.00	3.0	275	..	98	1.9	36	48.2	4,226	16.7
Turks and Caicos Islands	0.00	3.5	..	100	..	2.6	..	0.2	..	..
Tuvalu	0.00	0.2	..	98	85	1.0	..	..	..	..
Uganda	2.56	10.3	1,130	72	34	5.9	10	3.5	..	..
Ukraine	−0.21	3.6	1,162	98	94	−0.1	15	272.2	2,845	188.6
United Arab Emirates	−0.24	4.7	19	100	98	5.3	89	156.8	8,271	97.7
United Kingdom	−0.31	18.1	2,311	100	100	0.9	13	474.6	3,252	378.0
United States	−0.13	13.7	9,044	99	100	1.0	18	5,299.6	7,164	4,354.4
Uruguay	−2.14	0.3	17,515	100	100	0.5	112	7.9	1,241	10.8
Uzbekistan	−0.20	2.3	557	87	100	2.8	31	116.5	1,533	51.7
Vanuatu	0.00	0.5	..	90	57	3.7	14	0.1	..	..
Venezuela, RB	0.60	50.2	24,674	..	..	1.7	10	184.8	2,669	118.3
Vietnam	−1.65	4.6	4,092	95	76	3.1	54	142.3	681	94.9
Virgin Islands (U.S.)	0.80	1.5	..	..	..	0.1	..	..	..	..
West Bank and Gaza	−0.10	0.6	207	85	92	3.3	..	2.2	..	..
Yemen, Rep.	0.00	0.7	85	55	53	4.9	34	24.0	298	7.8
Zambia	0.33	36.0	5,952	61	48	5.3	27	2.0	628	11.3
Zimbabwe	1.88	28.0	961	80	40	2.7	34	8.9	764	8.1
World	**0.11** [w]	**11.9** [w]	**6,115** [s]	**88** [w]	**63** [w]	**2.1** [w]	**41** [w]	**32,042.2** [d,w]	**1,851** [w]	**21,448.9** [w]
Low income	0.61	10.0	5,125	65	37	3.6	54	229.8	363	197.4
Middle income	0.08	12.0	5,819	90	59	2.3	46	17,344.8	1,310	10,122.1
Lower middle income	0.31	8.8	3,121	87	47	2.6	53	3,884.9	667	2,138.2
Upper middle income	0.02	13.1	8,550	93	73	2.1	42	13,460.8	1,948	7,981.7
Low & middle income	0.15	11.6	5,722	86	56	2.4	47	17,574.2	1,210	10,344.7
East Asia & Pacific	* −0.44	13.3	4,446	90	66	2.9	55	8,936.9	1,520	4,888.8
Europe & Central Asia	−0.04	7.7	12,498	96	84	0.9	21	2,863.0	3,015	1,884.3
Latin America & Carib.	0.45	19.8	22,810	94	79	1.5	28	1,533.7	1,312	1,356.4
Middle East & N. Africa	−0.15	4.0	673	89	88	2.1	59	1,320.9	1,372	638.4
South Asia	−0.29	5.6	1,197	90	38	2.7	62	2,215.6	519	1,120.1
Sub-Saharan Africa	0.48	11.6	4,455	61	31	3.8	41	724.0	683	441.4
High income	−0.04	12.7	8,195	100	100	1.0	22	12,727.0	5,000	11,163.7
Euro area	−0.31	16.5	2,933	100	100	0.6	18	2,456.1	3,633	2,352.4

a. Negative values indicate an increase in forest area. b. River flows from other countries are not included because of data unreliability. c. Excludes South Sudan. d. Includes emissions not allocated to specific countries.

About the data

Environmental resources are needed to promote growth and poverty reduction, but growth can create new stresses on the environment. Deforestation, loss of biologically diverse habitat, depletion of water resources, pollution, urbanization, and ever increasing demand for energy production are some of the factors that must be considered in shaping development strategies.

Loss of forests

Forests provide habitat for many species and act as carbon sinks. If properly managed they also provide a livelihood for people who manage and use forest resources. FAO (2010) uses a uniform definition of forest to provide information on forest cover in 2010 and adjusted estimates of forest cover in 1990 and 2000. Data presented here do not distinguish natural forests from plantations, a breakdown the FAO provides only for developing countries. Thus, data may underestimate the rate at which natural forest is disappearing in some countries.

Habitat protection and biodiversity

Deforestation is a major cause of loss of biodiversity, and habitat conservation is vital for stemming this loss. Conservation efforts have focused on protecting areas of high biodiversity. The World Conservation Monitoring Centre (WCMC) and the United Nations Environment Programme (UNEP) compile data on protected areas. Differences in definitions, reporting practices, and reporting periods limit cross-country comparability. Nationally protected areas are defined using the six International Union for Conservation of Nature (IUCN) categories for areas of at least 1,000 hectares—scientific reserves and strict nature reserves with limited public access, national parks of national or international significance and not materially affected by human activity, natural monuments and natural landscapes with unique aspects, managed nature reserves and wildlife sanctuaries, protected landscapes (which may include cultural landscapes), and areas managed mainly for the sustainable use of natural systems to ensure long-term protection and maintenance of biological diversity—as well as terrestrial protected areas not assigned to an IUCN category. Designating an area as protected does not mean that protection is in force. For small countries with protected areas smaller than 1,000 hectares, the size limit in the definition leads to underestimation of protected areas. Due to variations in consistency and methods of collection, data quality is highly variable across countries. Some countries update their information more frequently than others, some have more accurate data on extent of coverage, and many underreport the number or extent of protected areas.

Freshwater resources

The data on freshwater resources are derived from estimates of runoff into rivers and recharge of groundwater. These estimates are derived from different sources and refer to different years, so cross-country comparisons should be made with caution. Data are collected intermittently and may hide substantial year-to-year variations in total renewable water resources. Data do not distinguish between seasonal and geographic variations in water availability within countries. Data for small countries and countries in arid and semiarid zones are less reliable than data for larger countries and countries with greater rainfall.

Water and sanitation

A reliable supply of safe drinking water and sanitary disposal of excreta are two of the most important means of improving human health and protecting the environment. Improved sanitation facilities prevent human, animal, and insect contact with excreta.

Data on access to an improved water source measure the percentage of the population with ready access to water for domestic purposes, based on surveys and estimates of service users provided by governments to the Joint Monitoring Programme of the World Health Organization (WHO) and the United Nations Children's Fund (UNICEF). The coverage rates are based on information from service users on household use rather than on information from service providers, which may include nonfunctioning systems. Access to drinking water from an improved source does not ensure that the water is safe or adequate, as these characteristics are not tested at the time of survey. While information on access to an improved water source is widely used, it is extremely subjective; terms such as "safe," "improved," "adequate," and "reasonable" may have different meanings in different countries despite official WHO definitions (see *Definitions*). Even in high-income countries treated water may not always be safe to drink. Access to an improved water source is equated with connection to a supply system; it does not account for variations in the quality and cost of the service.

Urbanization

There is no consistent and universally accepted standard for distinguishing urban from rural areas and, by extension, calculating their populations. Most countries use a classification related to the size or characteristics of settlements. Some define areas based on the presence of certain infrastructure and services. Others designate areas based on administrative arrangements. Because data are based on national definitions, cross-country comparisons should be made with caution.

Air pollution

Indoor and outdoor air pollution place a major burden on world health. More than half the world's people rely on dung, wood, crop waste, or coal to meet basic energy needs. Cooking and heating with these fuels on open fires or stoves without chimneys lead to indoor air pollution, which is responsible for 1.6 million deaths a year—one every 20 seconds. In many urban areas air pollution exposure is the main environmental threat to health. Long-term exposure to high levels of soot and small particles contributes to such health effects as respiratory diseases, lung cancer, and heart disease. Particulate pollution, alone or with sulfur dioxide, creates an enormous burden of ill health.

Data on particulate matter are estimated average annual concentrations in residential areas away from air pollution "hotspots," such as industrial districts and transport corridors. Data are estimates of annual ambient concentrations of particulate matter in cities of more than 100,000 people by the World Bank's Agriculture and Environmental Services Department.

Pollutant concentrations are sensitive to local conditions, and even monitoring sites in the same city may register different levels. Thus these data should be considered only a general indication of air quality, and comparisons should be made with caution. They allow for cross-country comparisons of the relative risk of particulate matter pollution facing urban residents. Major sources of urban outdoor particulate matter pollution are traffic and industrial emissions, but nonanthropogenic sources such as dust storms may also be a substantial contributor for some cities. Country technology and pollution controls are important determinants of particulate matter. Current WHO air quality guidelines are annual mean concentrations of 20 micrograms per cubic meter for particulate matter less than 10 microns in diameter.

Carbon dioxide emissions

Carbon dioxide emissions are the primary source of greenhouse gases, which contribute to global warming, threatening human and natural habitats. Fossil fuel combustion and cement manufacturing are the primary sources of anthropogenic carbon dioxide emissions, which the U.S. Department of Energy's Carbon Dioxide Information Analysis Center (CDIAC) calculates using data from the United Nations Statistics Division's World Energy Data Set and the U.S. Bureau of Mines's Cement Manufacturing Data Set. Carbon dioxide emissions, often calculated and reported as elemental carbon, were converted to actual carbon dioxide mass by multiplying them by 3.667 (the ratio of the mass of carbon to that of carbon dioxide). Although estimates of global carbon dioxide emissions are probably accurate within 10 percent (as calculated from global average fuel chemistry and use), country estimates may have larger error bounds. Trends estimated from a consistent time series tend to be more accurate than individual values. Each year the CDIAC recalculates the entire time series since 1949, incorporating recent findings and corrections. Estimates exclude fuels supplied to ships and aircraft in international transport because of the difficulty of apportioning the fuels among benefiting countries.

Energy use

In developing economies growth in energy use is closely related to growth in the modern sectors—industry, motorized transport, and urban areas—but also reflects climatic, geographic, and economic factors. Energy use has been growing rapidly in low- and middle-income economies, but high-income economies still use almost five times as much energy per capita.

Total energy use refers to the use of primary energy before transformation to other end-use fuels (such as electricity and refined petroleum products). It includes energy from combustible renewables and waste—solid biomass and animal products, gas and liquid from biomass, and industrial and municipal waste. Biomass is any plant matter used directly as fuel or converted into fuel, heat, or electricity. Data for combustible renewables and waste are often based on small surveys or other incomplete information and thus give only a broad impression of developments and are not strictly comparable across countries. The IEA reports include country notes that explain some of these differences (see *Data sources*). All forms of energy—primary energy and primary electricity—are converted into oil equivalents. A notional thermal efficiency of 33 percent is assumed for converting nuclear electricity into oil equivalents and 100 percent efficiency for converting hydroelectric power.

Electricity production

Use of energy is important in improving people's standard of living. But electricity generation also can damage the environment. Whether such damage occurs depends largely on how electricity is generated. For example, burning coal releases twice as much carbon dioxide—a major contributor to global warming—as does burning an equivalent amount of natural gas. Nuclear energy does not generate carbon dioxide emissions, but it produces other dangerous waste products.

The International Energy Agency (IEA) compiles data and data on energy inputs used to generate electricity. Data for countries that are not members of the Organisation for Economic Co-operation and Development (OECD) are based on national energy data adjusted to conform to annual questionnaires completed by OECD member governments. In addition, estimates are sometimes made to complete major aggregates from which key data are missing, and adjustments are made to compensate for differences in definitions. The IEA makes these estimates in consultation with national statistical offices, oil companies, electric utilities, and national energy experts. It occasionally revises its time series to reflect political changes. For example, the IEA has constructed historical energy statistics for countries of the former Soviet Union. In addition, energy statistics for other countries have undergone continuous changes in coverage or methodology in recent years as more detailed energy accounts have become available. Breaks in series are therefore unavoidable.

Definitions

• **Deforestation** is the permanent conversion of natural forest area to other uses, including agriculture, ranching, settlements, and infrastructure. Deforested areas do not include areas logged but intended for regeneration or areas degraded by fuelwood gathering, acid precipitation, or forest fires. • **Nationally protected areas** are terrestrial and marine protected areas as a percentage of total territorial area and include all nationally designated protected areas with known location and extent. All overlaps between different designations and categories, buffered points, and polygons are removed, and all undated protected areas are dated. • **Internal renewable freshwater resources** are the average annual flows of rivers and groundwater from rainfall in the country. Natural incoming flows originating outside a country's borders and overlapping water resources between surface runoff and groundwater recharge are excluded.

• **Access to an improved water source** is the percentage of the population with reasonable access to an adequate amount of water from an improved source, such as piped water into a dwelling, plot, or yard; public tap or standpipe; tubewell or borehole; protected dug well or spring; and rainwater collection. Unimproved sources include unprotected dug wells or springs, carts with small tank or drum, bottled water, and tanker trucks. Reasonable access is defined as the availability of at least 20 liters a person a day from a source within 1 kilometer of the dwelling • **Access to improved sanitation facilities** is the percentage of the population with at least adequate access to excreta disposal facilities (private or shared, but not public) that can effectively prevent human, animal, and insect contact with excreta (facilities do not have to include treatment to render sewage outflows innocuous). Improved facilities range from simple but protected pit latrines to flush toilets with a sewerage connection. To be effective, facilities must be correctly constructed and properly maintained. • **Urban population** is the midyear population of areas defined as urban in each country and reported to the United Nations divided by the World Bank estimate of total population. • **Particulate matter concentration** is fine suspended particulates of less than 10 microns in diameter (PM10) that are capable of penetrating deep into the respiratory tract and causing severe health damage. Data are urban-population-weighted PM10 levels in residential areas of cities with more than 100,000 residents. • **Carbon dioxide emissions** are emissions from the burning of fossil fuels and the manufacture of cement and include carbon dioxide produced during consumption of solid, liquid, and gas fuels and gas flaring. • **Energy use** refers to the use of primary energy before transformation to other end use fuels, which equals indigenous production plus imports and stock changes, minus exports and fuels supplied to ships and aircraft engaged in international transport. • **Electricity production** is measured at the terminals of all alternator sets in a station. In addition to hydropower, coal, oil, gas, and nuclear power generation, it covers generation by geothermal, solar, wind, and tide and wave energy as well as that from combustible renewables and waste. Production includes the output of electric plants designed to produce electricity only, as well as that of combined heat and power plants.

Data sources

Data on deforestation are from FAO (2010) and the FAO's data website. Data on protected areas, derived from the UNEP and WCMC online databases, are based on data from national authorities, national legislation, and international agreements. Data on freshwater resources are from the FAO's AQUASTAT database. Data on access to water and sanitation are from WHO and UNICEF (2012). Data on urban population are from the United Nations Population Division (2011). Data on particulate matter concentrations are World Bank estimates. Data on carbon dioxide emissions are from the CDIAC. Data on energy use and electricity production are from IEA electronic files and published in IEA's annual publications, *Energy Statistics of Non-OECD Countries, Energy Balances of Non-OECD Countries, Energy Statistics of OECD Countries,* and *Energy Balances of OECD Countries.*

References

CDIAC (Carbon Dioxide Information Analysis Center). n.d. Online database. http://cdiac.ornl.gov/home.html. Oak Ridge National Laboratory, Environmental Science Division, Oak Ridge, TN.

FAO (Food and Agriculture Organization of the United Nations). 2010. *Global Forest Resources Assessment 2010.* Rome.

———. n.d. AQUASTAT. Online database. www.fao.org/nr/water/aquastat/data/query/index.html. Rome.

IEA (International Energy Agency). Various years. *Energy Balances of Non-OECD Countries.* Paris.

———. Various years. *Energy Balances of OECD Countries.* Paris.

———. Various years. *Energy Statistics of Non-OECD Countries.* Paris.

———. Various years. *Energy Statistics of OECD Countries.* Paris.

UNEP (United Nations Environment Programme) and WCMC (World Conservation Monitoring Centre). 2012. Online databases www.unep-wcmc-apps.org/species/dbases/about.cfm. Nairobi.

United Nations Population Division. 2011. *World Urbanization Prospects: The 2011 Revision.* New York: United Nations, Department of Economic and Social Affairs.

WHO (World Health Organization). 2004. *Inheriting the World: The Atlas of Children's Health and the Environment.* www.who.int/ceh/publications/atlas/en/index.html. Geneva.

WHO (World Health Organization) and UNICEF (United Nations Children's Fund). 2012. *Progress on Sanitation and Drinking Water.* Geneva: WHO.

To access the World Development Indicators online tables, use the URL http://wdi.worldbank.org/table/ and the table number (for example, http://wdi.worldbank.org/table/3.1). To view a specific indicator online, use the URL http://data.worldbank.org/indicator/ and the indicator code (for example, http://data.worldbank.org/indicator/SP.RUR.TOTL.ZS).

3.1 Rural environment and land use

Rural population	SP.RUR.TOTL.ZS
Rural population growth	SP.RUR.TOTL.ZG
Land area	AG.LND.TOTL.K2
Forest area	AG.LND.FRST.ZS
Permanent cropland	AG.LND.CROP.ZS
Arable land, % of land area	AG.LND.ARBL.ZS
Arable land, hectares per person	AG.LND.ARBL.HA.PC

3.2 Agricultural inputs

Agricultural land, % of land area	AG.LND.AGRI.ZS
Agricultural land, % irrigated	AG.LND.IRIG.AG.ZS
Average annual precipitation	AG.LND.PRCP.MM
Land under cereal production	AG.LND.CREL.HA
Fertilizer consumption, % of fertilizer production	AG.CON.FERT.PT.ZS
Fertilizer consumption, kilograms per hectare of arable land	AG.CON.FERT.ZS
Agricultural employment	SL.AGR.EMPL.ZS
Tractors	AG.LND.TRAC.ZS

3.3 Agricultural output and productivity

Crop production index	AG.PRD.CROP.XD
Food production index	AG.PRD.FOOD.XD
Livestock production index	AG.PRD.LVSK.XD
Cereal yield	AG.YLD.CREL.KG
Agriculture value added per worker	EA.PRD.AGRI.KD

3.4 Deforestation and biodiversity

Forest area	AG.LND.FRST.K2
Average annual deforestation	..[a,b]
Threatened species, Mammals	EN.MAM.THRD.NO
Threatened species, Birds	EN.BIR.THRD.NO
Threatened species, Fishes	EN.FSH.THRD.NO
Threatened species, Higher plants	EN.HPT.THRD.NO
Terrestrial protected areas	ER.LND.PTLD.ZS
Marine protected areas	ER.MRN.PTMR.ZS

3.5 Freshwater

Internal renewable freshwater resources	ER.H2O.INTR.K3
Internal renewable freshwater resources, Per capita	ER.H2O.INTR.PC
Annual freshwater withdrawals, cu. m	ER.H2O.FWTL.K3
Annual freshwater withdrawals, % of internal resources	ER.H2O.FWTL.ZS

Annual freshwater withdrawals, % for agriculture	ER.H2O.FWAG.ZS
Annual freshwater withdrawals, % for industry	ER.H2O.FWIN.ZS
Annual freshwater withdrawals, % of domestic	ER.H2O.FWDM.ZS
Water productivity, GDP/water use	ER.GDP.FWTL.M3.KD
Access to an improved water source, % of rural population	SH.H2O.SAFE.RU.ZS
Access to an improved water source, % of urban population	SH.H2O.SAFE.UR.ZS

3.6 Energy production and use

Energy production	EG.EGY.PROD.KT.OE
Energy use	EG.USE.COMM.KT.OE
Energy use, Average annual growth	..[a,b]
Energy use, Per capita	EG.USE.PCAP.KG.OE
Fossil fuel	EG.USE.COMM.FO.ZS
Combustible renewable and waste	EG.USE.CRNW.ZS
Alternative and nuclear energy production	EG.USE.COMM.CL.ZS

3.7 Electricity production, sources, and access

Electricity production	EG.ELC.PROD.KH
Coal sources	EG.ELC.COAL.ZS
Natural gas sources	EG.ELC.NGAS.ZS
Oil sources	EG.ELC.PETR.ZS
Hydropower sources	EG.ELC.HYRO.ZS
Renewable sources	EG.ELC.RNWX.ZS
Nuclear power sources	EG.ELC.NUCL.ZS
Access to electricity	EG.ELC.ACCS.ZS

3.8 Energy dependency, efficiency and carbon dioxide emissions

Net energy imports	EG.IMP.CONS.ZS
GDP per unit of energy use	EG.GDP.PUSE.KO.PP.KD
Carbon dioxide emissions, Total	EN.ATM.CO2E.KT
Carbon dioxide emissions, Carbon intensity	EN.ATM.CO2E.EG.ZS
Carbon dioxide emissions, Per capita	EN.ATM.CO2E.PC
Carbon dioxide emissions, kilograms per 2005 PPP $ of GDP	EN.ATM.CO2E.PP.GD.KD

3.9 Trends in greenhouse gas emissions

Carbon dioxide emissions, Average annual growth	..[a,b]
Carbon dioxide emissions, % change	..[a,b]
Methane emissions, Total	EN.ATM.METH.KT.CE

Methane emissions, % change	..[a,b]
Methane emissions, From energy processes	EN.ATM.METH.EG.ZS
Methane emissions, Agricultural	EN.ATM.METH.AG.ZS
Nitrous oxide emissions, Total	EN.ATM.NOXE.KT.CE
Nitrous oxide emissions, % change	..[a,b]
Nitrous oxide emissions, Energy and industry	EN.ATM.NOXE.EI.ZS
Nitrous oxide emissions, Agriculture	EN.ATM.NOXE.AG.ZS
Other greenhouse gas emissions, Total	EN.ATM.GHGO.KT.CE
Other greenhouse gas emissions, % change	..[a,b]

3.10 Carbon dioxide emissions by sector

Electricity and heat production	EN.CO2.ETOT.ZS
Manufacturing industries and construction	EN.CO2.MANF.ZS
Residential buildings and commercial and public services	EN.CO2.BLDG.ZS
Transport	EN.CO2.TRAN.ZS
Other sectors	EN.CO2.OTHX.ZS

3.11 Climate variability, exposure to impact, and resilience

Average daily minimum/maximum temperature	..[b]
Projected annual temperature	..[b]
Projected annual cool days/cold nights	..[b]
Projected annual hot days/warm nights	..[b]
Projected annual precipitation	..[b]
Land area with an elevation of 5 meters or less	AG.LND.EL5M.ZS
Population living in areas with elevation of 5 meters or less	EN.POP.EL5M.ZS
Population affected by droughts, floods, and extreme temperatures	EN.CLC.MDAT.ZS
Disaster risk reduction progress score	EN.CLC.DRSK.XQ

3.12 Urbanization

Urban population	SP.URB.TOTL
Urban population, % of total population	SP.URB.TOTL.IN.ZS
Urban population, Average annual growth	SP.URB.GROW

Population in urban agglomerations of more than 1 million	EN.URB.MCTY.TL.ZS
Population in the largest city	EN.URB.LCTY.UR.ZS
Access to improved sanitation facilities, % of urban population	SH.STA.ACSN.UR
Access to improved sanitation facilities, % of rural population	SH.STA.ACSN.RU

3.13 Traffic and congestion

Motor vehicles, Per 1,000 people	IS.VEH.NVEH.P3
Motor vehicles, Per kilometer of road	IS.VEH.ROAD.K1
Passenger cars	IS.VEH.PCAR.P3
Road density	IS.ROD.DNST.K2
Road sector energy consumption, % of total consumption	IS.ROD.ENGY.ZS
Road sector energy consumption, Per capita	IS.ROD.ENGY.PC
Diesel fuel consumption	IS.ROD.DESL.PC
Gasoline fuel consumption	IS.ROD.SGAS.PC
Pump price for super grade gasoline	EP.PMP.SGAS.CD
Pump price for diesel	EP.PMP.DESL.CD
Urban-population-weighted particulate matter concentrations (PM10)	EN.ATM.PM10.MC.M3

3.14 Air pollution

This table provides air pollution data for major cities.	..[b]

3.15 Contribution of natural resources to gross domestic product

Total natural resources rents	NY.GDP.TOTL.RT.ZS
Oil rents	NY.GDP.PETR.RT.ZS
Natural gas rents	NY.GDP.NGAS.RT.ZS
Coal rents	NY.GDP.COAL.RT.ZS
Mineral rents	NY.GDP.MINR.RT.ZS
Forest rents	NY.GDP.FRST.RT.ZS

a. Derived from data elsewhere in the World Development Indicators database.
b. Available online only as part of the table, not as an individual indicator.

ECONOMY

The data in the *Economy* section provide a picture of the global economy and the economic activity of more than 200 countries and territories that produce, trade, and consume the world's output. They include measures of macroeconomic performance and stability and broader measures of income and savings adjusted for pollution, depreciation, and depletion of resources.

The world economy grew 2.3 percent in 2012, to reach $71 trillion, and the share from developing economies grew to 34.3 percent. Growth is expected to remain around 2.4 percent in 2013. Low- and middle-income economies, estimated to have grown 5.1 percent in 2012, are projected to expand 5.5 percent in 2013. Growth in high-income economies has been downgraded from earlier forecasts to 1.3 percent in 2012 and 2013.

Beginning in August 2012, the International Monetary Fund implemented the Balance of Payments Manual 6 (BPM6) framework in its major statistical publications. The World Bank will implement BPM6 in its online databases and publications in April 2013. Balance of payments data for 2005 onward will be presented in accord with the BPM6. The historical BPM5 data series will end with data for 2008, which can be accessed through the *World Development Indicators* archives.

The change to the BPM6 framework will affect some components of the balance of payments. In the current account, "merchanting"—the purchase of goods from a nonresident and the subsequent resale to another nonresident without the goods being present in the economy—has been reclassified from services to goods, while manufacturing services performed on physical inputs owned by others along with maintenance and repair services were reclassified from goods to services. In the capital account, reverse investment in direct investment has been reclassified to present assets and liabilities on a gross basis in the balance of payments and international investment position. No changes were made to the balances on current account, capital account, or financial account. Levels of reserves were not adjusted, nor were net errors and omissions.

For many economies changes to major aggregates and balancing items will be limited. The change in the methodology for "goods for processing" results in increases in imports and exports of services (equivalent to the amounts received or paid for manufacturing services) and larger reductions in gross imports and exports of goods (due to the elimination of imputed transactions in goods that do not change ownership), though net goods and services trade may not be affected. The change in the recording of reverse investment in foreign direct investment will result in substantial increases in both international investment position assets and liabilities for many economies under BPM6, though net international investment position is not affected by this change.

The complete balance of payments methodology can be accessed through the International Monetary Fund website (www.imf.org/external/np/sta/bop/bop.htm).

East Asia & Pacific: Service sector has potential for more growth

Value added in services as a share of GDP, 2010 (%)

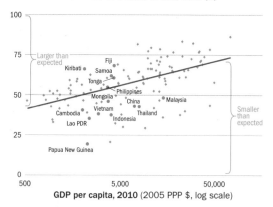

Source: World Development Indicators database.

The service sector contributed substantially to gross domestic product (GDP) growth in many East Asia and Pacific economies in recent years, constituting nearly half of GDP and contributing 3.7 percentage points to an overall growth rate of 8.5 percent. Reflecting strong domestic demand, continuing growth of services is consistent with long-term trends of rising incomes in other regions. But despite recent growth, the service sector in many East Asia and Pacific economies is smaller than expected based on average income. This reflects the relative success of manufacturing among the countries in the region. It may also be the result of limited adoption of high-value, modern services (information and communications technology, finance and professional business services). Few East Asia and Pacific countries besides the Philippines have developed robust industries focused on exporting modern services (World Bank 2012a; Asian Development Bank 2012).

Europe & Central Asia: Volatile food and energy prices pose a challenge

Net energy exports or imports, 2010 (% of energy use)

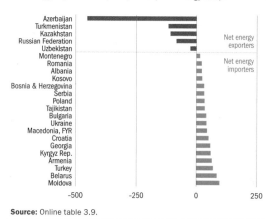

Source: Online table 3.9.

Europe and Central Asia is in general a net exporter of energy, but many economies in the region depend heavily on energy imports and are thus vulnerable to sudden price changes. Azerbaijan, Kazakhstan, the Russian Federation, Turkmenistan, and Uzbekistan, the main exporters, stand to benefit from rising world energy prices. But net energy imports account for 96 percent of energy use in Moldova, 84 percent in Belarus, 69 percent in Turkey, 64 percent in Armenia, and 59 percent in the Kyrgyz Republic. Most energy imports are oil, but Belarus, Croatia, Poland, and Serbia are also large importers of electricity. Some of these economies may face an acute deterioration of their balance of payments positions if oil prices rise. And some are also vulnerable to rising food prices, triggered by the substitution of crop-based fuels for petroleum-based fuels.

Latin America & Caribbean: Tracking global uncertainties

GDP growth (%)

Source: Online table 4.1.

GDP growth in Latin America and the Caribbean fell 1.7 percentage points from 2011 to 3.0 percent in 2012, the second largest drop among developing country regions after Europe and Central Asia, where growth fell 2.8 percentage points. The region's GDP growth decelerated due to slowing domestic demand and a weak external environment. The slowdown was particularly severe in Brazil, the region's largest economy, where global uncertainties and earlier fiscal, monetary, and credit policy tightening to contain inflation risks had a large impact, especially on private investment. In Chile growth remained buoyant and continued to expand briskly, if slightly slower than in 2011. Growth in Central America and the Caribbean slowed modestly, while growth in Mexico (the second largest economy in the region) rose slightly in 2012, to 4 percent, benefiting from the fairly strong recovery in U.S. manufacturing (De la Torre, Didier, and Pienknagura 2012; World Bank 2013).

Middle East & North Africa: Recovery has been slow

Macroeconomic fundamentals weakened in most Middle East and North Africa countries in 2011 and 2012, as growth slowed and governments responded to social pressures with expansionary fiscal policies. High oil prices heightened current account and fiscal deficits in oil importers, especially in places where governments subsidize energy use. Domestic pressures coupled with a challenging global environment and spillovers from regional events also weighed heavily on the economies of some oil importers such as Jordan, Lebanon, and Morocco. Postrevolutionary economies such as the Arab Republic of Egypt, Tunisia, and the Republic of Yemen are recovering after the Arab Spring turmoil. However, recovery has taken place in a weak global environment. The transition in these countries is far from complete, and uncertainty around the reform process continues to constrain private investment (World Bank 2012b).

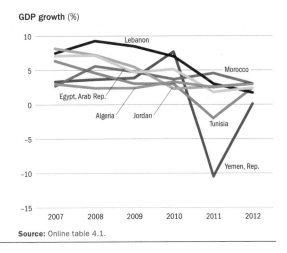

GDP growth (%)

Source: Online table 4.1.

South Asia: Revenues are low and stagnating

South Asian countries collect exceptionally low levels of tax revenue. Revenue collection by central governments in the region averages 10–15 percent of GDP, compared with 20 percent in similar developing economies and higher rates in more developed economies. In most South Asian countries the major source of revenue is the value added tax. Some are changing their tax structures—India is adopting a goods and services tax, for example—but the main problem remains low collection rates for the value added tax and income tax. Most South Asian countries have outdated tax laws and inadequate institutional arrangements unsuitable to the growing complexity of their economies. South Asian countries all need to upgrade their infrastructure and improve social services such as education and health care, which will require a substantial increase in fiscal spending and better sources of revenue (World Bank 2012c).

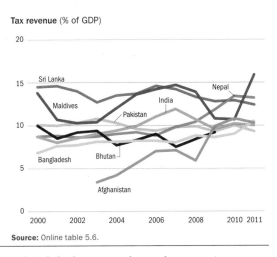

Tax revenue (% of GDP)

Source: Online table 5.6.

Sub-Saharan Africa: Resilient growth in an uncertain global economic environment

Despite a sluggish global economy, economic conditions in Sub-Saharan Africa held up well in 2011–12. Robust domestic demand, high commodity prices, rising export volumes (due to new capacity in the natural resources sector), and steady remittance flows supported growth in 2012. GDP in Sub-Saharan Africa expanded at an average of 4.9 percent a year over 2000–11 and rose an estimated 4.6 percent in 2012, the third most among developing regions. Excluding South Africa, the region's largest economy, GDP output rose 5.8 percent in 2012, with a third of countries growing at least 6 percent. Growth varied across the region, with steady expansion in most low-income countries but slow growth in middle-income countries, such as South Africa, that are more tightly integrated with the global economy and in some countries affected by political instability, such as Mali (IMF 2012; World Bank 2013).

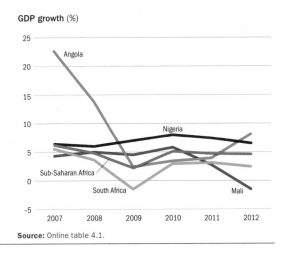

GDP growth (%)

Source: Online table 4.1.

	Gross domestic product			Gross savings	Adjusted net savings	Current account balance	Central government cash surplus or deficit	Central government debt	Consumer price index	Broad money
	average annual % growth	Estimate	Forecast	% of GDP	% of GNI	% of GDP	% of GDP	% of GDP	% growth	% of GDP
	2000–11	2011–12	2012–13	2011	2011	2011	2011	2011	2011	2011
Afghanistan	..	..	..	..	..	..	–0.6	..	5.7	35.8
Albania	5.2	0.8	1.6	12.7	0.9	–12.1	..	..	3.5	81.8
Algeria	3.7	3.0	3.4	48.4	25.3	10.4	–0.3	..	4.5	64.6
American Samoa	..	..	..	..	..	..	..	..	..	..
Andorra	5.9	..	..	..	..	..	..	..	..	..
Angola	12.2	8.1	7.2	20.2	–21.4	12.5	..	..	13.5	35.9
Antigua and Barbuda	2.7	1.7	2.4	26.8	..	–10.7	..	..	3.5	101.4
Argentina	..	..	..	22.3	11.3	0.0	..	..	..	28.8
Armenia	8.2	6.8	4.3	19.3	8.7	–10.8	–2.7	..	7.7	29.5
Aruba	..	..	..	..	..	..	..	..	4.4	..
Australia	3.1	..	..	22.9	6.8	–2.8	–3.7	30.7	3.4	105.8
Austria[a]	1.8	..	..	25.5	16.4	0.5	–2.2	75.0	3.3	..
Azerbaijan	16.0	2.0	4.2	45.9	7.5	27.0	1.4	6.4	7.9	27.8
Bahamas, The	0.5	..	..	11.5	..	–14.0	–3.5	..	3.2	80.5
Bahrain	6.3	..	..	30.1	9.6	3.4	..	..	–0.4	91.2
Bangladesh	6.0	6.1	6.0	36.5	25.0	0.2	–0.9	..	10.7	68.7
Barbados	0.9	..	..	16.9	..	–5.3	–8.6	104.4	9.4	152.3
Belarus	7.8	2.8	4.0	26.3	17.6	–10.5	1.9	44.2	53.2	40.5
Belgium[a]	1.5	..	..	22.3	14.1	–1.4	–3.6	91.0	3.5	..
Belize	3.7	4.0	2.8	..	..	–2.2	–1.6	..	–2.5	76.0
Benin	3.8	3.5	3.8	13.1	7.7	–8.1	–1.4	..	2.7	40.0
Bermuda	1.9	..	..	..	..	..	..	..	..	..
Bhutan	8.5	..	..	..	..	..	0.5	56.8	8.8	67.1
Bolivia	4.2	4.7	4.4	26.1	6.9	2.2	..	..	9.8	68.7
Bosnia and Herzegovina	4.2	..	..	13.1	..	–8.8	–1.2	..	3.7	56.7
Botswana	4.0	5.8	5.1	27.7	20.4	0.3	–1.7	..	8.9	37.8
Brazil	3.8	0.9	3.4	17.2	6.8	–2.1	–2.6	52.8	6.6	74.4
Brunei Darussalam	1.2	..	..	50.9	10.1	37.1	..	..	2.0	67.2
Bulgaria	4.3	0.8	1.8	23.6	13.7	0.4	–2.0	15.5	4.2	75.6
Burkina Faso	5.8	6.4	6.7	15.6	5.5	–4.6	–2.4	..	2.8	29.0
Burundi	3.5	4.1	4.3	1.7	–6.1	–12.2	..	..	9.7	24.2
Cambodia	8.4	6.6	6.7	10.6	3.4	–5.5	–4.2	..	5.5	39.1
Cameroon	3.2	4.6	4.8	12.2	0.8	–3.8	..	..	2.9	23.1
Canada	1.9	..	..	19.6	6.7	–2.8	–1.3	53.8	2.9	..
Cape Verde	6.2	4.8	4.9	22.2	16.7	–16.0	–3.7	..	4.5	77.0
Cayman Islands	..	..	..	..	..	..	..	..	..	..
Central African Republic	1.3	3.8	4.0	..	..	..	..	..	1.3	19.2
Chad	8.7	..	..	..	..	..	..	..	–4.9	13.8
Channel Islands	0.5	..	..	..	..	..	..	..	..	..
Chile	4.1	5.8	5.1	24.9	5.4	1.8	1.3	..	3.3	76.1
China	10.8	7.9	8.4	52.7	36.4	2.8	..	..	5.4	180.1
Hong Kong SAR, China	4.6	..	..	29.4	18.1	5.2	4.1	35.5	5.3	328.2
Macao SAR, China	12.5	..	..	55.9	..	42.7	25.0	..	5.8	101.9
Colombia	4.5	3.5	3.8	19.1	1.3	–3.0	0.3	53.2	3.4	39.9
Comoros	1.9	2.5	3.5	..	..	..	..	..	0.9	34.9
Congo, Dem. Rep.	5.6	6.6	8.2	..	..	..	3.8	..	..	16.8
Congo, Rep.	4.5	4.7	5.6	..	..	..	..	..	1.3	27.0

 Front | User guide | World view | People | Environment

	Gross domestic product			Gross savings	Adjusted net savings	Current account balance	Central government cash surplus or deficit	Central government debt	Consumer price index	Broad money
	average annual % growth	Estimate	Forecast	% of GDP	% of GNI	% of GDP	% of GDP	% of GDP	% growth	% of GDP
	2000–11	2011–12	2012–13	2011	2011	2011	2011	2011	2011	2011
Costa Rica	4.8	4.6	4.0	14.7	9.0	−5.3	−3.5	..	4.9	49.8
Côte d'Ivoire	1.0	8.2	7.0	12.7	4.1	2.0	..	..	4.9	40.5
Croatia	2.6	..	..	19.9	10.7	−0.7	−4.6	..	2.3	72.9
Cuba	6.1	..	..	..	..	..	..	..	..	..
Curaçao	..	..	..	..	..	..	..	..	..	..
Cyprusª	2.9ᵇ	..	..	8.8ᵇ	4.6ᵇ	−4.7	−6.3	114.0	3.3	..
Czech Republic	3.7	..	..	21.7	12.6	−2.9	−4.4	38.1	1.9	73.9
Denmark	0.8	..	..	23.5	15.0	5.7	−2.0	50.6	2.8	74.0
Djibouti	4.0	..	..	..	..	−6.8	..	..	4.4	89.7
Dominica	3.5	0.4	1.2	5.0	−3.7	−17.5	..	..	2.4	86.7
Dominican Republic	5.7	3.0	4.3	8.4	−1.7	−8.1	−2.9	..	8.5	33.4
Ecuador	4.8	4.5	3.9	22.8	−3.2	−0.4	..	..	4.5	35.6
Egypt, Arab Rep.	5.0	2.4	3.2	16.9	1.4	−2.4	−10.1	..	10.1	76.1
El Salvador	2.0	1.8	2.3	8.9	0.7	−4.6	−2.2	48.0	5.1	45.7
Equatorial Guinea	14.4	..	..	..	..	..	..	..	6.9	11.5
Eritrea	0.9	7.5	6.0	..	..	..	..	..	..	114.7
Estoniaª	3.9	..	..	25.1	16.3	2.2	1.0	7.1	5.0	59.8
Ethiopia	8.9	7.8	7.5	27.3	17.6	−2.6	−1.4	..	33.2	..
Faeroe Islands	..	..	..	..	..	−0.7	..	..	..	..
Fiji	1.2	..	..	..	..	−13.0	..	..	8.7	66.3
Finlandª	1.9	..	..	19.7	11.5	−1.2	−0.5	47.8	3.4	..
Franceª	1.2	..	..	17.9	9.0	−2.0	−5.2	93.9	2.1	..
French Polynesia	..	..	..	..	..	..	..	..	..	..
Gabon	2.4	4.7	3.5	..	..	..	..	..	1.3	22.1
Gambia, The	3.4	3.9	10.7	12.1	6.6	7.5	..	..	4.8	54.9
Georgia	6.6ᶜ	4.9ᶜ	5.1ᶜ	13.9ᶜ	4.9ᶜ	−11.8	−1.2	32.6	49.4	29.3
Germanyª	1.1	..	..	23.9	13.8	5.6	−0.4	55.6	2.1	..
Ghana	6.3	7.5	7.8	8.8	−6.6	−8.9	−4.0	..	8.7	30.8
Greeceª	1.8	..	..	5.4	−5.5	−9.9	−9.8	106.5	3.3	..
Greenland	1.7	..	..	..	..	..	..	..	..	..
Grenada	2.2	..	..	−5.7	..	−26.6	−3.0	..	3.0	94.3
Guam	..	..	..	..	..	..	..	..	..	..
Guatemala	3.6	3.1	3.2	10.7	0.9	−3.1	−2.8	24.6	6.2	45.5
Guinea	2.6	4.8	5.0	−6.5	−27.7	−22.8	..	..	21.4	36.4
Guinea-Bissau	2.5	−2.8	3.0	..	..	−8.5	..	..	5.0	40.5
Guyana	2.5	..	..	14.5	−1.3	−7.1	..	..	5.0	65.8
Haiti	0.7	2.2	6.0	24.6	17.0	−4.6	..	..	8.4	47.2
Honduras	4.4	3.3	3.7	17.9	11.0	−8.6	−2.6	..	6.8	52.2
Hungary	1.9	..	..	20.6	13.0	0.9	3.6	80.9	4.0	63.7
Iceland	2.7	..	..	7.3	0.9	−6.9	−5.3	119.3	4.0	96.3
India	7.8	5.5	5.9	34.6	22.5	−3.0	−3.7	48.5	8.9	76.7
Indonesia	5.4	6.1	6.3	31.8	17.1	0.2	−1.1	26.2	5.4	38.8
Iran, Islamic Rep.	5.4	..	..	..	..	..	0.5	..	20.6	45.0
Iraq	1.1	..	..	..	..	22.7	..	..	2.9	54.9
Irelandª	2.4	..	..	14.0	5.5	1.2	−13.5	106.0	2.6	..
Isle of Man	6.2	..	..	..	..	..	..	..	..	..
Israel	3.6	..	..	14.7	6.3	0.1	−4.4	..	3.5	104.5

	Gross domestic product			Gross savings	Adjusted net savings	Current account balance	Central government cash surplus or deficit	Central government debt	Consumer price index	Broad money
	average annual % growth			% of GDP	% of GNI	% of GDP	% of GDP	% of GDP	% growth	% of GDP
	2000–11	Estimate 2011–12	Forecast 2012–13	2011	2011	2011	2011	2011	2011	2011
Italy[a]	0.4	..	..	16.4	6.8	–3.1	–3.5	110.8	2.7	..
Jamaica	..	..	..	8.4	1.3	–14.3	–5.1	..	7.5	50.8
Japan	0.7	..	..	21.7	10.4	2.0	–8.3	175.0	–0.3	239.2
Jordan	6.5	3.0	3.3	13.4	5.8	–12.0	–6.8	61.9	4.4	129.6
Kazakhstan	8.0	5.0	5.5	29.7	–4.3	7.5	7.7	9.9	8.3	35.4
Kenya	4.4	4.3	4.9	13.5	11.3	–9.9	–4.6	..	14.0	51.0
Kiribati	0.4	..	..	..	..	..	..	..	..	..
Korea, Dem. Rep.	..	..	..	..	..	..	..	..	..	..
Korea, Rep.	4.0	..	..	31.5	22.2	2.4	1.8	..	4.0	78.1
Kosovo	5.2	..	..	..	..	..	..	..	7.3	41.0
Kuwait	6.0	..	..	48.7	12.2	29.6	25.0	..	4.7	56.9
Kyrgyz Republic	4.4	1.0	8.5	18.2	5.6	–6.1	–4.8	..	16.5	..
Lao PDR	7.3	8.2	7.5	16.3	–1.7	–2.5	–0.9	..	7.6	35.9
Latvia	4.1	5.3	3.0	26.1	18.5	–2.2	–2.9	42.5	4.4	47.0
Lebanon	5.0	1.7	2.8	11.5	0.8	–12.1	–5.9	..	4.0	242.0
Lesotho	3.8	4.3	5.2	15.1	..	–21.4	..	..	5.0	37.9
Liberia	6.0	..	..	30.4	23.0	–48.9	0.0	..	8.5	38.2
Libya	5.4	..	..	..	..	15.0	..	..	2.5	58.0
Liechtenstein	2.5	..	..	..	..	..	..	..	..	..
Lithuania	4.7	3.3	2.5	17.5	9.6	–1.4	–5.2	43.7	4.1	47.6
Luxembourg[a]	2.9	..	..	22.0	12.4	7.1	–0.4	16.8	3.4	..
Macedonia, FYR	3.3	0.0	1.0	25.6	14.9	–3.0	..	..	3.9	55.7
Madagascar	3.2	2.2	4.5	..	..	..	..	..	9.5	24.9
Malawi	5.1	4.1	5.4	13.5	9.8	–13.6	..	..	7.6	35.7
Malaysia	4.9	5.1	5.0	34.6	20.6	11.0	–4.8	51.8	3.2	138.5
Maldives	7.2	..	..	..	..	–23.9	–16.7	68.4	12.8	63.7
Mali	5.1	–1.5	3.5	8.5	–5.2	–12.6	–2.5	..	2.9	29.1
Malta[a]	1.8	..	..	9.5	..	–0.2	–2.8	86.5	2.7	..
Marshall Islands	1.5	..	..	..	..	..	..	..	..	..
Mauritania	5.6	4.8	5.2	..	..	..	..	..	5.7	32.8
Mauritius	3.9	3.3	3.6	13.8	4.8	–12.6	–1.1	36.3	6.5	103.3
Mexico	2.1	4.0	3.3	26.6	12.4	–1.0	..	..	3.4	31.4
Micronesia, Fed. Sts.	0.0	..	..	..	..	..	..	..	..	38.2
Moldova	5.1[d]	1.0[d]	3.0[d]	13.0[d]	10.2[d]	–11.3	–1.8	23.8	7.7	49.9
Monaco	4.3	..	..	..	..	..	..	..	..	..
Mongolia	7.4	11.8	16.2	31.1	–5.5	–31.5	–3.1	46.9	9.5	57.8
Montenegro	4.2	..	..	..	..	..	..	..	3.2	47.4
Morocco	4.8[e]	3.0[e]	4.4[e]	28.1[e]	20.2[e]	–8.0	–4.1	56.3	0.9	112.4
Mozambique	7.5	7.5	8.0	12.4	5.6	–19.1	..	..	10.4	38.8
Myanmar	..	..	..	..	..	..	..	..	5.0	..
Namibia	4.9	4.2	4.3	18.6	14.6	–1.2	..	..	5.0	66.6
Nepal	3.9	4.2	4.0	34.2	27.9	1.5	–1.0	33.8	9.5	75.7
Netherlands[a]	1.5	..	..	26.1	15.1	9.7	–3.9	66.0	2.4	..
New Caledonia	..	..	..	..	..	..	..	..	..	..
New Zealand	2.0	..	..	18.8	11.2	–4.2	–7.3	63.6	4.4	95.8
Nicaragua	3.2	4.0	4.2	19.0	11.2	–14.0	0.5	..	8.1	34.5
Niger	4.2	12.0	6.8	..	..	–25.1	..	..	2.9	21.4

	Gross domestic product			Gross savings	Adjusted net savings	Current account balance	Central government cash surplus or deficit	Central government debt	Consumer price index	Broad money
	average annual % growth	Estimate	Forecast	% of GDP	% of GNI	% of GDP	% of GDP	% of GDP	% growth	% of GDP
	2000–11	2011–12	2012–13	2011	2011	2011	2011	2011	2011	2011
Nigeria	6.8	6.5	6.6	..	..	3.6	..	..	10.8	33.6
Northern Mariana Islands	..	..	..	..	..	..	..	..	..	..
Norway	1.6	..	..	37.7	19.2	14.5	14.7	20.4	1.3	..
Oman	4.9	..	..	..	..	14.3	−0.8	5.1	4.1	35.7
Pakistan	4.9	3.8	3.9	20.4	9.3	−1.1	−6.5	..	11.9	38.0
Palau	0.3	..	..	..	..	..	..	..	..	..
Panama	7.2	10.0	7.5	17.7	9.4	−14.5	..	..	5.9	98.1
Papua New Guinea	4.3	8.0	4.0	20.3	..	−6.7	..	..	8.4	49.9
Paraguay	4.1	−1.0	8.5	10.6	3.6	−1.1	1.1	..	8.3	45.0
Peru	6.2	6.3	5.8	23.4	5.4	−1.9	1.3	19.5	3.4	35.8
Philippines	4.9	6.0	6.2	25.1	14.6	3.1	−1.8	..	4.6	59.8
Poland	4.3	..	..	16.9	9.2	−4.9	−4.3	..	4.2	58.0
Portugal[a]	0.5	..	..	11.7	−1.6	−6.5	−4.0	92.6	3.7	..
Puerto Rico	0.0	..	..	..	..	..	..	..	..	..
Qatar	13.6	..	..	..	..	..	2.9	..	1.9	49.2
Romania	4.4	0.6	1.6	24.8	14.4	−4.4	−4.9	..	5.8	37.3
Russian Federation	5.1	3.5	3.6	30.3	7.2	5.3	3.4	9.5	8.4	52.7
Rwanda	7.9	7.7	7.5	11.3	4.5	−7.5	..	..	5.7	..
Samoa	2.6	..	..	..	..	−11.9	..	..	5.2	47.2
San Marino	3.2	..	..	..	..	..	..	..	2.6	..
São Tomé and Príncipe	..	..	..	..	..	−43.5	..	..	11.9	35.8
Saudi Arabia	3.7	..	..	46.8	3.8	27.5	..	..	5.0	57.2
Senegal	4.1	3.7	4.8	21.8	17.3	−4.7	..	..	3.4	40.2
Serbia	3.7	..	..	16.4	..	−8.4	−4.2	..	11.1	44.7
Seychelles	2.9	3.3	4.2	..	..	−21.4	5.6	75.3	2.6	57.9
Sierra Leone	6.6	25.0	11.1	9.8	−6.0	−37.9	−4.6	..	16.2	21.6
Singapore	6.0	..	..	46.6	35.7	23.3	9.8	112.7	5.3	135.7
Sint Maarten	..	..	..	..	..	..	..	..	..	..
Slovak Republic[a]	5.1	..	..	16.5	7.2	0.0	−4.9	45.6	3.9	..
Slovenia[a]	2.9	..	..	21.4	13.2	0.0	−6.0	..	1.8	..
Solomon Islands	4.9	5.3	4.0	..	..	−30.1	..	..	7.3	40.8
Somalia	..	..	..	..	..	..	..	..	..	..
South Africa	3.7	2.4	2.7	16.4	1.5	−3.4	−4.4	..	5.0	76.1
South Sudan	..	−2.0	11.0	..	..	..	..	..	..	..
Spain[a]	2.1	..	..	18.2	9.1	−3.5	−3.5	55.2	3.2	..
Sri Lanka	5.8	6.1	6.8	22.1	13.4	−7.8	−6.4	..	6.7	38.1
St. Kitts and Nevis	2.5	..	..	23.4	..	−8.6	2.6	..	5.9	138.3
St. Lucia	2.9	0.7	1.2	11.8	..	−22.5	..	..	2.8	91.3
St. Martin	..	..	..	..	..	..	..	..	..	..
St. Vincent and Grenadines	3.1	1.2	1.5	−4.8	−12.2	−30.2	−3.7	..	4.0	67.8
Sudan	7.1[f]	3.0[f]	3.2[f]	20.9[f]	0.1[f]	0.2	..	..	13.0	24.5
Suriname	4.9	4.0	4.5	..	..	5.8	..	..	17.7	47.5
Swaziland	2.4	−2.0	1.0	−0.5	−5.1	−10.0	..	..	6.1	29.6
Sweden	2.3	..	..	26.2	18.7	6.5	0.5	38.2	3.0	86.6
Switzerland	1.9	..	..	32.1	22.0	7.5	..	..	0.2	167.8
Syrian Arab Republic	5.0	..	..	16.8	−5.7	−0.6	..	..	4.8	73.9
Tajikistan	8.0	..	..	23.2	16.4	−12.1	..	..	12.4	..

	Gross domestic product			Gross savings	Adjusted net savings	Current account balance	Central government cash surplus or deficit	Central government debt	Consumer price index	Broad money
	average annual % growth			% of GDP	% of GNI	% of GDP	% of GDP	% of GDP	% growth	% of GDP
		Estimate	Forecast							
	2000–11	2011–12	2012–13	2011	2011	2011	2011	2011	2011	2011
Tanzania[g]	7.0	6.5	6.8	20.3	10.5	−16.6	..	..	12.7	34.7
Thailand	4.2	4.7	5.0	31.0	20.8	4.1	−1.2	30.2	3.8	128.2
Timor-Leste	5.6	..	..	..	..	..	..	..	13.5	30.6
Togo	2.6	4.0	4.4	12.2	5.3	−6.3	−1.1	..	3.6	48.5
Tonga	1.0	..	..	3.9	..	−17.0	..	..	6.3	39.0
Trinidad and Tobago	5.6	..	..	..	..	19.9	−4.8	21.3	5.1	65.1
Tunisia	4.4	2.4	3.2	15.9	5.8	−7.3	−3.7	44.0	3.6	67.6
Turkey	4.7	2.9	4.0	14.1	4.0	−10.0	−1.3	45.9	6.5	54.7
Turkmenistan	8.7	..	..	..	..	..	..	..	..	..
Turks and Caicos Islands	..	..	..	..	..	..	..	..	..	..
Tuvalu	1.1	..	..	..	..	..	..	..	..	..
Uganda	7.7	3.4	6.2	20.8	11.2	−13.5	−3.9	42.7	18.7	26.5
Ukraine	4.3	0.5	2.2	16.0	6.2	−5.5	−2.3	27.1	8.0	52.1
United Arab Emirates	4.8	..	..	..	..	..	..	..	0.9	62.4
United Kingdom	1.7	..	..	12.9	2.7	−1.9	−7.7	101.2	4.5	165.7
United States	1.6	..	..	11.7	0.9	−3.2	−9.3	81.8	3.2	89.8
Uruguay	4.0	4.0	4.0	16.5	5.9	−3.1	−0.6	46.6	8.1	44.6
Uzbekistan	7.3	8.0	6.5	..	..	..	..	..	..	..
Vanuatu	3.9	2.0	2.5	..	..	−15.2	..	..	0.9	84.2
Venezuela, RB	4.4	5.2	1.8	30.7	1.4	8.6	..	..	26.1	36.6
Vietnam	7.3	5.2	5.5	33.1	17.4	0.2	..	..	18.7	109.3
Virgin Islands (U.S.)	..	..	..	..	..	..	..	..	..	..
West Bank and Gaza	..	..	..	..	..	..	..	..	2.8	..
Yemen, Rep.	3.6	0.1	4.0	8.3	−10.0	−3.0	..	..	16.4	30.1
Zambia	5.7	6.7	7.1	27.8	4.0	1.1	−1.5	..	6.4	23.4
Zimbabwe	−5.1	5.0	6.0	..	..	..	..	..	..	..
World	**2.7** [w]	**2.3** [w]	**2.4** [w]	**19.4** [w]	**6.7** [w]					
Low income	5.5	5.6	6.1	26.5	15.6					
Middle income	6.4	4.9	5.5	30.0	15.1					
Lower middle income	6.2	4.8	5.5	28.1	13.4					
Upper middle income	6.5	5.0	5.5	31.0	15.6					
Low & middle income	6.4	4.9	5.5	29.9	15.1					
East Asia & Pacific	9.4	7.5	7.9	47.7	30.3					
Europe & Central Asia	5.2	3.0	3.6	22.9	6.2					
Latin America & Carib.	3.9	3.0	3.6	21.5	8.6					
Middle East & N. Africa	4.7	0.2	2.4	..	..					
South Asia	7.3	5.4	5.7	33.3	21.2					
Sub-Saharan Africa	4.9	4.6	4.9	16.8	−2.4					
High income	1.6	1.3	1.3	17.6	5.7					
Euro area	1.2	−0.4	−0.1	20.1	8.6					

a. As members of the European Monetary Union, these countries share a single currency, the euro. b. Refers to the area controlled by the government of the Republic of Cyprus. c. Excludes Abkhazia and South Ossetia. d. Excludes Transnistria. e. Includes Former Spanish Sahara. f. Excludes South Sudan after July 9, 2011. g. Covers mainland Tanzania only.

About the data

Economic data are organized by several different accounting conventions: the system of national accounts, the balance of payments, government finance statistics, and international finance statistics. There has been progress in unifying the concepts in the system of national accounts, balance of payments, and government finance statistics, but there are many national variations in the implementation of these standards. For example, even though the United Nations recommends using the 2008 System of National Accounts (2008 SNA) methodology in compiling national accounts, many are still using earlier versions, some as old as 1968. The International Monetary Fund (IMF) has recently published a new balance of payments methodology (BPM6), but many countries are still using the previous version. Similarly, the standards and definitions for government finance statistics were updated in 2001, but several countries still report using the 1986 version. For individual country information about methodology used, refer to *Primary data documentation.*

Economic growth

An economy's growth is measured by the change in the volume of its output or in the real incomes of its residents. The 2008 SNA offers three plausible indicators for calculating growth: the volume of gross domestic product (GDP), real gross domestic income, and real gross national income. Only growth in GDP is reported here.

Growth rates of GDP and its components are calculated using the least squares method and constant price data in the local currency for countries and using constant price U.S. dollar series for regional and income groups. Local currency series are converted to constant U.S. dollars using an exchange rate in the common reference year. The growth rates are average annual and compound growth rates. Methods of computing growth are described in *Statistical methods.* Forecasts of growth rates come from World Bank (2013).

Rebasing national accounts

Rebasing of national accounts can alter the measured growth rate of an economy and lead to breaks in series that affect the consistency of data over time. When countries rebase their national accounts, they update the weights assigned to various components to better reflect current patterns of production or uses of output. The new base year should represent normal operation of the economy—it should be a year without major shocks or distortions. Some developing countries have not rebased their national accounts for many years. Using an old base year can be misleading because implicit price and volume weights become progressively less relevant and useful.

To obtain comparable series of constant price data for computing aggregates, the World Bank rescales GDP and value added by industrial origin to a common reference year. This year's *World Development Indicators* continues to use 2000 as the reference year. Because rescaling changes the implicit weights used in forming regional and income group aggregates, aggregate growth rates in this year's edition are not comparable with those from earlier editions with different base years.

Rescaling may result in a discrepancy between the rescaled GDP and the sum of the rescaled components. To avoid distortions in the growth rates, the discrepancy is left unallocated. As a result, the weighted average of the growth rates of the components generally does not equal the GDP growth rate.

Adjusted net savings

Adjusted net savings measure the change in a country's real wealth after accounting for the depreciation and depletion of a full range of assets in the economy. If a country's adjusted net savings are positive and the accounting includes a sufficiently broad range of assets, economic theory suggests that the present value of social welfare is increasing. Conversely, persistently negative adjusted net savings indicate that the present value of social welfare is decreasing, suggesting that an economy is on an unsustainable path.

Adjusted net savings are derived from standard national accounting measures of gross savings by making four adjustments. First, estimates of fixed capital consumption of produced assets are deducted to obtain net savings. Second, current public expenditures on education are added to net savings (in standard national accounting these expenditures are treated as consumption). Third, estimates of the depletion of a variety of natural resources are deducted to reflect the decline in asset values associated with their extraction and harvest. And fourth, deductions are made for damages from carbon dioxide emissions and local pollution. By accounting for the depletion of natural resources and the degradation of the environment, adjusted net savings goes beyond the definition of savings or net savings in the SNA.

Balance of payments

The balance of payments records an economy's transactions with the rest of the world. Balance of payments accounts are divided into two groups: the current account, which records transactions in goods, services, primary income, and secondary income, and the capital and financial account, which records capital transfers, acquisition or disposal of nonproduced, nonfinancial assets, and transactions in financial assets and liabilities. The current account balance is one of the most analytically useful indicators of an external imbalance.

A primary purpose of the balance of payments accounts is to indicate the need to adjust an external imbalance. Where to draw the line for analytical purposes requires a judgment concerning the imbalance that best indicates the need for adjustment. There are a number of definitions in common use for this and related analytical purposes. The trade balance is the difference between exports and imports of goods. From an analytical view it is arbitrary to distinguish goods from services. For example, a unit of foreign exchange earned by a freight company strengthens the balance of payments to the same extent as the foreign exchange earned by a goods exporter. Even so, the trade balance is useful because it is often the most timely indicator of trends in the current account balance. Customs authorities are typically able to provide data on trade in goods long before data on trade in services are available.

Beginning in August 2012, the International Monetary Fund implemented the Balance of Payments Manual 6 (BPM6) framework in its major statistical publications. The World Bank will implement BPM6 in its online databases and publications in April 2013. Balance of payments data for 2005 onward will be presented in accord with the BPM6. The historical BPM5 data series will end with data for 2008, which can be accessed through the *World Development Indicators* archives.

The complete balance of payments methodology can be accessed through the International Monetary Fund website (www.imf.org/external/np/sta/bop/bop.htm).

Government finance

Central government cash surplus or deficit, a summary measure of the ongoing sustainability of government operations, is comparable to the national accounting concept of savings plus net capital transfers receivable, or net operating balance in the 2001 update of the IMF's *Government Finance Statistics Manual.*

The 2001 manual, harmonized with the 1993 SNA, recommends an accrual accounting method, focusing on all economic events affecting assets, liabilities, revenues, and expenses, not just those represented by cash transactions. It accounts for all changes in stocks, so stock data at the end of an accounting period equal stock data at the beginning of the period plus flows over the period. The 1986 manual considered only debt stocks.

For most countries central government finance data have been consolidated into one account, but for others only budgetary central government accounts are available. Countries reporting budgetary data are noted in *Primary data documentation.* Because budgetary accounts may not include all central government units (such as social security funds), they usually provide an incomplete picture. In federal states the central government accounts provide an incomplete view of total public finance.

Data on government revenue and expense are collected by the IMF through questionnaires to member countries and by the Organisation for Economic Co-operation and Development (OECD). Despite IMF efforts to standardize data collection, statistics are often incomplete, untimely, and not comparable across countries.

Government finance statistics are reported in local currency. The indicators here are shown as percentages of GDP. Many countries report government finance data by fiscal year; see *Primary data documentation* for information on fiscal year end by country.

Financial accounts

Money and the financial accounts that record the supply of money lie at the heart of a country's financial system. There are several commonly used definitions of the money supply. The narrowest, M1, encompasses currency held by the public and demand deposits with banks. M2 includes M1 plus time and savings deposits with banks that require prior notice for withdrawal. M3 includes M2 as well as various money market instruments, such as certificates of deposit issued by banks, bank deposits denominated in foreign currency, and deposits with financial institutions other than banks. However defined, money is a liability of the banking system, distinguished from other bank liabilities by the special role it plays as a medium of exchange, a unit of account, and a store of value.

A general and continuing increase in an economy's price level is called inflation. The increase in the average prices of goods and services in the economy should be distinguished from a change in the relative prices of individual goods and services. Generally accompanying an overall increase in the price level is a change in the structure of relative prices, but it is only the average increase, not the relative price changes, that constitutes inflation. A commonly used measure of inflation is the consumer price index, which measures the prices of a representative basket of goods and services purchased by a typical household. The consumer price index is usually calculated on the basis of periodic surveys of consumer prices. Other price indices are derived implicitly from indexes of current and constant price series.

Consumer price indexes are produced more frequently and so are more current. They are constructed explicitly, using surveys of the cost of a defined basket of consumer goods and services. Nevertheless, consumer price indexes should be interpreted with caution. The definition of a household, the basket of goods, and the geographic (urban or rural) and income group coverage of consumer price surveys can vary widely by country. In addition, weights are derived from household expenditure surveys, which, for budgetary reasons, tend to be conducted infrequently in developing countries, impairing comparability over time. Although useful for measuring consumer price inflation within a country, consumer price indexes are of less value in comparing countries.

Definitions

• **Gross domestic product (GDP)** at purchaser prices is the sum of gross value added by all resident producers in the economy plus any product taxes (less subsidies) not included in the valuation of output. It is calculated without deducting for depreciation of fabricated capital assets or for depletion and degradation of natural resources. Value added is the net output of an industry after adding up all outputs and subtracting intermediate inputs. • **Gross savings** are the difference between gross national income and public and private consumption, plus net current transfers. • **Adjusted net savings** measure the change in value of a specified set of assets, excluding capital gains. Adjusted net savings are net savings plus education expenditure minus energy depletion, mineral depletion, net forest depletion, and carbon dioxide and particulate emissions damage. • **Current account balance** is the sum of net exports of goods and services, net primary income, and net secondary income. • **Central government cash surplus or deficit** is revenue (including grants) minus expense, minus net acquisition of nonfinancial assets. In editions before 2005 nonfinancial assets were included under revenue and expenditure in gross terms. This cash surplus or deficit is close to the earlier overall budget balance (still missing is lending minus repayments, which are included as a financing item under net acquisition of financial assets). • **Central government debt** is the entire stock of direct government fixed-term contractual obligations to others outstanding on a particular date. It includes domestic and foreign liabilities such as currency and money deposits, securities other than shares, and loans. It is the gross amount of government liabilities reduced by the amount of equity and financial derivatives held by the government. Because debt is a stock rather than a flow, it is measured as of a given date, usually the last day of the fiscal year. • **Consumer price index** reflects changes in the cost to the average consumer of acquiring a basket of goods and services that may be fixed or may change at specified intervals, such as yearly. The Laspeyres formula is generally used. • **Broad money** (IFS line 35L..ZK) is the sum of currency outside banks; demand deposits other than those of the central government; the time, savings, and foreign currency deposits of resident sectors other than the central government; bank and traveler's checks; and other securities such as certificates of deposit and commercial paper.

Data sources

Data on GDP for most countries are collected from national statistical organizations and central banks by visiting and resident World Bank missions; data for selected high-income economies are from the OECD. Data on gross savings are from World Bank national accounts data files. Data on adjusted net savings are based on a conceptual underpinning by Hamilton and Clemens (1999) and calculated using data on consumption of fixed capital from the United Nations Statistics Division's *National Accounts Statistics: Main Aggregates and Detailed Tables*, extrapolated to 2010; data on education expenditure from the United Nations Educational, Scientific, and Cultural Organization Institute for Statistics online database, with missing data estimated by World Bank staff; data on forest, energy, and mineral depletion based on sources and methods in World Bank (2011); data on carbon dioxide damage from Fankhauser (1994); data on local pollution damage from Pandey and others (2006). Data on current account balance are from the IMF's *Balance of Payments Statistics Yearbook* and *International Financial Statistics*. Data on central government finances are from the IMF's Government Finance Statistics database. Data on the consumer price index are from the IMF's *International Financial Statistics*. Data on broad money are from the IMF's monthly *International Financial Statistics* and annual *International Financial Statistics Yearbook*.

References

Asian Development Bank. 2012. *Asian Development Outlook 2012 Update: Services and Asia's Future Growth.* Manila.

De la Torre, Augusto, Tatiana Didier, and Samuel Pienknagura. 2012. *Latin America Copes with Volatility, the Dark Side of Globalization.* Washington, DC: World Bank.

Fankhauser, Samuel. 1994. "The Social Costs of Greenhouse Gas Emissions: An Expected Value Approach." *Energy Journal* 15 (2): 157–84.

Hamilton, Kirk, and Michael Clemens. 1999. "Genuine Savings Rates in Developing Countries." *World Bank Economic Review* 13 (2): 333–56.

IMF (International Monetary Fund). 2001. *Government Finance Statistics Manual.* Washington, DC.

———. 2012. *Regional Economic Outlook: Sub-Saharan Africa—Maintaining Growth in an Uncertain World, October 2012.* Washington, DC. www.imf.org/external/pubs/ft/reo/2012/afr/eng/sreo1012.htm.

Pandey, Kiran D., Katharine Bolt, Uwe Deichmann, Kirk Hamilton, Bart Ostro, and David Wheeler. 2006. "The Human Cost of Air Pollution: New Estimates for Developing Countries." World Bank, Development Research Group and Environment Department, Washington, DC.

United Nations Statistics Division. Various years. *National Accounts Statistics: Main Aggregates and Detailed Tables. Parts 1 and 2.* New York: United Nations.

World Bank. 2011. *The Changing Wealth of Nations: Measuring Sustainable Development for the New Millennium.* Washington, DC.

———. 2012a. *East Asia and Pacific Economic Update 2012, Volume 2: Remaining Resilient.* Washington, DC.

———. 2012b. *Middle East and North Africa Region Economic Developments and Prospects, October 2012: Looking Ahead After a Year in Transition.* Washington, DC.

———. 2012c. *South Asia Economic Focus—A Review of Economic Developments in South Asian Countries: Creating Fiscal Space through Revenue Mobilization.* Washington, DC.

———. 2013. *Global Economic Prospects, Volume 6, January 13: Assuring Growth over the Medium Term.* Washington, DC.

———. Various years. *World Development Indicators.* Washington, DC.

4 Economy

Online tables and indicators

To access the World Development Indicators online tables, use the URL http://wdi.worldbank.org/table/ and the table number (for example, http://wdi.worldbank.org/table/4.1). To view a specific indicator online, use the URL http://data.worldbank.org/indicator/ and the indicator code (for example, http://data.worldbank.org/indicator/NY.GDP.MKTP.KD.ZG).

4.1 Growth of output

Gross domestic product	NY.GDP.MKTP.KD.ZG
Agriculture	NV.AGR.TOTL.KD.ZG
Industry	NV.IND.TOTL.KD.ZG
Manufacturing	NV.IND.MANF.KD.ZG
Services	NV.SRV.TETC.KD.ZG

4.2 Structure of output

Gross domestic product	NY.GDP.MKTP.CD
Agriculture	NV.AGR.TOTL.ZS
Industry	NV.IND.TOTL.ZS
Manufacturing	NV.IND.MANF.ZS
Services	NV.SRV.TETC.ZS

4.3 Structure of manufacturing

Manufacturing value added	NV.IND.MANF.CD
Food, beverages and tobacco	NV.MNF.FBTO.ZS.UN
Textiles and clothing	NV.MNF.TXTL.ZS.UN
Machinery and transport equipment	NV.MNF.MTRN.ZS.UN
Chemicals	NV.MNF.CHEM.ZS.UN
Other manufacturing	NV.MNF.OTHR.ZS.UN

4.4 Structure of merchandise exports

Merchandise exports	TX.VAL.MRCH.CD.WT
Food	TX.VAL.FOOD.ZS.UN
Agricultural raw materials	TX.VAL.AGRI.ZS.UN
Fuels	TX.VAL.FUEL.ZS.UN
Ores and metals	TX.VAL.MMTL.ZS.UN
Manufactures	TX.VAL.MANF.ZS.UN

4.5 Structure of merchandise imports

Merchandise imports	TM.VAL.MRCH.CD.WT
Food	TM.VAL.FOOD.ZS.UN
Agricultural raw materials	TM.VAL.AGRI.ZS.UN
Fuels	TM.VAL.FUEL.ZS.UN
Ores and metals	TM.VAL.MMTL.ZS.UN
Manufactures	TM.VAL.MANF.ZS.UN

4.6 Structure of service exports

Commercial service exports	TX.VAL.SERV.CD.WT
Transport	TX.VAL.TRAN.ZS.WT
Travel	TX.VAL.TRVL.ZS.WT
Insurance and financial services	TX.VAL.INSF.ZS.WT
Computer, information, communications, and other commercial services	TX.VAL.OTHR.ZS.WT

4.7 Structure of service imports

Commercial service imports	TM.VAL.SERV.CD.WT
Transport	TM.VAL.TRAN.ZS.WT
Travel	TM.VAL.TRVL.ZS.WT
Insurance and financial services	TM.VAL.INSF.ZS.WT
Computer, information, communications, and other commercial services	TM.VAL.OTHR.ZS.WT

4.8 Structure of demand

Household final consumption expenditure	NE.CON.PETC.ZS
General government final consumption expenditure	NE.CON.GOVT.ZS
Gross capital formation	NE.GDI.TOTL.ZS
Exports of goods and services	NE.EXP.GNFS.ZS
Imports of goods and services	NE.IMP.GNFS.ZS
Gross savings	NY.GNS.ICTR.ZS

4.9 Growth of consumption and investment

Household final consumption expenditure	NE.CON.PRVT.KD.ZG
Household final consumption expenditure, Per capita	NE.CON.PRVT.PC.KD.ZG
General government final consumption expenditure	NE.CON.GOVT.KD.ZG
Gross capital formation	NE.GDI.TOTL.KD.ZG
Exports of goods and services	NE.EXP.GNFS.KD.ZG
Imports of goods and services	NE.IMP.GNFS.KD.ZG

4.10 Toward a broader measure of national income

Gross domestic product, $	NY.GDP.MKTP.CD
Gross national income, $	NY.GNP.MKTP.CD
Consumption of fixed capital	NY.ADJ.DKAP.GN.ZS
Natural resource depletion	NY.ADJ.DRES.GN.ZS
Adjusted net national income	NY.ADJ.NNTY.CD
Gross domestic product, % growth	NY.GDP.MKTP.KD.ZG
Gross national income, % growth	NY.GNP.MKTP.KD.ZG
Adjusted net national income	NY.ADJ.NNTY.KD.ZG

4.11 Toward a broader measure of savings

Gross savings	NY.ADJ.ICTR.GN.ZS
Consumption of fixed capital	NY.ADJ.DKAP.GN.ZS
Education expenditure	NY.ADJ.AEDU.GN.ZS
Net forest depletion	NY.ADJ.DFOR.GN.ZS
Energy depletion	NY.ADJ.DNGY.GN.ZS
Mineral depletion	NY.ADJ.DMIN.GN.ZS
Carbon dioxide damage	NY.ADJ.DCO2.GN.ZS
Local pollution damage	NY.ADJ.DPEM.GN.ZS
Adjusted net savings	NY.ADJ.SVNG.GN.ZS

4.12 Central government finances

Revenue	GC.REV.XGRT.GD.ZS
Expense	GC.XPN.TOTL.GD.ZS
Cash surplus or deficit	GC.BAL.CASH.GD.ZS
Net incurrence of liabilities, Domestic	GC.FIN.DOMS.GD.ZS
Net incurrence of liabilities, Foreign	GC.FIN.FRGN.GD.ZS
Debt and interest payments, Total debt	GC.DOD.TOTL.GD.ZS
Debt and interest payments, Interest	GC.XPN.INTP.RV.ZS

4.13 Central government expenditure

Goods and services	GC.XPN.GSRV.ZS
Compensation of employees	GC.XPN.COMP.ZS
Interest payments	GC.XPN.INTP.ZS
Subsidies and other transfers	GC.XPN.TRFT.ZS
Other expense	GC.XPN.OTHR.ZS

4.14 Central government revenues

Taxes on income, profits and capital gains	GC.TAX.YPKG.RV.ZS
Taxes on goods and services	GC.TAX.GSRV.RV.ZS
Taxes on international trade	GC.TAX.INTT.RV.ZS
Other taxes	GC.TAX.OTHR.RV.ZS
Social contributions	GC.REV.SOCL.ZS
Grants and other revenue	GC.REV.GOTR.ZS

4.15 Monetary indicators

Broad money	FM.LBL.BMNY.ZG
Claims on domestic economy	FM.AST.DOMO.ZG.M3
Claims on central governments	FM.AST.CGOV.ZG.M3
Interest rate, Deposit	FR.INR.DPST
Interest rate, Lending	FR.INR.LEND
Interest rate, Real	FR.INR.RINR

4.16 Exchange rates and price

Official exchange rate	PA.NUS.FCRF
Purchasing power parity (PPP) conversion factor	PA.NUS.PPP
Ratio of PPP conversion factor to market exchange rate	PA.NUS.PPPC.RF
Real effective exchange rate	PX.REX.REER
GDP implicit deflator	NY.GDP.DEFL.KD.ZG
Consumer price index	FP.CPI.TOTL.ZG
Wholesale price index	FP.WPI.TOTL

4.17 Balance of payments current account

Goods and services, Exports	BX.GSR.GNFS.CD
Goods and services, Imports	BM.GSR.GNFS.CD
Balance on primary income	BN.GSR.FCTY.CD
Balance on secondary income	BN.TRF.CURR.CD
Current account balance	BN.CAB.XOKA.CD
Total reserves	FI.RES.TOTL.CD

STATES AND MARKETS

States and markets includes indicators of private sector investment and performance, the role of the public sector in nurturing investment and growth, and the quality and availability of infrastructure essential for growth and development. These indicators measure the business environment, the functions of government, financial system development, infrastructure, information and communication technology, science and technology, performance of governments and their policies, and conditions in fragile countries with weak institutions.

Measures of investment in infrastructure projects with private participation show the private sector's contributions to providing public services and easing fiscal constraints. For example, private investment in the dynamic telecommunications sector has increased more than 50 percent since 2006, reaching $158.5 billion in 2011.

Data on access to finance, availability of credit, cost of service, and stock markets help improve understanding of the state of financial development. In 2011 people had greater access to finance in Europe and Central Asia, with 19 commercial bank branches and 47 automated teller machines per 100,000 people, than in other developing regions. Stock market measures show the effects of the global financial crises: the market capitalization of listed companies dropped from $64.6 trillion in 2007 to $34.9 trillion in 2008, recovering to only $46.8 trillion in 2011.

Economic health is measured not only in macroeconomic terms but also by laws, regulations, and institutional arrangements. Firms evaluating investment options, governments interested in improving business conditions, and economists seeking to explain economic performance have all grappled with defining and measuring the business environment and how constraints affect productivity and job creation. The World Development Indicators database includes results from enterprise surveys and expert assessments of the business environment from the Doing Business project.

States and markets also includes data on the size of the transportation and power sectors, as well as the spread of new information technology. To become competitive suppliers to the rest of the world, many developing countries need to improve their road, rail, port, and air transport facilities. Expanding electricity supply to meet the growing demand of increasingly urban and industrialized economies without unacceptable social, economic, and environmental costs is one of the greatest challenges facing developed and developing countries. Data on electric power consumption per capita show that consumption in developing countries has doubled since 1995, to 1,660 kilowatt-hours in 2010.

With rapid growth of mobile telephony and the global expansion of the Internet, information and communication technologies are increasingly recognized as essential for development. *World Development Indicators* includes data showing the rapid changes in this sector. For instance, mobile cellular subscriptions increased from 16 percent of the global population in 2001 to 85 percent in 2011, and Internet users from 8 percent to 33 percent over the same period.

Highlights

East Asia & Pacific: Patent applications are rising, especially in China

Patent applications, 2011 (thousands)

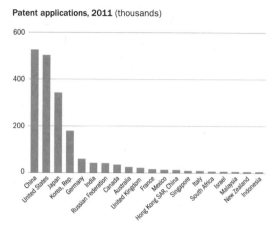

Source: Online table 5.13.

While the global economy continued to underperform, intellectual property filings worldwide grew strongly in 2011. Demand for patents rose from 800,000 applications in the early 1980s to 2.14 million in 2011, topping 2 million for the first time. After dropping 4 percent in 2009, patent applications rebounded strongly in 2010 and 2011, averaging 7 percent growth a year. In 2011 China's patent office became the world's largest, measured by patent applications received, according to World Intellectual Property Organization (2012). China received 526,412 applications, compared with 503,582 for the United States and 342,610 for Japan. Of the 20 busiest patent offices, 7 were in East Asia and Pacific, accounting for 58 percent of total applications filed worldwide in 2011.

Europe & Central Asia: Container traffic picks up

Container port traffic (millions of twenty-foot equivalent units)

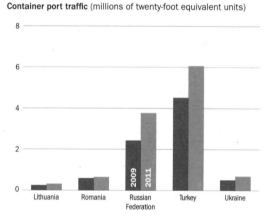

Source: Online table 5.10.

Measures of port container traffic, much of it commodity shipments of medium to high value added, give some indication of a country's economic status, though much of the economic benefit from transshipments goes to the terminal operator and ancillary services for ships and containers rather than to the country more broadly. After the 2008 fiscal crisis, worldwide container shipments fell to 472 million in 2009, an almost 9 percent drop from 2008, affecting all ports, operators, and countries. But shipments rebounded in 2010, growing 15 percent and reaching precrisis levels. Most of the growth came from intercontinental shipments by developing countries. In 2011 the Russian Federation (3.8 million) and Turkey (6.1 million) led the market in container shipments in Europe and Central Asia.

Latin America & Caribbean: Homicide rates mount

Intentional homicides, 2011 or latest available (per 100,000 people)

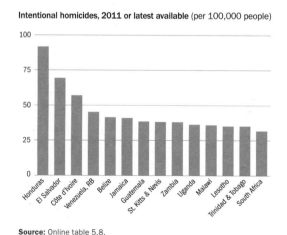

Source: Online table 5.8.

Homicide rates are very high in Latin America and the Caribbean and Sub-Saharan Africa, where they add to the death toll caused by armed conflicts. According to the Geneva Declaration on Armed Violence and Development (2011), a quarter of all violent deaths occur in just 14 countries, averaging more than 30 violent deaths per 100,000 people a year, half of them in Latin America and the Caribbean. In many of these countries, homicides, not armed conflicts, account for the majority of violent deaths. The links between violent death rates and socioeconomic development show that homicide rates are higher where income disparity, extreme poverty, and hunger are high. Countries that have strengthened their rule of law have seen a decline in homicide rates.

 Front | User guide | World view | People | Environment

Middle East & North Africa: Military spending share continues to rise

Demanding open government and good governance from their head of states, citizens of countries in the Middle East and North Africa brought about the Arab Spring in late 2010 and 2011. Although it is still too soon to estimate the effects of the turbulent years, there are signs of higher military spending and arms imports. From 2010 to 2011 all regions except the Middle East and North Africa reduced military spending as a share of gross domestic product (GDP). Algeria increased military spending from 3.5 percent of GDP in 2010 to 4.6 percent in 2011, and Tunisia from 1.2 percent of GDP in 2010 to 1.3 percent in 2011. Saudi Arabia (8.4 percent of GDP) and Israel (6.8 percent), both high-income economies, spend the most on the military, followed by Iraq (5.1 percent), Jordan (4.7 percent), and Lebanon (4.4 percent).

Military spending (% of GDP)

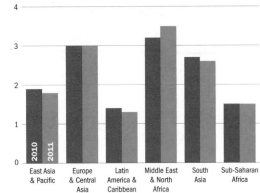

Source: Online table 5.7.

South Asia: Mobile phone access growing rapidly

Mobile phone subscriptions have roughly doubled every two years since 2002 and now exceed the number of fixed-line subscriptions in 2002. By the end of 2011 there were 5.9 billion mobile phone subscriptions worldwide, almost one for every person if distributed equally. Developing economies have lagged behind, but they are catching up. Sub-Saharan Africa, where 53 per 100 people have mobile phone subscriptions, started far behind but has reached the same subscription rate as high-income economies did 11 years ago. South Asia is only eight years behind. In recent years South Asia has had the largest growth in mobile subscription coverage among developing regions, with 69 mobile phone subscriptions per 100 people in 2011, up from 8 in 2005.

Mobile phone subscriptions (per 100 people)

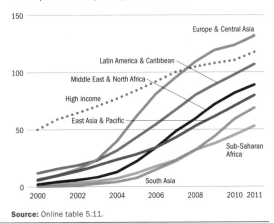

Source: Online table 5.11.

Sub-Saharan Africa: Growth with good policies

The World Bank's Country Policy and Institutional Assessment (CPIA) score reflects country performance in promoting economic growth and reducing poverty. Data for Sub-Saharan countries show a positive association between average CPIA score and average GDP growth over 2006–11. In 2011 the region's average CPIA score for International Development Association countries was 3.2 on a scale of 1 (low) to 6 (high). The regional average masks the wide variation across countries, from 2.2 in Eritrea and Zimbabwe to 4.0 in Cape Verde. For several countries the policy environment is the best in recent years. Thirteen countries saw an improvement in the 2011 score by at least 0.1, 20 countries saw no change, and 5 saw a decline of 0.1 or more (World Bank 2012).

Average GDP growth, 2006–11 (%)

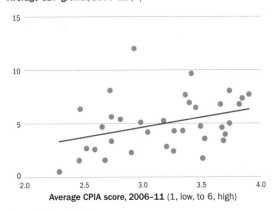

Average CPIA score, 2006–11 (1, low, to 6, high)

Source: Online table 5.9.

5 States and markets

	Business entry density per 1,000 people ages 15–64 2011	Time required to start a business days June 2012	Stock market capitalization % of GDP 2011	Domestic credit provided by banking sector % of GDP 2011	Tax revenue collected by central government % of GDP 2011	Military expenditures % of GDP 2011	Electric power consumption per capita kilowatt-hours 2010	Mobile cellular subscriptions[a] per 100 people 2011	Individuals using the Internet[a] % of population 2011	High-technology exports % of manufactured exports 2011
Afghanistan	0.12	7	..	−2.9	8.7	4.7	..	54	5	..
Albania	0.96	4	..	69.1	..	1.5	1,770	96	49	0.5
Algeria	0.19	25	..	−4.7	39.4[b]	4.6	1,026	99	14	0.2
American Samoa	..	..	..	..	..	..	..	..	..	..
Andorra	..	..	..	..	..	..	..	75	81	..
Angola	..	68	..	17.9	..	3.5	248	48	15	..
Antigua and Barbuda	..	21	..	101.4	..	..	..	196	82	0.0
Argentina	0.46	26	9.8	31.3	..	0.7	2,904	135	48	8.0
Armenia	1.12	8	0.4	36.0	17.0	4.0	1,606	104	32	2.6
Aruba	..	..	..	..	..	..	..	123	57	4.6
Australia	6.17	2	86.9	145.1	20.6[b]	1.9	10,286	108	79	13.0
Austria	0.56	25	19.7	135.3	18.4[b]	0.9	8,356	155	80	11.9
Azerbaijan	0.63	8	..	20.0	12.7	4.9	1,603	109	50	1.3
Bahamas, The	..	31	..	108.1	16.8	..	..	86	65	0.0
Bahrain	..	9	89.0	75.2	..	3.4	9,814	128	77	0.2
Bangladesh	0.10	19	21.0	70.4	10.0	1.3	279	56	5	..
Barbados	..	18	124.1	136.3	27.2	..	..	127	72	13.7
Belarus	0.91	5	..	34.4	16.3	1.1	3,564	112	40	2.6
Belgium	3.00	4	44.8	116.9	24.6[b]	1.1	8,388	117	78	10.0
Belize	4.54	44	..	66.9	22.3	1.1	..	70	14	0.4
Benin	..	26	..	21.7	15.7[b]	1.0	90	85	4	0.5
Bermuda	..	..	26.6	..	..	..	..	136	88	..
Bhutan	0.06	36	..	49.2	9.2	..	..	66	21	0.1
Bolivia	0.48	50	17.2	48.6	..	1.5	616	83	30	13.7
Bosnia and Herzegovina	0.71	37	..	57.7	20.9[b]	1.4	3,110	85	60	3.0
Botswana	9.44	61	23.7	7.1	20.8	2.1	1,586	143	7	0.9
Brazil	2.38	119	49.6	98.3	15.7	1.4	2,384	124	45	9.7
Brunei Darussalam	..	101	..	8.1	..	2.5	8,759	109	56	..
Bulgaria	7.20	18	15.4	71.4	19.1	1.5	4,476	141	51	7.5
Burkina Faso	0.11	13	..	17.6	14.2[b]	1.3	..	45	3	5.9
Burundi	..	8	..	28.3	..	2.7	..	22	1	8.5
Cambodia	0.22	85	..	24.2	10.0[b]	1.5	146	96	3	0.1
Cameroon	..	15	..	14.0	..	1.4	271	52	5	4.9
Canada	7.56	5	109.8	177.6	11.9[b]	1.4	15,137	80	83	13.4
Cape Verde	..	11	..	80.6	19.8	0.5	..	79	32	0.6
Cayman Islands	..	..	..	..	..	..	..	168	69	..
Central African Republic	..	22	..	25.4	..	2.6	..	41	2	0.0
Chad	..	62	..	7.0	..	2.3	..	32	2	..
Channel Islands	..	..	..	..	..	..	..	..	..	..
Chile	4.13	8	108.7	71.2	19.1[b]	3.2	3,297	130	54	4.6
China	..	33	46.3	145.5	10.5	2.0[c]	2,944	73	38	25.8
Hong Kong SAR, China	27.67	3	357.8	207.1	13.5[b]	..	5,923	215	75	13.7
Macao SAR, China	..	..	..	−28.1	37.9[b]	..	..	243	58	0.0
Colombia	1.80	13	60.4	65.6	13.9[b]	3.3	1,012	98	40	4.3
Comoros	..	20	..	21.2	..	..	..	29	6	..
Congo, Dem. Rep.	..	58	..	3.3	13.7	1.5	95	23	1	..
Congo, Rep.	..	161	..	−16.1	..	1.1	145	94	6	3.7

 Front User guide World view People Environment

	Business entry density per 1,000 people ages 15–64 2011	Time required to start a business days June 2012	Stock market capitalization % of GDP 2011	Domestic credit provided by banking sector % of GDP 2011	Tax revenue collected by central government % of GDP 2011	Military expenditures % of GDP 2011	Electric power consumption per capita kilowatt-hours 2010	Mobile cellular subscriptions[a] per 100 people 2011	Individuals using the Internet[a] % of population 2011	High-technology exports % of manufactured exports 2011
Costa Rica	17.64	60	3.5	53.3	13.8[b]	..	1,855	92	42	40.8
Côte d'Ivoire	..	32	26.1	25.3	..[b]	1.5	210	86	2	15.1
Croatia	2.39	9	34.9	90.3	18.4	1.7	3,813	116	71	7.6
Cuba	..	..	..	..	..	3.3	1,299	12	23	..
Curaçao	..	..	..	..	..	..	..	..	..	..
Cyprus	24.73	8	11.6	330.1	26.1[b]	2.2	4,675	98	58	27.3
Czech Republic	2.84	20	17.7	67.4	13.7	1.1	6,321	123	73	16.0
Denmark	4.55	6	53.8	205.4	33.8[b]	1.5	6,327	128	90	13.9
Djibouti	..	37	..	32.3	..	3.7	..	21	7	0.1
Dominica	3.30	13	..	57.9	..	..	..	164	51	0.0
Dominican Republic	0.96	19	..	43.8	12.7[b]	0.6	1,442	87	36	2.2
Ecuador	..	56	8.8	28.3	..	3.5	1,055	105	31	3.2
Egypt, Arab Rep.	0.13	7	21.2	74.9	14.1	1.9	1,608	101	39	0.7
El Salvador	0.46	17	23.7	66.5	13.5[b]	1.0	855	134	18	5.8
Equatorial Guinea	..	135	..	−3.0	..	..	..	59	6	..
Eritrea	..	84	..	104.0	..	..	52	4	6	..
Estonia	8.10	7	7.3	85.8	16.0[b]	1.7	6,464	139	77	13.4
Ethiopia	0.03	15	..	37.1	9.3	1.1	54	17	1	2.0
Faeroe Islands	..	..	..	..	..	..	..	122	81	0.6
Fiji	..	58	35.9	114.3	..	1.6	..	84	28	4.5
Finland	3.60	14	54.4	101.6	20.6[b]	1.5	16,483	166	89	9.3
France	3.13	7	56.6	133.5	21.3[b]	2.2	7,729	95	80	23.7
French Polynesia	..	..	..	..	..	..	..	81	49	15.8
Gabon	4.27	58	..	12.2	..	0.9	1,004	117	8	3.0
Gambia, The	..	27	..	43.8	..	..	..	79	11	3.3
Georgia	4.49	2	5.5	34.3	23.9	3.0	1,743	102	37	1.8
Germany	1.35	15	32.9	124.8	11.8[b]	1.3	7,215	132	83	15.0
Ghana	1.09	12	7.9	27.7	15.0	0.3	298	85	14	1.4
Greece	0.85	11	11.6	153.2	21.3[b]	2.8	5,242	106	53	9.7
Greenland	..	..	..	..	..	..	..	103	64	..
Grenada	..	15	..	91.3	18.3	..	..	117	33	11.1
Guam	..	..	..	..	..	..	..	..	51	..
Guatemala	0.64	40	..	39.2	11.0	0.4	567	140	12	4.4
Guinea	..	35	..	32.3	..	..	..	44	1	0.1
Guinea-Bissau	..	9	..	13.6	..	..	..	56	3	..
Guyana	..	20	17.1	51.0	..	1.2	..	70	32	0.1
Haiti	..	105	..	17.4	..	..	24	41	8	..
Honduras	..	14	..	53.3	15.0[b]	1.1	671	104	16	1.3
Hungary	7.63	5	13.4	75.7	21.0[b]	1.0	3,876	117	59	22.7
Iceland	7.94	5	14.4	148.2	22.3	0.1	51,440	106	95	20.9
India	0.09	27	54.2	74.1	10.4	2.5	616	72	10	6.9
Indonesia	0.27	47	46.1	38.5	11.8	0.7	641	103	18	8.3
Iran, Islamic Rep.	..	13	19.1	37.4	9.3	1.9	2,652	75	21	4.5
Iraq	0.11	74	..	−0.8	..	5.1	1,183	78	5	..
Ireland	4.78	10	16.3	225.7	23.1[b]	0.6	6,025	108	77	21.2
Isle of Man	11.65	..	..	..	..	..	..	..	..	..
Israel	4.46	21	59.7	85.9	24.5[b]	6.8	6,856	122	70	14.0

5 States and markets

	Business entry density per 1,000 people ages 15–64 2011	Time required to start a business days June 2012	Stock market capitalization % of GDP 2011	Domestic credit provided by banking sector % of GDP 2011	Tax revenue collected by central government % of GDP 2011	Military expenditures % of GDP 2011	Electric power consumption per capita kilowatt-hours 2010	Mobile cellular subscriptions[a] per 100 people 2011	Individuals using the Internet[a] % of population 2011	High-technology exports % of manufactured exports 2011
Italy	1.63	6	19.7	157.0	22.5[b]	1.6	5,384	158	57	7.4
Jamaica	1.10	7	50.0	49.6	25.6[b]	0.8	1,223	108	32	0.6
Japan	1.10	23	60.3	341.7	9.8[b]	1.0	8,394	105	80	17.5
Jordan	0.83	12	94.3	106.7	15.0	4.7	2,226	118	35	2.5
Kazakhstan	1.64	19	23.0	40.3	22.5	1.0	4,728	156	45	29.9
Kenya	0.85	32	30.3	52.0	19.9	1.5	156	67	28	5.7
Kiribati	0.11	31	..	..	..	..	..	14	10	42.7
Korea, Dem. Rep.	..	..	..	..	..	..	749	4	0	..
Korea, Rep.	1.83	7	89.1	102.7	15.6	2.8	9,744	109	84	25.7
Kosovo	0.92	52	..	20.8	..	..	2,650	..	..	..
Kuwait	..	32	57.1	50.0	0.7	3.2	18,320	175	74	0.5
Kyrgyz Republic	0.95	10	2.7	..	16.1	4.2	1,375	116	20	3.0
Lao PDR	0.10	92	..	26.5	13.6	0.2	..	87	9	..
Latvia	11.18	16	3.8	79.3	13.3	1.0	3,026	103	72	8.2
Lebanon	..	9	25.3	173.7	17.0[b]	4.4	3,569	79	52	2.4
Lesotho	1.22	24	..	0.7	58.9	2.4	..	56	4	0.3
Liberia	..	6	..	30.9	0.2	0.7	..	49	3	..
Libya	..	..	..	−65.9	..	1.2	4,270	156	17	..
Liechtenstein	25.11	..	..	..	..	..	..	102	85	..
Lithuania	2.18	20	9.5	57.5	13.4[b]	1.0	3,271	151	65	10.3
Luxembourg	7.31	19	114.2	172.4	24.3	..	16,834	148	91	9.7
Macedonia, FYR	4.12	2	24.0	45.5	19.1	1.3	3,591	107	57	3.9
Madagascar	0.08	8	..	11.7	13.0[b]	0.7	..	41	2	8.4
Malawi	0.08	39	24.6	38.0	..	..	..	26	3	3.2
Malaysia	2.42	6	137.2	128.7	15.3	1.6	4,117	127	61	43.4
Maldives	3.09	9	..	82.5	11.0	..	..	166	34	..
Mali	..	8	..	16.6	14.6[b]	1.8	..	68	2	2.4
Malta	9.52	40	38.5	159.2	27.7	0.7	4,151	125	69	47.2
Marshall Islands	..	17	..	..	..	..	..	..	4	..
Mauritania	..	19	..	42.4	..	3.8	..	94	5	..
Mauritius	7.88	6	58.1	110.0	18.4	0.1	..	99	35	0.8
Mexico	0.87	9	35.4	45.5	..	0.5	1,990	82	36	16.5
Micronesia, Fed. Sts.	..	16	..	−18.3	..	..	..	25	20	..
Moldova	1.32	9	..	39.5	18.3	0.3	1,049	105	38	6.3
Monaco	..	..	..	..	..	..	..	90	75	..
Mongolia	..	12	18.0	40.3	21.9	0.9	1,530	105	20	..
Montenegro	10.44	10	73.9	61.8	..	2.0	5,547	185	40	..
Morocco	1.28	12	60.0	110.9	23.6[b]	3.3	781	113	51	7.7
Mozambique	..	13	..	25.0	..	0.9	444	33	4	26.5
Myanmar	..	..	..	..	..	..	131	3	1	0.0
Namibia	..	66	9.2	50.9	..	3.4	1,479	96	12	1.6
Nepal	..	29	24.0	66.6	13.2	1.4	93	44	9	0.3
Netherlands	3.20	5	71.1	211.4	21.7[b]	1.4	7,010	115	92	19.8
New Caledonia	..	..	..	..	..	..	..	89	50	15.4
New Zealand	14.53	1	44.9	155.8	27.5[b]	1.1	9,566	109	86	9.3
Nicaragua	..	39	..	46.1	15.2	0.6	473	82	11	5.3
Niger	0.00	17	..	14.7	..	0.9	..	30	1	4.5

	Business entry density per 1,000 people ages 15–64 2011	Time required to start a business days June 2012	Stock market capitalization % of GDP 2011	Domestic credit provided by banking sector % of GDP 2011	Tax revenue collected by central government % of GDP 2011	Military expenditures % of GDP 2011	Electric power consumption per capita kilowatt-hours 2010	Mobile cellular subscriptions[a] per 100 people 2011	Individuals using the Internet[a] % of population 2011	High-technology exports % of manufactured exports 2011
Nigeria	0.83	34	16.1	37.5	0.3	1.0	136	59	28	1.1
Northern Mariana Islands	..	..	..	..	..	..	..	..	..	..
Norway	4.94	7	45.1	..	28.4[b]	1.6	25,175	116	94	18.5
Oman	1.67	8	27.5	32.3	2.2	6.0	5,933	169	68	2.6
Pakistan	0.03	21	15.6	43.3	9.3	3.0	457	62	9	1.8
Palau	..	28	..	..	..	..	..	75	..	..
Panama	0.08	7	39.9	104.9	..	..	1,832	189	43	35.4
Papua New Guinea	..	51	69.6	27.8	..	0.5	..	34	2	..
Paraguay	..	35	4.0	34.7	13.2	1.1	1,134	99	24	7.3
Peru	2.54	26	44.8	18.7	15.9	1.2	1,106	110	37	6.2
Philippines	0.19	36	73.6	51.8	12.3	1.1	643	99	29	46.4
Poland	0.52	32	26.9	66.2	17.0[b]	1.9	3,783	131	65	5.9
Portugal	3.92	5	26.0	204.1	21.5[b]	2.0	4,929	115	55	3.5
Puerto Rico	..	6	..	..	..	..	..	83	48	..
Qatar	..	9	72.5	70.2	14.4	2.2	14,997	123	86	0.0
Romania	4.41	10	11.2	52.1	17.2[b]	1.1	2,392	109	44	10.2
Russian Federation	0.83	18	42.9	39.5	15.4[b]	3.9	6,431	179	49	8.0
Rwanda	0.78	3	..	..	..	1.2	..	41	7	3.4
Samoa	1.37	9	..	47.3	..	..	..	91	7	0.2
San Marino	..	..	..	..	22.3	..	..	112	50	..
São Tomé and Príncipe	2.56	7	..	39.5	..	..	..	68	20	14.0
Saudi Arabia	..	21	58.7	–4.8	..	8.4	7,967	191	48	0.7
Senegal	0.19	5	..	31.5	..	1.6	195	73	18	0.6
Serbia	1.66	12	18.3	54.1	20.5	2.1	4,359	125	42	..
Seychelles	..	39	..	45.8	31.7	0.9	..	146	43	3.4
Sierra Leone	0.38	12	..	12.9	11.1	0.9	..	36	0	..
Singapore	8.45	3	128.6	93.6	14.1	3.6	8,307	150	71	45.2
Sint Maarten	..	..	..	..	..	..	..	..	..	..
Slovak Republic	4.81	16	4.9	54.1	12.7[b]	1.1	5,164	109	74	7.1
Slovenia	4.04	6	12.8	94.7	17.9	1.4	6,521	107	72	5.9
Solomon Islands	..	9	..	15.0	..	..	..	50	6	..
Somalia	..	..	..	..	..	..	..	7	1	..
South Africa	0.77	19	209.6	175.0	25.7[b]	1.3	4,803	127	21	5.1
South Sudan	0.31	..	..	..	..	2.9	..	..	..	..
Spain	2.59	28	69.8	230.9	9.5[b]	1.0	6,155	113	68	6.4
Sri Lanka	0.58	7	32.8	46.2	12.4	2.6	449	87	15	1.0
St. Kitts and Nevis	5.69	19	85.8	123.3	19.7	..	..	153	76	0.1
St. Lucia	3.00	15	..	114.6	..	..	..	123	42	16.9
St. Martin	..	..	..	..	..	..	..	..	..	..
St. Vincent and Grenadines	..	10	..	56.6	22.2	..	..	121	43	0.0
Sudan	..	36	..	23.0	..	..	141	56	19	29.4
Suriname	1.02	694	..	24.1	..	..	..	179	32	6.5
Swaziland	..	56	..	25.8	..	3.0	..	64	18	..
Sweden	7.17	16	87.1	142.3	21.9[b]	1.3	14,939	119	91	13.3
Switzerland	2.52	18	141.4	185.1	10.4	0.8	8,175	131	85	24.4
Syrian Arab Republic	0.05	13	..	47.7	..	3.9	1,905	63	23	1.3
Tajikistan	0.29	24	..	..	..	..	2,004	91	13	..

	Business entry density per 1,000 people ages 15–64 2011	Time required to start a business days June 2012	Stock market capitalization % of GDP 2011	Domestic credit provided by banking sector % of GDP 2011	Tax revenue collected by central government % of GDP 2011	Military expenditures % of GDP 2011	Electric power consumption per capita kilowatt-hours 2010	Mobile cellular subscriptions[a] per 100 people 2011	Individuals using the Internet[a] % of population 2011	High-technology exports % of manufactured exports 2011
Tanzania	..	26	6.4	24.2	..	1.1	78	56	12	5.4
Thailand	0.59	29	77.7	159.0	17.6[b]	1.6	2,243	112	24	20.7
Timor-Leste	..	94	..	−26.5	..	2.6	..	53	1	..
Togo	0.11	38	..	35.4	17.1[b]	1.6	107	50	4	0.2
Tonga	1.96	16	..	29.0	..	..	..	53	25	0.0
Trinidad and Tobago	..	41	65.5	32.3	26.2	..	5,894	136	55	0.1
Tunisia	0.63	11	20.8	82.1	20.9	1.3	1,350	117	39	5.6
Turkey	0.96	6	26.0	69.3	20.1[b]	2.3	2,477	89	42	1.8
Turkmenistan	..	..	..	..	..	..	2,403	69	5	..
Turks and Caicos Islands	..	..	..	..	..	..	..	..	..	2.1
Tuvalu	..	..	..	..	..	..	..	22	30	..
Uganda	0.72	33	46.0	18.7	16.1	1.6	..	48	13	21.9
Ukraine	0.60	22	15.5	73.4	18.3	2.5	3,550	123	31	4.4
United Arab Emirates	1.37	8	26.0	81.4	..	5.4	11,044	149	70	3.2
United Kingdom	10.41	13	118.7	212.6	27.4[b]	2.6	5,733	131	82	21.3
United States	..	6	104.3	234.9	10.1[b]	4.7	13,394	93	78	18.1
Uruguay	3.36	7	0.4	29.9	19.6	1.9	2,763	141	51	5.8
Uzbekistan	0.82	12	..	..	..	..	1,648	92	30	..
Vanuatu	2.18	35	..	70.5	..	..	..	56	8	..
Venezuela, RB	..	144	1.6	29.3	..	0.8	3,287	98	40	2.5
Vietnam	..	34	14.8	120.7	..	2.2	1,035	143	35	8.6
Virgin Islands (U.S.)	..	..	..	..	..	..	..	..	27	..
West Bank and Gaza	..	48	..	..	..	..	..	46	41	..
Yemen, Rep.	..	40	..	22.7	..	4.4	249	47	15	0.3
Zambia	1.26	17	20.9	18.0	16.6	1.6	623	61	12	24.8
Zimbabwe	..	90	112.9	..	..	1.6	1,022	72	16	1.0
World	**3.42** [u]	**30** [u]	**68.7** [w]	**164.9** [w]	**14.8** [w]	**2.5** [w]	**2,975** [w]	**85** [w]	**33** [w]	**17.6** [w]
Low income	0.32	30	..	40.4	11.6	1.6	242	42	6	..
Middle income	2.30	35	47.7	92.4	13.2	2.0	1,823	86	27	17.1
Lower middle income	1.01	31	43.2	58.9	11.9	2.0	698	80	16	9.3
Upper middle income	3.50	40	48.8	101.3	13.6	2.0	2,942	92	38	18.6
Low & middle income	2.01	34	47.4	91.6	13.2	2.0	1,661	80	24	17.0
East Asia & Pacific	1.04	37[d]	50.6	132.5	10.9	1.8	2,337	81	34	26.0
Europe & Central Asia	2.82	15[d]	32.9	49.2	17.1	3.0	4,059	132	42	6.3
Latin America & Carib.	2.84	58[d]	42.0	68.5	..	1.3	1,973	107	39	10.9
Middle East & N. Africa	0.36	25[d]	..	53.6	23.8	3.5	1,658	89	27	2.9
South Asia	0.16	19[d]	48.2	69.7	10.3	2.5	555	69	9	6.4
Sub-Saharan Africa	1.99	32[d]	..	74.7	..	1.5	553	53	13	2.8
High income	6.38	18	78.6	203.2	14.6	2.8	9,415	114	76	17.9
Euro area	5.10	13	41.9	153.5	17.6	1.5	6,847	125	73	14.9

a. Data are from the International Telecommunication Union's (ITU) World Telecommunication/ICT Indicators database. Please cite ITU for third party use of these data. b. Data were reported on a cash basis and have been adjusted to the accrual framework of the International Monetary Fund's *Government Finance Statistics Manual 2001*. c. Differs from the official value published by the government of China (1.3 percent; see National Bureau of Statistics of China, www.stats.gov.cn). d. Differs from data reported on the Doing Business website because the regional aggregates on the Doing Business website include developed economies.

 Front User guide  World view People Environment

About the data

Entrepreneurial activity

The rate new businesses are added to an economy is a measure of its dynamism and entrepreneurial activity. Data on business entry density are from the World Bank's 2012 Entrepreneurship Database, which includes indicators for more than 150 countries for 2004–11. Survey data are used to analyze firm creation, its relationship to economic growth and poverty reduction, and the impact of regulatory and institutional reforms. Data on total registered businesses were collected from national registrars of companies. For cross-country comparability, only limited liability corporations that operate in the formal sector are included. For additional information on sources, methodology, calculation of entrepreneurship rates, and data limitations see http://www.doingbusiness.org/data/exploretopics/entrepreneurship.

Data on time required to start a business are from the Doing Business database, whose indicators measure business regulation, gauge regulatory outcomes, and measure the extent of legal protection of property, the flexibility of employment regulation, and the tax burden on businesses. The fundamental premise is that economic activity requires good rules and regulations that are efficient, accessible, and easy to implement. Some indicators give a higher score for more regulation, such as stricter disclosure requirements in related-party transactions, and others give a higher score for simplified regulations, such as a one-stop shop for completing business startup formalities. There are 11 sets of indicators covering starting a business, registering property, dealing with construction permits, getting electricity, enforcing contracts, getting credit, protecting investors, paying taxes, trading across borders, resolving insolvency, and employing workers. The indicators are available at www.doingbusiness.org.

Doing Business data are collected with a standardized survey that uses a simple business case to ensure comparability across economies and over time—with assumptions about the legal form of the business, its size, its location, and nature of its operation. Surveys in 185 countries are administered through more than 9,000 local experts, including lawyers, business consultants, accountants, freight forwarders, government officials, and other professionals who routinely administer or advise on legal and regulatory requirements.

The Doing Business methodology has limitations that should be considered when interpreting the data. First, the data collected refer to businesses in the economy's largest city and may not represent regulations in other locations of the economy. To address this limitation, subnational indicators are being collected for selected economies; they point to significant differences in the speed of reform and the ease of doing business across cities in the same economy. Second, the data often focus on a specific business form—generally a limited liability company of a specified size—and may not represent regulation for other types of businesses such as sole proprietorships. Third, transactions described in a standardized business case refer to a specific set of issues and may not represent all the issues a business encounters. Fourth, the time measures involve an element of judgment by the expert respondents. When sources indicate different estimates, the Doing Business time indicators represent the median values of several responses given under the assumptions of the standardized case. Fifth, the methodology assumes that a business has full information on what is required and does not waste time when completing procedures. In constructing the indicators, it is assumed that entrepreneurs know about all regulations and comply with them. In practice, entrepreneurs may not be aware of all required procedures or may avoid legally required procedures altogether.

Financial systems

Stock markets and banking systems both enhance growth, the main factor in poverty reduction. At low levels of economic development commercial banks tend to dominate the financial system, while at higher levels domestic stock markets become more active and efficient.

Open economies with sound macroeconomic policies, good legal systems, and shareholder protection attract capital and thus have larger financial markets. The table includes market capitalization as a share of gross domestic product (GDP) as a measure of stock market size. Market size can be measured in other ways that may produce a different ranking of countries. Recent research on stock market development shows that modern communications technology and increased financial integration have resulted in more cross-border capital flows, a stronger presence of financial firms around the world, and the migration of trading activities to international exchanges. Many firms in emerging markets now cross-list on international exchanges, which provides them with lower cost capital and more liquidity-traded shares. However, this also means that exchanges in emerging markets may not have enough financial activity to sustain them. Comparability across countries may be limited by conceptual and statistical weaknesses, such as inaccurate reporting and differences in accounting standards.

Standard & Poor's (S&P) Indices provides regular updates on 21 emerging stock markets and 36 frontier markets. The S&P Global Equity Indices, S&P Indices's leading emerging markets index, is designed to be sufficiently investable to support index tracking portfolios in emerging market stocks that are legally and practically open to foreign portfolio investment. The S&P Frontier Broad Market Index measures the performance of 36 smaller and less liquid markets. These indexes are widely used benchmarks for international portfolio management. See www.spindices.com for further information on the indexes.

Because markets included in S&P's emerging markets category vary widely in level of development, it is best to look at the entire category to identify the most significant market trends. And it is useful to remember that stock market trends may be distorted by currency conversions, especially when a currency has registered a significant devaluation (Demirgüç-Kunt and Levine 2006; Beck and Levine 2001; and Claessens, Klingebiel, and Schmukler 2002).

Domestic credit provided by the banking sector as a share of GDP measures banking sector depth and financial sector development in terms of size. Data are taken from the banking survey of the International Monetary Fund's (IMF) *International Financial Statistics* or, when unavailable, from its monetary survey. The monetary survey includes monetary authorities (the central bank), deposit money banks, and other banking institutions, such as finance companies, development banks, and savings and loan institutions. In a few countries governments may hold international reserves as deposits in the banking system rather than in the central bank. Claims on the central government are a net item (claims on the central government minus central government deposits) and thus may be negative, resulting in a negative value for domestic credit provided by the banking sector.

Tax revenues

Taxes are the main source of revenue for most governments. Tax revenue as a share of GDP provides a quick overview of the fiscal obligations and incentives facing the private sector across countries. The table shows only central government data, which may significantly understate the total tax burden, particularly in countries where provincial and municipal governments are large or have considerable tax authority.

Low ratios of tax revenue to GDP may reflect weak administration and large-scale tax avoidance or evasion. Low ratios may also reflect a sizable parallel economy with unrecorded and undisclosed incomes. Tax revenue ratios tend to rise with income, with higher income countries relying on taxes to finance a much broader range of social services and social security than lower income countries are able to.

Military expenditures

Although national defense is an important function of government, high expenditures for defense or civil conflicts burden the economy and may impede growth. Military expenditures as a share of GDP are a rough indicator of the portion of national resources used for military activities. As an "input" measure, military expenditures are not directly related to the "output" of military activities, capabilities, or security. Comparisons across countries should take into account many factors, including historical and cultural traditions, the length of borders that need defending, the quality of relations with neighbors, and the role of the armed forces in the body politic.

Data are from the Stockholm International Peace Research Institute (SIPRI), whose primary source of military expenditure data is official data provided by national governments. These data are derived from budget documents, defense white papers, and other public documents from official government agencies, including government responses to questionnaires sent by SIPRI, the United Nations Office for Disarmament Affairs, or the Organization for Security and Co-operation in Europe. Secondary sources include international statistics, such as those of the North Atlantic Treaty Organization (NATO) and the IMF's *Government Finance Statistics Yearbook*. Other secondary sources include country reports of the Economist Intelligence Unit, country reports by IMF staff, and specialist journals and newspapers.

In the many cases where SIPRI cannot make independent estimates, it uses country-provided data. Because of differences in definitions and the difficulty of verifying the accuracy and completeness of data,

data are not always comparable across countries. However, SIPRI puts a high priority on ensuring that the data series for each country is comparable over time. More information on SIPRI's military expenditure project can be found at www.sipri.org/research/armaments/milex.

Infrastructure

The quality of an economy's infrastructure, including power and communications, is an important element in investment decisions and economic development. The International Energy Agency (IEA) collects data on electric power consumption from national energy agencies and adjusts the values to meet international definitions. Consumption by auxiliary stations, losses in transformers that are considered integral parts of those stations, and electricity produced by pumping installations are included. Where data are available, electricity generated by primary sources of energy—coal, oil, gas, nuclear, hydro, geothermal, wind, tide and wave, and combustible renewables—are included. Consumption data do not capture the reliability of supplies, including breakdowns, load factors, and frequency of outages.

The International Telecommunication Union (ITU) estimates that there were 5.9 billion mobile subscriptions globally in 2011. No technology has ever spread faster around the world. Mobile communications have a particularly important impact in rural areas. The mobility, ease of use, flexible deployment, and relatively low and declining rollout costs of wireless technologies enable them to reach rural populations with low levels of income and literacy. The next billion mobile subscribers will consist mainly of the rural poor.

Operating companies have traditionally been the main source of telecommunications data, so information on subscriptions has been widely available for most countries. This gives a general idea of access, but a more precise measure is the penetration rate—the share of households with access to telecommunications. During the past few years more information on information and communication technology use has become available from household and business surveys. Also important are data on actual use of telecommunications services. The quality of data varies among reporting countries as a result of differences in regulations covering data provision and availability.

High-technology exports

The method for determining high-technology exports was developed by the Organisation for Economic Co-operation and Development in collaboration with Eurostat. It takes a "product approach" (rather than a "sectoral approach") based on research and development intensity (expenditure divided by total sales) for groups of products from Germany, Italy, Japan, the Netherlands, Sweden, and the United States. Because industrial sectors specializing in a few high-technology products may also produce low-technology products, the product approach is more appropriate for international trade. The method takes only research and development intensity into account, but other characteristics of high technology are also important, such as knowhow, scientific personnel, and technology embodied in patents. Considering these characteristics would yield a different list (see Hatzichronoglou 1997).

Definitions

• **Business entry density** is the number of newly registered limited liability corporations per 1,000 people ages 15–64. • **Time required to start a business** is the number of calendar days to complete the procedures for legally operating a business using the fastest procedure, independent of cost. • **Stock market capitalization** (also known as market value) is the share price times the number of shares outstanding. • **Domestic credit provided by banking sector** is all credit to various sectors on a gross basis, except to the central government, which is net. The banking sector includes monetary authorities, deposit money banks, and other banking institutions for which data are available. • **Tax revenue collected by central government** is compulsory transfers to the central government for public purposes. Certain compulsory transfers such as fines, penalties, and most social security contributions are excluded. Refunds and corrections of erroneously collected tax revenue are treated as negative revenue. The analytic framework of the IMF's *Government Finance Statistics Manual 2001* (GFSM 2001) is based on accrual accounting and balance sheets. For countries still reporting government finance data on a cash basis, the IMF adjusts reported data to the GFSM 2001 accrual framework. These countries are footnoted in the table. • **Military expenditures** are SIPRI data derived from NATO's former definition (in use until 2002), which includes all current and capital expenditures on the armed forces, including peacekeeping forces; defense ministries and other government agencies engaged in defense projects; paramilitary forces, if judged to be trained and equipped for military operations; and military space activities. Such expenditures include military and civil personnel, including retirement pensions and social services for military personnel; operation and maintenance; procurement; military research and development; and military aid (in the military expenditures of the donor country). Excluded are civil defense and current expenditures for previous military activities, such as for veterans benefits, demobilization, and weapons conversion and destruction. This definition cannot be applied for all countries, however, since that would require more detailed information than is available about military budgets and off-budget military expenditures (for example, whether military budgets cover civil defense, reserves and auxiliary forces, police and paramilitary forces, and military pensions). • **Electric power consumption per capita** is the production of power plants and combined heat and power plants less transmission, distribution, and transformation losses and own use by heat and power plants, divided by midyear population. • **Mobile cellular subscriptions** are the number of subscriptions to a public mobile telephone service that provides access to the public switched telephone network using cellular technology. Postpaid subscriptions and active prepaid accounts (that is, accounts that have been used during the last three months) are included. The indicator applies to all mobile cellular subscriptions that offer voice communications and excludes subscriptions for data cards or USB modems, subscriptions to public mobile data services, private-trunked mobile radio, telepoint, radio paging, and telemetry services. • **Individuals using the Internet** are the percentage of individuals who have used the Internet (from any location) in the last 12 months. Internet can be used via a computer, mobile phone, personal digital assistant, games machine, digital television, or similar device. • **High-technology exports** are products with high research and development intensity, such as in aerospace, computers, pharmaceuticals, scientific instruments, and electrical machinery.

Data sources

Data on business entry density are from the World Bank's Entrepreneurship Database (www.doingbusiness.org/data/exploretopics/ entrepreneurship). Data on time required to start a business are from the World Bank's Doing Business project (www.doingbusiness .org). Data on stock market capitalization are from Standard & Poor's (2012). Data on domestic credit are from the IMF's *International Financial Statistics*. Data on central government tax revenue are from the IMF's *Government Finance Statistics*. Data on military expenditures are from SIPRI's Military Expenditure Database (www.sipri.org/databases/milex). Data on electricity consumption are from the IEA's *Energy Statistics of Non-OECD Countries, Energy Balances of Non-OECD Countries,* and *Energy Statistics of OECD Countries* and from the United Nations Statistics Division's *Energy Statistics Yearbook*. Data on mobile cellular phone subscriptions and individuals using the Internet are from the ITU's World Telecommunication/ICT Indicators database and TeleGeography. Data on high-technology exports are from the United Nations Statistics Division's Commodity Trade (Comtrade) database.

References

Beck, Thorsten, and Ross Levine. 2001. "Stock Markets, Banks, and Growth: Correlation or Causality?" Policy Research Working Paper 2670, World Bank, Washington, DC.

Claessens, Stijn, Daniela Klingebiel, and Sergio L. Schmukler. 2002. "Explaining the Migration of Stocks from Exchanges in Emerging Economies to International Centers." Policy Research Working Paper 2816, World Bank, Washington, DC.

Demirgüç-Kunt, Asli, and Ross Levine. 1996. "Stock Market Development and Financial Intermediaries: Stylized Facts." *World Bank Economic Review* 10 (2): 291–321.

Geneva Declaration on Armed Violence and Development. 2011. *Global Burden of Armed Violence.* Geneva.

Hatzichronoglou, Thomas. 1997. "Revision of the High-Technology Sector and Product Classification." STI Working Paper 1997/2. Organisation for Economic Co-operation and Development, Directorate for Science, Technology, and Industry, Paris.

Standard & Poors. 2012. *Global Stock Markets Factbook 2012.* New York.

WIPO (World Intellectual Property Organization). 2012. *World Intellectual Property Indicators 2012.* Geneva.

World Bank. 2012. *CPIA Africa: Accessing Africa's Policies and Institutions.* Washington, DC.

5 States and markets

To access the World Development Indicators online tables, use the URL http://wdi.worldbank.org/table/ and the table number (for example, http://wdi.worldbank.org/table/5.1). To view a specific indicator online, use the URL http://data.worldbank.org/indicator/ and the indicator code (for example, http://data.worldbank.org/indicator/IE.PPI.TELE.CD).

5.1 Private sector in the economy

Telecommunications investment	IE.PPI.TELE.CD
Energy investment	IE.PPI.ENGY.CD
Transport investment	IE.PPI.TRAN.CD
Water and sanitation investment	IE.PPI.WATR.CD
Domestic credit to private sector	FS.AST.PRVT.GD.ZS
Businesses registered, New	IC.BUS.NREG
Businesses registered, Entry density	IC.BUS.NDNS.ZS

5.2 Business environment: enterprise surveys

Time dealing with officials	IC.GOV.DURS.ZS
Average number of times meeting with tax officials	IC.TAX.METG
Time required to obtain operating license	IC.FRM.DURS
Informal payments to public officials	IC.FRM.CORR.ZS
Losses due to theft, robbery, vandalism, and arson	IC.FRM.CRIM.ZS
Firms competing against unregistered firms	IC.FRM.CMPU.ZS
Firms with female top manager	IC.FRM.FEMM.ZS
Firms using banks to finance investment	IC.FRM.BNKS.ZS
Value lost due to electrical outages	IC.FRM.OUTG.ZS
Internationally recognized quality certification ownership	IC.FRM.ISOC.ZS
Average time to clear exports through customs	IC.CUS.DURS.EX
Firms offering formal training	IC.FRM.TRNG.ZS

5.3 Business environment: Doing Business indicators

Number of procedures to start a business	IC.REG.PROC
Time required to start a business	IC.REG.DURS
Cost to start a business	IC.REG.COST.PC.ZS
Number of procedures to register property	IC.PRP.PROC
Time required to register property	IC.PRP.DURS
Number of procedures to build a warehouse	IC.WRH.PROC
Time required to build a warehouse	IC.WRH.DURS
Time required to get electricity	IC.ELC.TIME
Number of procedures to enforce a contract	IC.LGL.PROC
Time required to enforce a contract	IC.LGL.DURS
Business disclosure index	IC.BUS.DISC.XQ
Time required to resolve insolvency	IC.ISV.DURS

5.4 Stock markets

Market capitalization, $	CM.MKT.LCAP.CD
Market capitalization, % of GDP	CM.MKT.LCAP.GD.ZS
Value of shares traded	CM.MKT.TRAD.GD.ZS
Turnover ratio	CM.MKT.TRNR
Listed domestic companies	CM.MKT.LDOM.NO

S&P/Global Equity Indices	CM.MKT.INDX.ZG

5.5 Financial access, stability, and efficiency

Strength of legal rights index	IC.LGL.CRED.XQ
Depth of credit information index	IC.CRD.INFO.XQ
Depositors with commercial banks	FB.CBK.DPTR.P3
Borrowers from commercial banks	FB.CBK.BRWR.P3
Commercial bank branches	FB.CBK.BRCH.P5
Automated teller machines	FB.ATM.TOTL.P5
Bank capital to assets ratio	FB.BNK.CAPA.ZS
Ratio of bank non-performing loans to total gross loans	FB.AST.NPER.ZS
Domestic credit provided by banking sector	FS.AST.DOMS.GD.ZS
Interest rate spread	FR.INR.LNDP
Risk premium on lending	FR.INR.RISK

5.6 Tax policies

Tax revenue collected by central government	GC.TAX.TOTL.GD.ZS
Number of tax payments by businesses	IC.TAX.PAYM
Time for businesses to prepare, file and pay taxes	IC.TAX.DURS
Business profit tax	IC.TAX.PRFT.CP.ZS
Business labor tax and contributions	IC.TAX.LABR.CP.ZS
Other business taxes	IC.TAX.OTHR.CP.ZS
Total business tax rate	IC.TAX.TOTL.CP.ZS

5.7 Military expenditures and arms transfers

Military expenditure, % of GDP	MS.MIL.XPND.GD.ZS
Military expenditure, % of central government expenditure	MS.MIL.XPND.ZS
Arm forces personnel	MS.MIL.TOTL.P1
Arm forces personnel, % of total labor force	MS.MIL.TOTL.TF.ZS
Arms transfers, Exports	MS.MIL.XPRT.KD
Arms transfers, Imports	MS.MIL.MPRT.KD

5.8 Fragile situations

International Development Association Resource Allocation Index	IQ.CPA.IRAI.XQ
Peacekeeping troops, police, and military observers	VC.PKP.TOTL.UN
Battle related deaths	VC.BTL.DETH
Intentional homicides	VC.IHR.PSRC.P5
Military expenditures	MS.MIL.XPND.GD.ZS
Losses due to theft, robbery, vandalism, and arson	IC.FRM.CRIM.ZS
Firms formally registered when operations started	IC.FRM.FREG.ZS

Children in employment ♀♂	SL.TLF.0714.ZS
Refugees, By country of origin	SM.POP.REFG.OR
Refugees, By country of asylum	SM.POP.REFG
Internally displaced persons	VC.IDP.TOTL.HE
Access to an improved water source	SH.H2O.SAFE.ZS
Access to improved sanitation facilities	SH.STA.ACSN
Maternal mortality ratio, National estimate	SH.STA.MMRT.NE
Maternal mortality ratio, Modeled estimate	SH.STA.MMRT
Under-five mortality rate ♀♂	SH.DYN.MORT
Depth of food deficit	SN.ITK.DFCT
Primary gross enrollment ratio ♀♂	SE.PRM.ENRR

5.9 Public policies and institutions

International Development Association Resource Allocation Index	IQ.CPA.IRAI.XQ
Macroeconomic management	IQ.CPA.MACR.XQ
Fiscal policy	IQ.CPA.FISP.XQ
Debt policy	IQ.CPA.DEBT.XQ
Economic management, Average	IQ.CPA.ECON.XQ
Trade	IQ.CPA.TRAD.XQ
Financial sector	IQ.CPA.FINS.XQ
Business regulatory environment	IQ.CPA.BREG.XQ
Structural policies, Average	IQ.CPA.STRC.XQ
Gender equality	IQ.CPA.GNDR.XQ
Equity of public resource use	IQ.CPA.PRES.XQ
Building human resources	IQ.CPA.HRES.XQ
Social protection and labor	IQ.CPA.PROT.XQ
Policies and institutions for environmental sustainability	IQ.CPA.ENVR.XQ
Policies for social inclusion and equity, Average	IQ.CPA.SOCI.XQ
Property rights and rule-based governance	IQ.CPA.PROP.XQ
Quality of budgetary and financial management	IQ.CPA.FINQ.XQ
Efficiency of revenue mobilization	IQ.CPA.REVN.XQ
Quality of public administration	IQ.CPA.PADM.XQ
Transparency, accountability, and corruption in the public sector	IQ.CPA.TRAN.XQ
Public sector management and institutions, Average	IQ.CPA.PUBS.XQ

5.10 Transport services

Total road network	IS.ROD.TOTL.KM
Paved roads	IS.ROD.PAVE.ZS
Road passengers carried	IS.ROD.PSGR.K6
Road goods hauled	IS.ROD.GOOD.MT.K6
Rail lines	IS.RRS.TOTL.KM
Railway passengers carried	IS.RRS.PASG.KM
Railway goods hauled	IS.RRS.GOOD.MT.K6
Port container traffic	IS.SHP.GOOD.TU
Registered air carrier departures worldwide	IS.AIR.DPRT
Air passengers carried	IS.AIR.PSGR

Air freight	IS.AIR.GOOD.MT.K1

5.11 Power and communications

Electric power consumption per capita	EG.USE.ELEC.KH.PC
Electric power transmission and distribution losses	EG.ELC.LOSS.ZS
Fixed telephone subscriptions	IT.MLT.MAIN.P2
Mobile cellular subscriptions	IT.CEL.SETS.P2
Fixed telephone international voice traffic	..[a]
Mobile cellular network international voice traffic	..[a]
Population covered by mobile cellular network	..[a]
Fixed telephone sub-basket	..[a]
Mobile cellular sub-basket	..[a]
Telecommunications revenue	..[a]
Mobile cellular and fixed-line subscribers per employee	..[a]

5.12 The information age

Households with television	..[a]
Households with a computer	..[a]
Individuals using the Internet	..[a]
Fixed (wired) broadband Internet subscriptions	IT.NET.BBND.P2
International Internet bandwidth	..[a]
Fixed broadband sub-basket	..[a]
Secure Internet servers	IT.NET.SECR.P6
Information and communications technology goods, Exports	TX.VAL.ICTG.ZS.UN
Information and communications technology goods, Imports	TM.VAL.ICTG.ZS.UN
Information and communications technology services, Exports	BX.GSR.CCIS.ZS

5.13 Science and technology

Research and development (R&D), Researchers	SP.POP.SCIE.RD.P6
Research and development (R&D), Technicians	SP.POP.TECH.RD.P6
Scientific and technical journal articles	IP.JRN.ARTC.SC
Expenditures for R&D	GB.XPD.RSDV.GD.ZS
High-technology exports, $	TX.VAL.TECH.CD
High-technology exports, % of manufactured exports	TX.VAL.TECH.MF.ZS
Charges for the use of intellectual property, Receipts	BX.GSR.ROYL.CD
Charges for the use of intellectual property, Payments	BM.GSR.ROYL.CD
Patent applications filed, Residents	IP.PAT.RESD
Patent applications filed, Nonresidents	IP.PAT.NRES
Trademark applications filed, Total	IP.TMK.TOTL

♀♂ Data disaggregated by sex are available in the World Development Indicators database.
a. Available online only as part of the table, not as an individual indicator.

GLOBAL LINKS

The world economy is bound together by trade in goods and services, financial flows, and the movement of people. As national economies develop, their links expand and grow more complex. The indicators in this section measure the size and direction of these flows and document the effects of policy interventions and aid flows on the world economy.

The optimistic economic momentum at the beginning of 2011 slowed over the course of the year. The adverse effects of the tsunami in Japan coupled with intensification of the sovereign debt crisis in the euro area shook confidence at the global level. The slowdown became more pronounced in high-income economies, reducing the growth in capital inflows to developing countries.

Net debt and equity inflows to developing economies in 2011 were $1.1 trillion—or 8 percent lower than in 2010 and below the level reached before the global financial crisis. The downturn was driven by the collapse of portfolio equity, again the most volatile of capital flows. Equity flows to emerging markets with good growth prospects, such as China, Brazil, and India, dropped substantially. Low- and middle-income economies recorded net inflows of only $8.3 billion in 2011, compared with $130 billion in 2010.

Debt net inflows to developing countries in 2011 were $437 billion—down 9 percent from 2010. The slowdown was led by a drop in lending by official creditors from $77 billion in 2010 to $30 billion in 2011. However, commercial bank financing tripled to $110 billion, and the private sector created more liquidity through bond issuances, reaching their highest stock level of $1.5 trillion. Net inflows of short-term debt shrank 27 percent in 2011 after being the fastest growing debt component the previous year.

Global foreign direct investment (FDI) rose 22.7 percent in 2011, to its pre-crisis level. Some 40 percent of those investments were directed to developing economies. In 2011 many developing countries continued to implement policy changes to further liberalize and facilitate FDI entry and operations and to regulate FDI. The largest recipients of FDI inflows were Brazil, China, India, and the Russian Federation, accounting for more than half of inflows to developing economies. China was the largest recipient, with net FDI inflows of $220 billion, a decline of 10 percent compared with 2010.

In 2011 world merchandise exports to developing countries increased 27 percent from 2010, while exports to high-income countries increased 20 percent. Brazil, China, India, and the Russian Federation were among the top traders, with China accounting for 70 percent of East Asia and Pacific's merchandise trade.

Official development assistance, a stable source of development financing and buffer against the impact of several financial crises, was $134 billion in 2011, or 0.58 percent of developing countries' combined gross national income, down from 0.65 percent in 2010.

Worldwide tourism continues to grow and has become one of the largest and fastest growing economic sectors in the world. The number of international tourist arrivals in 2011 reached a record high of over 1 billion, and inbound tourism expenditures increased 12 percent to $1.3 trillion from 2010. The only developing region that saw a drop in tourist arrivals in 2011 was the Middle East and North Africa, due to political instability and armed conflict in the region.

Highlights

East Asia & Pacific: Equity investment drops

Equity inflows to East Asia and Pacific ($ billions)

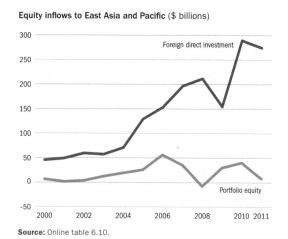

Source: Online table 6.10.

After recovering from a 2009 low by 2010, equity investment in East Asia and Pacific fell again in 2011. Turmoil in the euro area and the natural disaster in Japan caused a large withdrawal of foreign equity. Foreign direct investment (FDI) net inflows combined with portfolio equity inflows in 2011 were 17 percent lower than in 2010. Net FDI flows declined 5 percent, while portfolio equity inflows fell to a fifth their 2010 level. China, the largest recipient of capital flows into the region (with 80 percent), recorded a 10 percent decline of FDI inflows compared with 2010 and portfolio equity inflows a sixth of their 2010 level. Investments in the service sector in China maintained their growth rate.

Europe & Central Asia: Remittance flows diverge

Remittance inflows ($ billions)

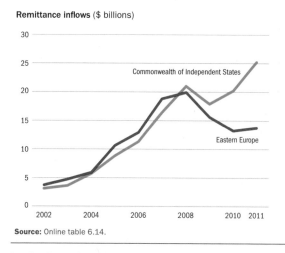

Source: Online table 6.14.

High unemployment in the developed countries of the European Union impaired employment prospects of existing migrants and limited their ability to send money home. Remittance flows to developing countries in Eastern Europe dropped sharply in 2009 and have yet to recover. Romania, one of the largest recipients of remittances in the European Union, experienced an annual average decrease of 30 percent over the last three years. In contrast, remittances to almost all the member countries of the Commonwealth of Independent States rebounded strongly. Rising employment and higher real wages in the Russian Federation gave migrants the opportunity to increase their remittances. Tajikistan, with the most emigrants to the Russian Federation, depends on remittances as a major source of external finance. In 2011 it received $3.2 billion in remittances, equivalent to 46 percent of GDP.

Latin America & Caribbean: More trade with developing countries

Share of total merchandise exports (%)

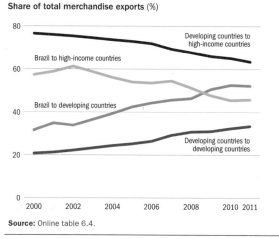

Source: Online table 6.4.

Trade between developing countries continues to grow. Between 2000 and 2010 merchandise exports between developing countries grew more than 600 percent, while developing country exports to high-income countries grew half that amount. By 2011 a third of developing country trade went to other developing countries, while the share of merchandise exports from developing countries to high-income countries fell from 77 percent in 2000 to about 63 percent. In Latin America and the Caribbean, Brazil is a leading example. Since 2009 Brazil's merchandise exports to developing countries have exceeded those to high-income countries—largely due to Brazil's increased natural resource exports to Asia, particularly to China. In addition, intraregional trade has increased since 2009, especially between Common Market of the South members (Argentina, Brazil, Paraguay, Uruguay, and Venezuela), surpassing the level reached before the global financial crisis.

 Front | User guide | World view | People | Environment

Middle East & North Africa: Tourist arrivals fall due to instability

Despite increased worldwide tourism, tourist arrivals fell in the Middle East and North Africa in 2011 due to political instability and armed conflict in the region (World Tourism Organization 2012b). "The Arab Spring," as it has come to be known, began in Tunisia with mass demonstrations and riots at the end of 2010. As a result, international tourist arrivals to Tunisia fell 31 percent, from 6.9 million in 2010 to 4.8 million in 2011, the lowest level since 1998, and tourist expenditures fell from $3.5 billion to $2.5 billion. In February 2011 Egypt's government was overthrown. Egypt experienced a 32 percent drop in tourist arrivals in 2011 after an 18 percent increase in 2010. Heavily dependent on tourism, it saw tourist expenditures fall from $51.2 billion in 2010 to $43.1 billion in 2011.

International tourist arrivals (millions)

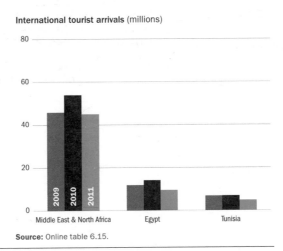

Source: Online table 6.15.

South Asia: Encouraging investment in China and India

China and India, the two largest and fastest growing economies in the developing world, have altered their regulatory systems to attract and keep inflows of foreign direct investment (FDI). China started first. It began opening its economy in 1979 and continued through to its membership in the World Trade Organization in 2001, reassuring investors of its increasing reliability. While FDI in China was driven by export-oriented policies, India pursued an import substitution policy, promoting domestic firms and limiting the rights of foreign investors. It was not until the 1990s that India started significantly liberalizing FDI, and it only recently liberalized the FDI policies of its retail sector. Before the financial crisis net FDI inflows as a share of GDP to India began to catch up with those to China. After bottoming out in 2010, they began to recover, while net FDI inflows as a share of GDP to China dropped again.

Net inflows of foreign direct investment (% of GDP)

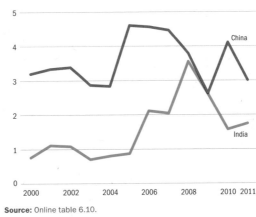

Source: Online table 6.10.

Sub-Saharan Africa: Less official development assistance in 2011

Official development assistance to Sub-Saharan Africa as a share of the region's gross national income fell in 2011. But aid to three of the five largest recipients, the Democratic Republic of Congo, São Tomé and Príncipe, and Rwanda, rose. The Democratic Republic of Congo was second among all countries receiving aid from Development Assistance Committee (DAC) members (after Afghanistan). But this distinction is likely to be short lived. Like Liberia in 2010, the Democratic Republic of Congo benefited from debt forgiveness after reaching the completion point under the enhanced Heavily Indebted Poor Countries initiative in July 2010 and the subsequent Paris Club rescheduling agreement at the end of 2010. As its two major Paris Club creditors, the United States and France were also the top DAC donors to the Democratic Republic of Congo, increasing their aid to the country from $278 million to $1.3 billion and from $135 million to $1.1 billion respectively from 2010.

Net official development assistance from all donors (% of GNI)

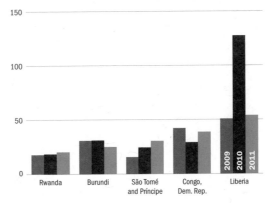

Source: Online table 6.12.

6 Global links

	Merchandise trade	Net barter terms of trade index	Inbound tourism expenditure	Net official development assistance	Net migration	Personal transfers and compensation of employees, received	Foreign direct investment	Portfolio equity	Total external debt stock	Total debt service
	% of GDP	2000 = 100	% of exports	% of GNI	thousands	$ millions	Net inflow $ millions	Net inflow $ millions	$ millions	% of exports of goods, services, and primary income[a]
	2011	2011	2011	2011	2005–10	2011	2011	2011	2011	2011
Afghanistan	33.1	146.3	..	35.0	–381	..	83	..	2,623	..
Albania	56.6	94.1	41.7	2.4	–48	1,162	1,370	2	5,938	9.3
Algeria	63.5	199.1	0.4	0.1	–140	203	2,721	0	6,072	0.8
American Samoa	..	129.0								
Andorra	..	..	..	..		..	..	..	..	..
Angola	82.9	244.7	1.0	0.2	82	0	–3,024	0	21,115	4.3
Antigua and Barbuda	47.0	75.1	58.1	1.4	..	20	58	..	..	..
Argentina	35.5	135.2	6.2	0.0	–200	686	8,671	–174	114,704	15.3
Armenia	53.5	128.5	20.2	3.5	–75	1,994	663	0	7,383	25.4
Aruba	..	118.5	19.8	..	4	5	544	0	..	..
Australia	37.3	200.7	..	..	1,125	1,871	67,638	–3,308	..	..
Austria	88.8	89.0	9.6	..	160	2,674	15,734	483	..	..
Azerbaijan	71.3	187.6	4.0	0.5	53	1,893	4,485	0	8,427	4.9
Bahamas, The	46.4	108.6	66.0	..	6	..	595	..	..	..
Bahrain	..	128.5	7.7	..	448	..	781	982	..	..
Bangladesh	54.2	54.8	0.4	1.2	–2,908	12,068	798	–10	27,043	5.5
Barbados	62.7	111.0	..	..	0	82	334	..	..	..
Belarus	156.3	103.8	1.9	0.2	–50	814	4,002	0	29,120	4.5
Belgium	182.4	100.1	3.0	..	200	10,912	102,000	–4,200	..	..
Belize	86.4	104.4	26.7	2.3	–1	76	95	..	1,278	13.9
Benin	61.7	125.1	..	9.3	50	185	118	..	1,423	..
Bermuda	..	72.4	..	..	..	1,253	111	–3	..	..
Bhutan	90.6	151.5	..	8.7	17	10	16	0	1,035	11.1
Bolivia	66.8	175.4	5.5	3.3	–165	1,043	859	0	6,474	4.9
Bosnia and Herzegovina	93.4	101.5	9.8	2.3	–10	1,958	380	..	10,729	10.9
Botswana	74.7	82.4	..	0.7	19	63	587	..	2,396	..
Brazil	19.9	135.8	2.3	0.0	–500	2,798	71,539	7,174	404,317	19.4
Brunei Darussalam	94.7	200.6	..	..	4	..	1,208	..	..	..
Bulgaria	112.3	110.7	12.7	..	–50	1,483	2,588	–42	39,930	12.2
Burkina Faso	42.3	141.2	..	9.5	–125	111	7	..	2,420	..
Burundi	36.1	172.6	1.6	24.8	370	45	3	..	628	3.4
Cambodia	126.7	70.6	24.1	6.5	–255	160	902	0	4,336	1.0
Cameroon	44.0	149.6	..	2.5	–19	115	360	..	3,074	..
Canada	52.7	122.5	3.7	..	1,098	..	39,510	21,313	..	..
Cape Verde	53.7	106.0	55.5	13.3	–17	177	105	..	1,025	5.0
Cayman Islands	..	77.6	..	..	..	..	7,408	..	..	..
Central African Republic	24.6	82.4	..	12.4	5	..	109	..	573	..
Chad	64.3	208.8	..	4.9	–75	..	1,855	..	1,821	..
Channel Islands	..	..	..	..	5	..	..	..	..	..
Chile	62.3	213.3	..	0.0	30	4	17,299	4,477	96,245	15.2
China	49.8	72.8	2.6	0.0	–1,884	40,483	220,143	5,308	685,418	3.6
Hong Kong SAR, China	388.9	95.9	6.0	..	176	357	95,352	9,814	..	..
Macao SAR, China	24.2	87.1	..	..	51	48	2,116	0	..	..
Colombia	33.5	142.4	4.9	0.4	–120	4,205	13,605	1,969	76,918	15.6
Comoros	49.5	76.1	..	8.5	–10	..	7	..	278	..
Congo, Dem. Rep.	77.3	146.7	..	38.4	–24	115	1,596	..	5,448	2.4
Congo, Rep.	110.2	214.5	..	2.4	50	..	2,931	..	2,523	..

 Front User guide World view  People Environment

	Merchandise trade	Net barter terms of trade index	Inbound tourism expenditure	Net official development assistance	Net migration	Personal transfers and compensation of employees, received	Foreign direct investment	Portfolio equity	Total external debt stock	Total debt service
										% of exports of goods, services, and primary income[a]
	% of GDP	2000 = 100	% of exports	% of GNI	thousands	$ millions	Net inflow $ millions	Net inflow $ millions	$ millions	
	2011	2011	2011	2011	2005–10	2011	2011	2011	2011	2011
Costa Rica	65.2	78.1	15.4	0.1	76	520	2,157	0	10,292	13.5
Côte d'Ivoire	74.0	159.0	..	6.2	–360	373	344	..	12,012	..
Croatia	57.7	99.0	36.6	0.0	10	1,378	1,265	17	..	..
Cuba	..	165.6	..	..	–190	..	110	..	..	..
Curaçao	..	99.9	..	..	..	34	70	0	..	..
Cyprus	42.1	103.1	25.5	..	44	127	1,080	429	..	..
Czech Republic	144.6	104.0	5.2	..	240	1,815	5,380	–2	..	..
Denmark	63.3	106.2	3.4	..	90	1,273	13,106	–2,250	..	..
Djibouti	..	77.8	4.6	..	0	32	79	0	767	..
Dominica	54.1	104.3	58.9	5.2	..	23	34	..	284	9.8
Dominican Republic	47.1	92.4	31.4	0.4	–140	3,650	2,295	0	15,395	10.4
Ecuador	70.7	130.4	3.4	0.3	–120	2,681	568	2	16,497	9.7
Egypt, Arab Rep.	39.0	159.4	19.8	0.2	–347	14,324	–483	–711	35,001	7.4
El Salvador	66.9	90.5	11.3	1.3	–292	3,665	247	0	11,995	21.7
Equatorial Guinea	98.5	226.4	..	0.2	20	..	737	..	..	..
Eritrea	49.8	81.9	..	6.3	55	..	19	..	1,055	..
Estonia	155.0	141.9	7.6	..	0	407	436	–112	..	..
Ethiopia	38.1	136.5	34.4	11.8	–300	513	627	..	8,597	6.1
Faeroe Islands	..	103.1	..	..	..	146	..	..	..	..
Fiji	82.8	107.8	..	2.0	–29	158	204	..	861	..
Finland	61.8	74.8	5.3	..	73	751	–5,758	–5	..	..
France	47.3	95.6	8.0	..	500	19,307	45,209	3,608	..	..
French Polynesia	..	83.1	..	..	0	700	40	..	..	..
Gabon	95.6	218.6	..	0.5	5	..	728	..	2,879	..
Gambia, The	48.8	91.7	32.4	15.6	–14	91	36	..	466	7.5
Georgia	64.4	133.8	20.2	3.9	–150	1,537	1,154	–7	11,124	26.9
Germany	75.8	99.5	3.0	..	550	13,160	39,067	7,778	..	..
Ghana	71.4	185.3	5.4	4.8	–51	152	3,222	1	11,289	2.4
Greece	30.9	93.9	22.0	..	154	1,186	1,092	–354	..	..
Greenland	..	72.4	..	..	..	..	..	..	..	..
Grenada	42.4	101.9	57.0	1.6	–5	29	41	..	567	13.3
Guam	..	85.0	..	..	0	..	..	..	..	..
Guatemala	57.7	90.9	10.5	0.9	–200	4,508	1,081	0	16,286	15.6
Guinea	73.7	109.9	0.1	4.5	–300	65	896	..	3,139	11.2
Guinea-Bissau	54.8	80.6	..	12.3	–10	46	19	..	284	..
Guyana	114.5	130.0	..	6.2	–40	373	165	..	1,846	..
Haiti	49.8	64.5	15.9	23.2	–240	1,551	181	0	783	0.5
Honduras	97.2	89.8	8.5	3.8	–100	2,811	1,043	0	4,642	16.0
Hungary	152.9	94.1	5.5	..	75	2,441	9,629	–203	..	..
Iceland	72.5	90.3	9.0	..	10	21	1,107	–11	..	..
India	40.5	135.9	..	0.2	–3,000	63,818	32,190	–4,137	334,331	6.5
Indonesia	44.6	134.1	4.1	0.1	–1,293	6,924	18,160	–326	213,541	14.5
Iran, Islamic Rep.	..	180.9	..	..	–186	1,330	4,150	..	19,113	1.4
Iraq	119.0	211.8	1.9	1.7	–150	386	1,396	94	..	..
Ireland	88.9	86.2	4.2	..	100	755	11,506	86,184	..	..
Isle of Man	..	..	..	..	..	..	..	..	..	..
Israel	58.7	95.0	6.2	..	274	595	11,374	–821	..	..

	Merchandise trade	Net barter terms of trade index	Inbound tourism expenditure	Net official development assistance	Net migration	Personal transfers and compensation of employees, received	Foreign direct investment	Portfolio equity	Total external debt stock	Total debt service
							Net inflow $ millions	Net inflow $ millions		% of exports of goods, services, and primary income[a]
	% of GDP	2000 = 100	% of exports	% of GNI	thousands	$ millions	$ millions	$ millions	$ millions	
	2011	2011	2011	2011	2005–10	2011	2011	2011	2011	2011
Italy	49.2	95.6	7.2	..	1,999	7,025	28,003	5,978	..	..
Jamaica	55.4	68.6	48.1	0.4	−100	2,106	173	0	14,350	36.5
Japan	28.6	60.1	1.3	..	270	2,132	79	5,645	..	..
Jordan	91.1	76.5	29.4	3.4	203	3,453	1,469	109	17,634	6.7
Kazakhstan	67.1	219.9	1.6	0.1	7	180	13,227	39	124,437	34.6
Kenya	61.1	90.7	18.6	7.4	−189	934	335	20	10,258	4.2
Kiribati	78.0	90.1	..	27.2	..	..	4	..	..	..
Korea, Dem. Rep.	..	79.6	..	..	0	..	55	..	..	..
Korea, Rep.	96.7	63.1	2.7	..	−30	8,494	4,661	−7,479	..	..
Kosovo	..	..	..	9.9	..	1,122	546	0	1,531	8.9
Kuwait	69.9	219.2	..	..	278	..	400	1,099	..	..
Kyrgyz Republic	105.1	109.4	20.3	9.7	−132	1,709	694	5	5,486	11.8
Lao PDR	60.9	125.0	17.2	5.2	−75	110	301	11	6,158	..
Latvia	103.0	110.4	6.7	..	−10	695	1,502	38	38,255	47.0
Lebanon	65.9	98.1	27.5	1.1	−13	7,322	3,476	240	24,767	19.9
Lesotho	152.5	73.7	2.1	9.0	−20	649	132	0	792	..
Liberia	90.7	162.0	18.6	53.6	300	360	1,313	..	448	..
Libya	..	185.4	..	..	−20	..	200	0	..	..
Liechtenstein	..	..	..	..	..	..	..	..	..	..
Lithuania	139.5	102.3	4.3	..	−36	1,956	1,443	9	29,988	20.1
Luxembourg	85.6	98.5	5.3	..	42	1,740	18,366	32,486	..	..
Macedonia, FYR	112.8	86.7	4.5	1.6	2	434	495	−8	6,286	18.9
Madagascar	45.3	74.7	..	4.2	−5	..	907	..	2,769	2.1
Malawi	62.8	98.2	2.7	14.5	−20	17	92	−1	1,202	1.3
Malaysia	144.0	100.7	7.4	0.0	84	1,198	12,001	..	94,468	3.9
Maldives	88.3	100.1	80.3	2.7	0	3	282	0	983	..
Mali	52.7	177.3	..	12.3	−101	473	178	..	2,931	..
Malta	120.2	53.6	16.1	..	5	37	467	−7	..	..
Marshall Islands	100.8	107.2	..	38.2	..	..	7	..	..	..
Mauritania	125.1	131.5	..	9.2	10	..	45	..	2,709	3.6
Mauritius	69.3	71.5	30.5	1.7	0	1	273	9,387	1,435	1.4
Mexico	61.6	107.9	3.4	0.1	−1,805	23,588	20,823	−6,244	287,037	11.2
Micronesia, Fed. Sts.	62.8	97.3	..	41.2	−9	..	8	..	..	..
Moldova	105.9	105.9	8.3	6.0	−172	1,600	294	5	5,452	12.8
Monaco	..	..	..	..	..	..	..	..	..	..
Mongolia	129.1	226.8	4.7	4.3	−15	279	4,715	9	2,564	2.1
Montenegro	70.6	..	..	1.6	−3	343	558	−15	2,093	10.2
Morocco	65.1	140.6	25.7	1.3	−675	7,256	2,521	166	29,049	9.9
Mozambique	77.6	106.8	7.0	16.3	−20	157	2,079	0	4,097	1.6
Myanmar	..	104.5	3.3	..	−500	127	1,001	..	7,765	..
Namibia	85.5	116.7	12.1	2.4	−1	15	969	4	..	..
Nepal	35.5	77.9	22.3	4.7	−100	4,217	94	..	3,956	9.5
Netherlands	150.7	..	..	..	8	..	..	..	..	..
New Caledonia	..	230.2	..	..	6	519	1,745	0	..	..
New Zealand	46.8	132.6	11.3	..	65	875	4,285	1,594	..	..
Nicaragua	80.4	82.8	8.0	7.6	−200	914	968	0	7,121	14.8
Niger	60.7	163.9	..	10.9	−29	102	1,014	..	1,408	..

	Merchandise trade	Net barter terms of trade index	Inbound tourism expenditure	Net official development assistance	Net migration	Personal transfers and compensation of employees, received	Foreign direct investment	Portfolio equity	Total external debt stock	Total debt service % of exports of goods, services, and primary income[a]
	% of GDP 2011	2000 = 100 2011	% of exports 2011	% of GNI 2011	thousands 2005–10	$ millions 2011	Net inflow $ millions 2011	Net inflow $ millions 2011	$ millions 2011	2011
Nigeria	71.3	211.4	0.7	0.8	−300	20,619	8,842	2,571	13,108	0.4
Northern Mariana Islands	..	86.2	..	..	..	..	0	..	..	..
Norway	51.4	156.6	3.2	..	171	765	7,281	1,708	..	..
Oman	98.6	230.9	3.3	..	153	39	788	−447	..	..
Pakistan	33.2	52.4	3.6	1.6	−2,000	12,263	1,309	−37	60,182	9.2
Palau	76.1	104.2	..	20.7	..	..	2	..	..	..
Panama	133.3	86.4	12.2	0.4	11	388	3,223	0	12,583	3.6
Papua New Guinea	92.4	166.0	..	4.9	0	11	−309	..	12,582	15.8
Paraguay	74.8	107.5	2.3	0.4	−40	893	412	0	6,011	3.6
Peru	47.6	159.0	5.8	0.4	−725	2,697	8,233	147	44,872	6.5
Philippines	49.9	64.7	6.0	−0.1	−1,233	22,973	1,869	1,038	76,043	17.6
Poland	76.8	99.7	5.0	..	56	7,641	15,296	3,052	..	..
Portugal	58.6	86.8	17.3	..	150	3,778	13,074	−10,557	..	..
Puerto Rico	..	..	..	..	−145	..	..	..	..	..
Qatar	83.4	213.3	..	..	857	574	−87	−903	..	..
Romania	77.2	98.3	2.9	..	−100	3,889	2,557	−37	129,822	27.5
Russian Federation	45.5	234.2	3.0	..	1,136	4,951	52,878	−9,707	542,977	10.5
Rwanda	33.1	225.7	..	20.2	15	103	106	..	1,103	..
Samoa	62.7	77.5	67.9	16.6	−16	139	15	..	368	5.8
San Marino	..	..	..	..	..	..	..	..	..	..
São Tomé and Príncipe	57.6	120.3	54.2	30.2	−7	7	35	0	231	5.4
Saudi Arabia	82.6	215.8	2.5	..	1,056	244	16,308	..	..	..
Senegal	59.1	105.4	..	7.5	−133	1,478	286	..	4,320	..
Serbia	69.7	..	7.2	1.3	0	3,271	2,700	69	31,569	31.5
Seychelles	115.1	75.0	34.6	2.1	..	26	139	0	1,780	3.2
Sierra Leone	68.6	61.7	8.1	14.7	60	59	715	..	1,049	3.8
Singapore	323.4	81.2	..	..	722	..	64,003	−3,754	..	..
Sint Maarten	..	..	..	..	..	11	−48	..	..	..
Slovak Republic	163.0	87.4	3.0	..	37	1,753	3,658	39	..	..
Slovenia	141.6	86.1	8.0	..	22	433	818	222	..	..
Solomon Islands	104.3	87.9	..	49.6	0	2	146	..	256	2.0
Somalia	..	100.3	..	..	−300	..	102	..	3,050	..
South Africa	53.5	154.1	9.1	0.3	700	1,158	5,889	−3,769	113,512	5.3
South Sudan	..	..	..	..	..	..	..	..	..	..
Spain	44.7	99.0	14.9	..	2,250	9,907	31,419	2,978	..	..
Sri Lanka	51.0	72.1	10.4	1.0	−250	5,153	956	−623	23,984	9.3
St. Kitts and Nevis	42.1	66.8	40.8	2.5	..	48	114	..	..	..
St. Lucia	69.9	94.8	56.7	3.0	−1	29	81	..	448	7.8
St. Martin	..	..	..	..	..	..	..	..	..	..
St. Vincent and Grenadines	53.8	107.2	48.3	2.8	−5	29	110	..	283	15.2
Sudan	28.3	229.4	..	2.0	135	1,420	1,936	..	21,169	..
Suriname	96.3	141.8	2.6	..	−5	4	145	0	..	..
Swaziland	97.8	105.3	..	3.2	−6	55	95	..	605	1.9
Sweden	67.1	87.2	6.2	..	266	776	3,054	2,146	..	..
Switzerland	67.1	79.8	5.0	..	183	3,307	10,077	7,543	..	..
Syrian Arab Republic	..	143.7	..	..	−56	2,079	1,060	..	4,968	..
Tajikistan	68.1	102.4	3.4	5.5	−296	3,060	11	0	3,323	..

	Merchandise trade	Net barter terms of trade index	Inbound tourism expenditure	Net official development assistance	Net migration	Personal transfers and compensation of employees, received	Foreign direct investment	Portfolio equity	Total external debt stock	Total debt service
							Net inflow	Net inflow		% of exports of goods, services, and primary income[a]
	% of GDP	2000 = 100	% of exports	% of GNI	thousands	$ millions	$ millions	$ millions	$ millions	
	2011	2011	2011	2011	2005–10	2011	2011	2011	2011	2011
Tanzania	66.3	151.4	19.9	10.4	−300	76	1,095	3	10,044	2.0
Thailand	132.3	93.9	..	−0.1	492	4,554	7,780	875	80,039	3.8
Timor-Leste	30.4	..	..	..	−50	131	47	..	..	..
Togo	77.3	30.4	..	15.5	−5	337	54	..	643	..
Tonga	44.7	81.2	..	21.1	−8	72	10	..	191	8.8
Trinidad and Tobago	103.2	152.6	..	..	−20	91	574	..	..	..
Tunisia	91.2	95.0	11.2	1.5	−20	2,005	433	−44	22,335	10.7
Turkey	48.5	88.6	15.4	0.1	−50	1,087	16,049	−986	307,007	30.2
Turkmenistan	72.7	221.2	..	0.2	−55	..	3,186	..	445	..
Turks and Caicos Islands	..	73.4	..	..	..	..	97	..	..	..
Tuvalu	70.7	..	..	76.9	..	..	2	..	..	..
Uganda	45.0	119.7	24.2	9.6	−135	949	797	106	3,858	1.7
Ukraine	91.4	124.0	6.1	0.5	−40	7,822	7,207	519	134,481	30.8
United Arab Emirates	136.0	178.3	..	..	3,077	..	7,679	..	..	..
United Kingdom	45.4	101.4	5.9	..	1,020	1,796	36,244	−16,894	..	..
United States	25.0	94.6	8.8	..	4,955	5,810	257,528	27,350	..	..
Uruguay	40.1	100.9	18.7	0.0	−50	102	2,177	..	14,350	11.1
Uzbekistan	51.2	178.0	..	0.5	−518	..	1,403	..	8,382	..
Vanuatu	47.4	91.9	71.2	12.4	0	22	58	0	202	1.6
Venezuela, RB	44.3	258.7	0.9	0.0	40	138	5,226	..	67,908	6.4
Vietnam	164.8	99.9	5.3	3.0	−431	8,600	7,430	1,064	57,841	3.2
Virgin Islands (U.S.)	..	..	..	..	−4	..	..	..	..	..
West Bank and Gaza	..	..	..	..	−90	1,545	..	..	..	..
Yemen, Rep.	59.0	157.5	9.2	1.5	−135	1,404	−713	0	6,418	2.8
Zambia	83.3	192.8	1.6	6.1	−85	46	1,982	11	4,360	2.1
Zimbabwe	81.8	110.5	..	7.4	−900	..	387	..	6,275	..
World	**51.8**	**..**	**5.4[b]**	**0.2[c]**	**..**	**479,246**	**1,654,419**	**183,598**	**..**	**..**
Low income	58.1	..	12.0[b]	8.8[c]	−6,808	27,628	18,331	124	133,292	4.6
Middle income	51.4	..	4.7[b]	0.2[c]	−16,352	330,766	629,613	8,474	4,742,871	8.9
Lower middle income	53.2	..	6.5[b]	0.8[c]	−12,699	202,300	108,774	−349	1,170,790	9.5
Upper middle income	50.9	..	4.3[b]	0.1[c]	−3,653	128,466	520,838	8,822	3,572,081	8.8
Low & middle income	51.5	..	4.8[b]	0.6[c]	−23,160	358,394	647,943	8,598	4,876,163	8.8
East Asia & Pacific	57.2	..	3.4[b]	0.1[c]	−5,221	85,943	274,550	7,980	1,242,633	4.7
Europe & Central Asia	57.0	..	5.7[b]	0.2[c]	−595	42,960	119,394	−10,115	1,484,186	17.8
Latin America & Carib.	38.2	..	4.7[b]	0.2[c]	−5,088	59,532	161,618	7,351	1,233,484	13.4
Middle East & N. Africa	67.3	..	11.1[b]	..	−1,628	41,339	16,309	−145	166,124	5.1
South Asia	40.7	..	6.5[b]	0.7[c]	−8,622	97,532	35,728	−4,807	454,138	6.7
Sub-Saharan Africa	62.7	..	6.5[b]	3.9[c]	−2,006	31,088	40,345	8,334	295,598	3.4
High income	51.9	..	5.7[b]	0.0[c]	22,906	120,853	1,006,476	175,000	..	..
Euro area	70.8	..	6.1[b]	0.0[c]	6,336	75,712	320,055	128,811	..	..

a. The numerator refers to 2011, whereas the denominator is a three-year average of 2009–11 data. b. Calculated using the World Bank's weighted aggregation methodology (see *Statistical methods*) and thus may differ from data reported by the World Tourism Organization. c. Based on the World Bank classification of economies and thus may differ from data reported by the Organisation for Economic Co-operation and Development.

 Front | User guide | World view | People | Environment

About the data

Starting with *World Development Indicators 2013,* the World Bank is changing its presentation of balance of payments data to conform to the International Monetary Fund's (IMF) Balance of Payments Manual, 6th edition (BPM6). The historical data series based on BPM5 ends with data for 2005. Balance of payments data from 2005 forward have been presented in accord with the BPM6 methodology, which can be accessed at www.imf.org/external/np/sta/bop/bop.htm.

Trade in goods

Data on merchandise trade are from customs reports of goods moving into or out of an economy or from reports of financial transactions related to merchandise trade recorded in the balance of payments. Because of differences in timing and definitions, trade flow estimates from customs reports and balance of payments may differ. Several international agencies process trade data, each correcting unreported or misreported data, leading to other differences. The most detailed source of data on international trade in goods is the United Nations Statistics Division's Commodity Trade Statistics (Comtrade) database. The IMF and the World Trade Organization also collect customs-based data on trade in goods.

The "terms of trade" index measures the relative prices of a country's exports and imports. The most common way to calculate terms of trade is the net barter (or commodity) terms of trade index, or the ratio of the export price index to the import price index. When a country's net barter terms of trade index increases, its exports have become more expensive or its imports cheaper.

Tourism

Tourism is defined as the activity of people traveling to and staying in places outside their usual environment for no more than one year for leisure, business, and other purposes not related to an activity remunerated from within the place visited. Data on inbound and outbound tourists refer to the number of arrivals and departures, not to the number of unique individuals. Thus a person who makes several trips to a country during a given period is counted each time as a new arrival. Data on inbound tourism show the arrivals of nonresident tourists (overnight visitors) at national borders. When data on international tourists are unavailable or incomplete, the table shows the arrivals of international visitors, which include tourists, same-day visitors, cruise passengers, and crew members. The aggregates are calculated using the World Bank's weighted aggregation methodology (see *Statistical methods*) and differ from the World Tourism Organization's aggregates.

For tourism expenditure, the World Tourism Organization uses balance of payments data from the IMF supplemented by data from individual countries. These data, shown in the table, include travel and passenger transport items as defined by the Balance of Payments. When the IMF does not report data on passenger transport items, expenditure data for travel items are shown.

Official development assistance

Data on official development assistance received refer to aid to eligible countries from members of the Organisation of Economic Co-operation and Development's (OECD) Development Assistance Committee (DAC), multilateral organizations, and non-DAC donors. Data do not reflect aid given by recipient countries to other developing countries or distinguish among types of aid (program, project, or food aid; emergency assistance; or postconflict peacekeeping assistance), which may have different effects on the economy.

Ratios of aid to gross national income (GNI), gross capital formation, imports, and government spending measure a country's dependency on aid. Care must be taken in drawing policy conclusions. For foreign policy reasons some countries have traditionally received large amounts of aid. Thus aid dependency ratios may reveal as much about a donor's interests as about a recipient's needs. Increases in aid dependency ratios can reflect events affecting both the numerator (aid) and the denominator (GNI).

Data are based on information from donors and may not be consistent with information recorded by recipients in the balance of payments, which often excludes all or some technical assistance—particularly payments to expatriates made directly by the donor. Similarly, grant commodity aid may not always be recorded in trade data or in the balance of payments. DAC statistics exclude aid for military and antiterrorism purposes. The aggregates refer to World Bank classifications of economies and therefore may differ from those reported by the OECD.

Migration, personal transfers, and compensation of employees

The movement of people, most often through migration, is a significant part of global integration. Migrants contribute to the economies of both their host country and their country of origin. Yet reliable statistics on migration are difficult to collect and are often incomplete, making international comparisons a challenge.

Since data on emigrant stock is difficult for countries to collect, the United Nations Population Division provides data on net migration, taking into account the past migration history of a country or area, the migration policy of a country, and the influx of refugees in recent periods to derive estimates of net migration. The data to calculate these estimates come from various sources, including border statistics, administrative records, surveys, and censuses. When there are insufficient data, net migration is derived through the difference between the growth rate of a country's population over a certain period and the rate of natural increase of that population (itself being the difference between the birth rate and the death rate).

Migrants often send funds back to their home countries, which are recorded as personal transfers in the balance of payments. Personal transfers thus include all current transfers between resident and nonresident individuals, independent of the source of income of the sender (irrespective of whether the sender receives income from labor, entrepreneurial or property income, social benefits, or any other types of transfers or disposes of assets) and the relationship between the households (irrespective of whether they are related or unrelated individuals).

Compensation of employees refers to the income of border, seasonal, and other short-term workers who are employed in an economy where they are not resident and of residents employed by nonresident entities. Compensation of employees has three main components: wages and salaries in cash, wages and salaries in kind, and employers' social contributions.

Equity flows

Equity flows comprise foreign direct investment (FDI) and portfolio equity. The internationally accepted definition of FDI (from BPM6) includes the following components: equity investment, including investment associated with equity that gives rise to control or influence; investment in indirectly influenced or controlled enterprises; investment in fellow enterprises; debt (except selected debt); and reverse investment. The Framework for Direct Investment Relationships provides criteria for determining whether cross-border ownership results in a direct investment relationship, based on control and influence.

Direct investments may take the form of greenfield investment, where the investor starts a new venture in a foreign country by constructing new operational facilities; joint venture, where the investor enters into a partnership agreement with a company abroad to establish a new enterprise; or merger and acquisition, where the investor acquires an existing enterprise abroad. The IMF suggests that investments should account for at least 10 percent of voting stock to be counted as FDI. In practice many countries set a higher threshold. Many countries fail to report reinvested earnings, and the definition of long-term loans differs among countries.

Portfolio equity investment is defined as cross-border transactions and positions involving equity securities, other than those included in direct investment or reserve assets. Equity securities are equity instruments that are negotiable and designed to be traded, usually on organized exchanges or "over the counter." The negotiability of securities facilitates trading, allowing securities to be held by different parties during their lives. Negotiability allows investors to diversify their portfolios and to withdraw their investment readily. Included in portfolio investment are investment fund shares or units (that is, those issued by investment funds) that are evidenced by securities and that are not reserve assets or direct investment. Although they are negotiable instruments, exchange-traded financial derivatives are not included in portfolio investment because they are in their own category.

External debt

External indebtedness affects a country's creditworthiness and investor perceptions. Data on external debt are gathered through the World Bank's Debtor Reporting System (DRS). Indebtedness is calculated using loan-by-loan reports submitted by countries on long-term public and publicly guaranteed borrowing and using information on short-term debt collected by the countries, from creditors through the reporting systems of the Bank for International Settlements, or based on national data from the World Bank's *Quarterly External Debt Statistics.* These data are supplemented by information from major multilateral banks and official lending agencies in major creditor countries. Currently, 128 developing countries report to the DRS. Debt data are reported in the currency of repayment and compiled and published in U.S. dollars. End-of-period exchange rates are used for the compilation of stock figures (amount of debt outstanding), and projected debt service and annual average exchange rates are used for the flows. Exchange rates are taken from the IMF's *International Financial Statistics.* Debt repayable in multiple currencies, goods, or services and debt with a provision for maintenance of the value of the currency of repayment are shown at book value.

While data related to public and publicly guaranteed debt are reported to the DRS on a loan-by-loan basis, data on long-term private nonguaranteed debt are reported annually in aggregate by the country or estimated by World Bank staff for countries. Private nonguaranteed debt is estimated based on national data from the World Bank's *Quarterly External Debt Statistics.*

Total debt service as a share of exports of goods, services, and primary income provides a measure of a country's ability to service its debt out of export earnings.

Definitions

• **Merchandise trade** includes all trade in goods and excludes trade in services. • **Net barter terms of trade index** is the percentage ratio of the export unit value indexes to the import unit value indexes, measured relative to the base year 2000. • **Inbound tourism expenditure** is expenditures by international inbound visitors, including payments to national carriers for international transport and any other prepayment made for goods or services received in the destination country. They may include receipts from same-day visitors, except when these are important enough to justify separate classification. Data include travel and passenger transport items as defined by Balance of Payments. When passenger transport items are not reported, expenditure data for travel items are shown. Exports refer to all transactions between residents of a country and the rest of the world involving a change of ownership from residents to nonresidents of general merchandise, goods sent for processing and repairs, nonmonetary gold, and services. • **Net official development assistance** is flows (net of repayment of principal) that meet the DAC definition of official development assistance and are made to countries and territories on the DAC list of aid recipients, divided by World Bank estimates of GNI. • **Net migration** is the net total of migrants (immigrants less emigrants, including both citizens and noncitizens) during the period. Data are five-year estimates. • **Personal transfers and compensation of employees, received,** are the sum of personal transfers (current transfers in cash or in kind made or received by resident households to or from nonresident households) and compensation of employees (remuneration for the labor input to the production process contributed by an individual in an employer-employee relationship with the enterprise). • **Foreign direct investment** is cross-border investment associated with a resident in one economy having control or a significant degree of influence on the management of an enterprise that is resident in another economy. • **Portfolio equity** is net inflows from equity securities other than those recorded as direct investment or reserve assets, including shares, stocks, depository receipts, and direct purchases of shares in local stock markets by foreign investors • **Total external debt stock** is debt owed to nonresident creditors and repayable in foreign currency, goods, or services by public and private entities in the country. It is the sum of long-term external debt, short-term debt, and use of IMF credit. • **Total debt service** is the sum of principal repayments and interest actually paid in foreign currency, goods, or services on long-term debt; interest paid on short-term debt; and repayments (repurchases and charges) to the IMF. Exports of goods and services and primary income are the total value of exports of goods and services, receipts of compensation of nonresident workers, and primary investment income from abroad.

Data sources

Data on merchandise trade are from the World Trade Organization. Data on trade indexes are from the United Nations Conference on Trade and Development's (UNCTAD) annual *Handbook of Statistics*. Data on tourism expenditure are from the World Tourism Organization's *Yearbook of Tourism Statistics* and World Tourism Organization (2012a) and updated from its electronic files. Data on net official development assistance are compiled by the OECD (http://stats.oecd.org). Data on net migration are from United Nations Population Division (2011). Data on personal transfers and compensation of employees are from the IMF's *Balance of Payments Statistics Yearbook* supplemented by World Bank staff estimates. Data on FDI are World Bank staff estimates based on IMF balance of payments statistics and UNCTAD data (http://unctadstat.unctad.org/ReportFolders/reportFolders.aspx). Data on portfolio equity are from the IMF's *Balance of Payments Statistics Yearbook*. Data on external debt are mainly from reports to the World Bank through its DRS from member countries that have received International Bank for Reconstruction and Development loans or International Development Assistance credits, with additional information from the files of the World Bank, the IMF, the African Development Bank and African Development Fund, the Asian Development Bank and Asian Development Fund, and the Inter-American Development Bank. Summary tables of the external debt of developing countries are published annually in the World Bank's *International Debt Statistics* and International Debt Statistics database.

References

IMF (International Monetary Fund). Various issues. *International Financial Statistics*. Washington, DC.

———. Various years. *Balance of Payments Statistics Yearbook. Parts 1 and 2*. Washington, DC.

UNCTAD (United Nations Conference on Trade and Development). Various years. *Handbook of Statistics*. New York and Geneva.

United Nations Population Division. 2011. *World Population Prospects: The 2010 Revision*. New York: United Nations, Department of Economic and Social Affairs.

World Bank. Various years. *International Debt Statistics*. Washington, DC.

World Tourism Organization. 2012a. *Compendium of Tourism Statistics 2012*. Madrid.

———. 2012b *Tourism Highlights: 2012 Edition*. Madrid.

———. Various years. *Yearbook of Tourism Statistics. Vols. 1 and 2*. Madrid.

6 Global links

To access the World Development Indicators online tables, use the URL http://wdi.worldbank.org/table/ and the table number (for example, http://wdi.worldbank.org/table/6.1). To view a specific indicator online, use the URL http://data.worldbank.org/indicator/ and the indicator code (for example, http://data.worldbank.org/indicator/TX.QTY.MRCH.XD.WD).

6.1 Growth of merchandise trade

Export volume	TX.QTY.MRCH.XD.WD
Import volume	TM.QTY.MRCH.XD.WD
Export value	TX.VAL.MRCH.XD.WD
Import value	TM.VAL.MRCH.XD.WD
Net barter terms of trade index	TT.PRI.MRCH.XD.WD

6.2 Direction and growth of merchandise trade

This table provides estimates of the flow of trade in goods between groups of economies.	..ᵃ

6.3 High-income economy trade with low- and middle-income economies

This table illustrates the importance of developing economies in the global trading system.	..ᵃ

6.4 Direction of trade of developing economies

Exports to developing economies within region	TX.VAL.MRCH.WR.ZS
Exports to developing economies outside region	TX.VAL.MRCH.OR.ZS
Exports to high-income economies	TX.VAL.MRCH.HI.ZS
Imports from developing economies within region	TM.VAL.MRCH.WR.ZS
Imports from developing economies outside region	TM.VAL.MRCH.OR.ZS
Imports from high-income economies	TM.VAL.MRCH.HI.ZS

6.5 Primary commodity prices

This table provides historical commodity price data.	..ᵃ

6.6 Tariff barriers

All products, Binding coverage	TM.TAX.MRCH.BC.ZS
Simple mean bound rate	TM.TAX.MRCH.BR.ZS
Simple mean tariff	TM.TAX.MRCH.SM.AR.ZS
Weighted mean tariff	TM.TAX.MRCH.WM.AR.ZS
Share of tariff lines with international peaks	TM.TAX.MRCH.IP.ZS
Share of tariff lines with specific rates	TM.TAX.MRCH.SR.ZS
Primary products, Simple mean tariff	TM.TAX.TCOM.SM.AR.ZS
Primary products, Weighted mean tariff	TM.TAX.TCOM.WM.AR.ZS
Manufactured products, Simple mean tariff	TM.TAX.MANF.SM.AR.ZS
Manufactured products, Weighted mean tariff	TM.TAX.MANF.WM.AR.ZS

6.7 Trade facilitation

Logistics performance index	LP.LPI.OVRL.XQ
Burden of customs procedures	IQ.WEF.CUST.XQ
Lead time to export	LP.EXP.DURS.MD
Lead time to import	LP.IMP.DURS.MD
Documents to export	IC.EXP.DOCS
Documents to import	IC.IMP.DOCS
Liner shipping connectivity index	IS.SHP.GCNW.XQ
Quality of port infrastructure	IQ.WEF.PORT.XQ

6.8 External debt

Total external debt, $	DT.DOD.DECT.CD
Total external debt, % of GNI	DT.DOD.DECT.GN.ZS
Long-term debt, Public and publicly guaranteed	DT.DOD.DPPG.CD
Long-term debt, Private nonguaranteed	DT.DOD.DPNG.CD
Short-term debt, $	DT.DOD.DSTC.CD
Short-term debt, % of total debt	DT.DOD.DSTC.ZS
Short-term debt, % of total reserves	DT.DOD.DSTC.IR.ZS
Total debt service	DT.TDS.DECT.EX.ZS
Present value of debt, % of GNI	DT.DOD.PVLX.GN.ZS
Present value of debt, % of exports of goods, services and primary income	DT.DOD.PVLX.EX.ZS

6.9 Global private financial flows

Foreign direct investment net inflows, $	BX.KLT.DINV.CD.WD
Foreign direct investment net inflows, % of GDP	BX.KLT.DINV.WD.GD.ZS
Portfolio equity	BX.PEF.TOTL.CD.WD
Bonds	DT.NFL.BOND.CD
Commercial banks and other lendings	DT.NFL.PCBO.CD

6.10 Net official financial flows

Net financial flows from bilateral sources	DT.NFL.BLAT.CD
Net financial flows from multilateral sources	DT.NFL.MLAT.CD
World Bank, IDA	DT.NFL.MIDA.CD
World Bank, IBRD	DT.NFL.MIBR.CD
IMF, Concessional	DT.NFL.IMFC.CD
IMF, Non concessional	DT.NFL.IMFN.CD
Regional development banks, Concessional	DT.NFL.RDBC.CD
Regional development banks, Nonconcessional	DT.NFL.RDBN.CD
Regional development banks, Other institutions	DT.NFL.MOTH.CD

6.11 Aid dependency

Net official development assistance (ODA)	DT.ODA.ODAT.CD
Net ODA per capita	DT.ODA.ODAT.PC.ZS

Grants, excluding technical cooperation	BX.GRT.EXTA.CD.WD
Technical cooperation grants	BX.GRT.TECH.CD.WD
Net ODA, % of GNI	DT.ODA.ODAT.GN.ZS
Net ODA, % of gross capital formation	DT.ODA.ODAT.GI.ZS
Net ODA, % of imports of goods and services and income	DT.ODA.ODAT.MP.ZS
Net ODA, % of central government expenditure	DT.ODA.ODAT.XP.ZS

6.12 Distribution of net aid by Development Assistance Committee members

Net bilateral aid flows from DAC donors	DC.DAC.TOTL.CD
United States	DC.DAC.USAL.CD
EU institutions	DC.DAC.CECL.CD
Germany	DC.DAC.DEUL.CD
France	DC.DAC.FRAL.CD
United Kingdom	DC.DAC.GBRL.CD
Japan	DC.DAC.JPNL.CD
Netherlands	DC.DAC.NLDL.CD
Australia	DC.DAC.AUSL.CD
Canada	DC.DAC.CANL.CD
Norway	DC.DAC.NORL.CD
Other DAC donors	..[a,b]

6.13 Movement of people

Net migration	SM.POP.NETM
International migrant stock	SM.POP.TOTL
Emigration rate of tertiary educated to OECD countries	SM.EMI.TERT.ZS
Refugees by country of origin	SM.POP.REFG.OR
Refugees by country of asylum	SM.POP.REFG
Personal transfers and compensation of employees, Received	BX.TRF.PWKR.CD.DT
Personal transfers and compensation of employees, Paid	BM.TRF.PWKR.CD.DT

6.14 Travel and tourism

International inbound tourists	ST.INT.ARVL
International outbound tourists	ST.INT.DPRT
Inbound tourism expenditure, $	ST.INT.RCPT.CD
Inbound tourism expenditure, % of exports	ST.INT.RCPT.XP.ZS
Outbound tourism expenditure, $	ST.INT.XPND.CD
Outbound tourism expenditure, % of imports	ST.INT.XPND.MP.ZS

a. Available online only as part of the table, not as an individual indicator.
b. Derived from data elsewhere in the World Development Indicators database.

Front | User guide | World view | People | Environment

Primary data documentation

As a major user of socioeconomic data, the World Bank recognizes the importance of data documentation to inform users of differences in the methods and conventions used by primary data collectors—usually national statistical agencies, central banks, and customs services—and by international organizations, which compile the statistics that appear in the World Development Indicators database. These differences may give rise to significant discrepancies over time, both within countries and across them. Delays in reporting data and the use of old surveys as the base for current estimates may further compromise the quality of data reported here.

This section provides information on sources, methods, and reporting standards of the principal demographic, economic, and environmental indicators in *World Development Indicators*. Additional documentation is available from the World Bank's Bulletin Board on Statistical Capacity at http://data.worldbank.org.

The demand for good-quality statistical data is ever increasing. Statistics provide the evidence needed to improve decisionmaking, document results, and heighten public accountability. The need for improved statistics to monitor the Millennium Development Goals and the parallel effort to support a culture of results-based management has stimulated a decade-long effort to improve statistics. The results have been impressive, but more needs to done.

The "Statistics for Transparency, Accountability, and Results: A Busan Action Plan for Statistics" was endorsed by the Busan Partnership for Effective Development Cooperation at the Fourth High-level Forum for Aid Effectiveness held November 29–December 1, 2011, in Busan, Republic of Korea. This plan builds on the progress made under the first global plan to improve national and international statistics, the 2004 Marrakech Action Plan for Statistics, but goes beyond it in many ways. The main objectives of the plan are to integrate statistics into decisionmaking, promote open access to statistics within government and for all other uses, and increase resources for statistical systems, both for investment in new capacity and for maintaining current operations.

Primary data documentation

	Currency	National accounts						Balance of payments and trade			Government finance	IMF data dissemination standard
		Base year	Reference year	System of National Accounts	SNA price valuation	Alternative conversion factor	PPP survey year	Balance of Payments Manual in use	External debt	System of trade	Accounting concept	
Afghanistan	Afghan afghani	2002/03		1993	B				A	G	C	G
Albania	Albanian lek	[a]	1996	1993	B		Rolling	6	A	G	C	G
Algeria	Algerian dinar	1980		1968	B			6	A	S	B	G
American Samoa	U.S. dollar			1968						S		
Andorra	Euro	1990		1968						S		
Angola	Angolan kwanza	2002		1993	P	1991–96	2005	6	A	S		G
Antigua and Barbuda	East Caribbean dollar	2006		1968	B			6		G		G
Argentina	Argentine peso	1993		1993	B	1971–84	2005	6	A	S	C	S
Armenia	Armenian dram	[a]	1996	1993	B	1990–95	2005	6	A	S	C	S
Aruba	Aruban florin	1995		1993				6		S		
Australia	Australian dollar	[a]	2009	2008	B		2008	6		G	C	S
Austria	Euro	2005		1993	B		Rolling	6		S	C	S
Azerbaijan	New Azeri manat	[a]	2003	1993	B	1992–95	2005	6	A	G	B	G
Bahamas, The	Bahamian dollar	2006		1993	B			6		G	B	G
Bahrain	Bahraini dinar	1985		1968	P		2005	6		G	B	G
Bangladesh	Bangladeshi taka	1995/96		1993	B		2005	6	A	G	C	G
Barbados	Barbados dollar	1974		1968	B			6		G	B	G
Belarus	Belarusian rubel	[a]	2000	1993	B	1990–95	2005	6	A	G	C	S
Belgium	Euro	2005		1993	B		Rolling	6		S	C	S
Belize	Belize dollar	2000		1993	B			6	A	G	B	G
Benin	CFA franc	1985		1968	P	1992	2005	6	A	S	B	G
Bermuda	Bermuda dollar	2006		1993	B			6		G		
Bhutan	Bhutanese ngultrum	2000		1993	B		2005	6	A	G	C	G
Bolivia	Bolivian Boliviano	1990		1968	B	1960–85	2005	6	A	G	C	G
Bosnia and Herzegovina	Bosnia and Herzegovina convertible mark	[a]	1996	1993	B		Rolling	6	A	S	C	
Botswana	Botswana pula	1993/94		1993	B		2005	6	A	G	B	G
Brazil	Brazilian real	2000		1993	B		2005	6	A	G	C	S
Brunei Darussalam	Brunei dollar	2000		1993	P		2005			S		G
Bulgaria	Bulgarian lev	[a]	2002	1993	B	1978–89, 1991–92	Rolling	6	A	S	C	S
Burkina Faso	CFA franc	1999		1993	B	1992–93	2005	6	A	G	B	G
Burundi	Burundi franc	2008		1993	B		2005	6	A	S	C	G
Cambodia	Cambodian riel	2000		1993	B		2005	6	A	S	C	G
Cameroon	CFA franc	2000		1993	B		2005	6	A	S	B	G
Canada	Canadian dollar	2005		1993	B		2008	6		G	C	S
Cape Verde	Cape Verde escudo	1980		1968	P		2005	6	A	G	C	G
Cayman Islands	Cayman Islands dollar			1993						G		
Central African Republic	CFA franc	2000		1968	B		2005	6	P	S	B	G
Chad	CFA franc	1995		1993	B		2005	6	E	S		G
Channel Islands	Pound sterling	2003	2007	1968	B							
Chile	Chilean peso	2003		1993	B		2008	6	A	S	C	S
China	Chinese yuan	2000		1993	P	1978–93	2005	6	P	S	B	S
Hong Kong SAR, China	Hong Kong dollar	2009		1993	B		2005	6		G	C	S
Macao SAR, China	Macao pataca	2009		1993	B		2005	6		G	C	G
Colombia	Colombian peso	2005		1993	B	1992–94	2005	6	A	G	B	S
Comoros	Comorian franc	1990		1968	P		2005		A	S		
Congo, Dem. Rep.	Congolese franc	2000		1968	B	1999–2001	2005	6	A	S	C	G
Congo, Rep.	CFA franc	1990		1968	P	1993	2005	6	P	S	C	G
Costa Rica	Costa Rican colon	1991		1993	B			6	A	S	C	S
Côte d'Ivoire	CFA franc	1996		1968	P		2005	6	A	S	C	G
Croatia	Croatian kuna	[a]	2005	1993	B		Rolling	6		G	C	S
Cuba	Cuban peso	2005		1993	B					S		
Curaçao	Netherlands Antilles guilder			1993								
Cyprus	Euro	[a]	2000	1993	B		Rolling	6		G	C	S
Czech Republic	Czech koruna	2005		1993	B		Rolling	6		S	C	S

 Front | User guide | World view | People | Environment

	Latest population census	Latest demographic, education, or health household survey	Source of most recent income and expenditure data	Vital registration complete	Latest agricultural census	Latest industrial data	Latest trade data	Latest water withdrawal data
Afghanistan	1979	MICS, 2010/11	IHS, 2008		2013/14		2011	2000
Albania	2011	DHS, 2009	LSMS, 2008	Yes		2009	2011	2006
Algeria	2008	MICS, 2012	IHS, 1995				2011	2001
American Samoa	2010			Yes	2007			
Andorra	2011[b]			Yes			2006	
Angola	1970	MIS, 2011; IBEP, 2008/09	IHS, 2000		1964/65		1991	2005
Antigua and Barbuda	2011			Yes	2007		2011	2005
Argentina	2010	MICS, 2011	IHS, 2011	Yes	2013	2002	2011	2000
Armenia	2011	DHS, 2010	IHS, 2010	Yes	2013/14		2011	2007
Aruba	2010			Yes			2011	
Australia	2011		ES/BS, 1994	Yes	2011	2006	2011	2000
Austria	2011[b]		IS, 2000	Yes	2010	2009	2011	2002
Azerbaijan	2009	DHS, 2006	ES/BS, 2008	Yes		2009	2011	2005
Bahamas, The	2010						2011	
Bahrain	2010			Yes			2011	2003
Bangladesh	2011	DHS, 2011	IHS, 2010		2008		2007	2008
Barbados	2010	MICS, 2012		Yes			2011	2005
Belarus	2009	MICS, 2012	ES/BS, 2009	Yes		2009	2011	2000
Belgium	2011		IHS, 2000	Yes	2010	2009	2011	2007
Belize	2010	MICS, 2011	ES/BS, 2011				2011	2000
Benin	2002	DHS, 2011/12	CWIQ, 2007		2011/12		2010	2001
Bermuda	2010			Yes			2011	
Bhutan	2005	MICS, 2010	IHS, 2010		2009		2011	2008
Bolivia	2012	DHS, 2008	IHS, 2009		2013	2001	2011	2000
Bosnia and Herzegovina	1991	MICS, 2011/12	LSMS, 2007	Yes			2011	2009
Botswana	2011	DHS, 1988	ES/BS, 2008			2009	2011	2000
Brazil	2010	LSMS, 1996/97	LFS, 2009		2006	2007	2011	2006
Brunei Darussalam	2011			Yes			2006	1994
Bulgaria	2011	LSMS, 2007	ES/BS, 2007	Yes	2010	2009	2011	2009
Burkina Faso	2006	DHS, 2011	CWIQ, 2009		2010		2011	2001
Burundi	2008	DHS, 2010	CWIQ, 2006				2010	2000
Cambodia	2008	DHS, 2010	IHS, 2008	–	2013	2000	2011	2006
Cameroon	2005	DHS, 2011	PS, 2007		1984	2002	2011	2000
Canada	2011		LFS, 2000	Yes	2011	2008	2011	1986
Cape Verde	2010	DHS, 2005	ES/BS, 2007	Yes			2011	2001
Cayman Islands	2010			Yes				
Central African Republic	2003	MICS, 2010	PS, 2008				2011	2005
Chad	2009	MICS, 2010	PS, 2002/03		2011		1995	2005
Channel Islands	2009, 2011[c]							
Chile	2012		IHS, 2009	Yes	2007	2008	2011	2007
China	2010	NSS, 2007	IHS, 2008		2007	2007	2011	2005
Hong Kong SAR, China	2011[d]			Yes		2009	2011	
Macao SAR, China	2011			Yes		2009	2007	
Colombia	2006	DHS, 2010	IHS, 2011		2013	2005	2011	2000
Comoros	2003	DHS, 2012	IHS, 2004				2007	1999
Congo, Dem. Rep.	1984	MICS, 2010	1-2-3, 2004/05		1990		1987	2005
Congo, Rep.	2007	DHS, 2011/12	CWIQ/PS, 2011		1985/86	2009	2010	2002
Costa Rica	2011	MICS, 2011	LFS, 2011	Yes	1973	2009	2011	1997
Côte d'Ivoire	1998	DHS, 2012	IHS, 2008		2001		2011	2005
Croatia	2011		ES/BS, 2008	Yes	2010		2011	2010
Cuba	2012	MICS, 2010/11		Yes			2006	2007
Curaçao								
Cyprus	2011			Yes	2010	2009	2011	2009
Czech Republic	2011	RHS, 1993	IS, 1996	Yes	2010	2007	2011	2007

	Currency	National accounts						Balance of payments and trade			Government finance	IMF data dissem- ination standard
		Base year	Reference year	System of National Accounts	SNA price valuation	Alternative conversion factor	PPP survey year	Balance of Payments Manual in use	External debt	System of trade	Accounting concept	
Denmark	Danish krone	2005		1993	B		Rolling	6		S	C	S
Djibouti	Djibouti franc	1990		1968	B		2005	6	A	G		G
Dominica	East Caribbean dollar	2006		1993	B			6	A	S		G
Dominican Republic	Dominican peso	1991		1993	B			6	A	G	C	G
Ecuador	U.S. dollar	2000		1993	B		2005	6	A	G	B	S
Egypt, Arab Rep.	Egyptian pound	1991/92		1993	B		2005	6	A	G	C	S
El Salvador	U.S. dollar	1990		1968	B			6	A	S	C	S
Equatorial Guinea	CFA franc	2000		1968	B	1965–84	2005			G		
Eritrea	Eritrean nakfa	2000		1968	B			6	E			
Estonia	Euro	2005		1993	B	1987–95	Rolling	6		S	C	S
Ethiopia	Ethiopian birr	1999/2000		1993	B		2005	6	A	G	B	G
Faeroe Islands	Danish krone			1993	B			6		G		
Fiji	Fijian dollar	2005		1993	B		2005	6	A	G	B	G
Finland	Euro	2005		1993	B		Rolling	6		G	C	S
France	Euro	a	2005	1993	B		Rolling	6		S	C	S
French Polynesia	CFP franc	1990/91		1993						S		
Gabon	CFA franc	1991		1993	P	1993	2005	6	A	S		G
Gambia, The	Gambian dalasi	2004		1993	P		2005	6	A	G	C	G
Georgia	Georgian lari	a	1996	1993	B	1990–95	2005	6	A	G	C	S
Germany	Euro	2005		1993	B		Rolling	6		S	C	S
Ghana	New Ghanaian cedi	2006		1993	B	1973–87	2005	6	A	G	B	G
Greece	Euro	a	2005	1993	B		Rolling	6		S	C	S
Greenland	Danish krone	1990		1993						G		
Grenada	East Caribbean dollar	2006		1968	B			6	A	S	B	G
Guam	U.S. dollar			1993						G		
Guatemala	Guatemalan quetzal	2001		1993	B			6	A	S	B	G
Guinea	Guinean franc	2003		1993	B		2005	6	P	S	B	G
Guinea-Bissau	CFA franc	2005		1993	B		2005	6	E	G		G
Guyana	Guyana dollar	2006		1993	B			6	A	S		G
Haiti	Haitian gourde	1986/87		1968	B	1991		6	A	G		G
Honduras	Honduran lempira	2000		1993	B	1988–89		6	A	S	C	G
Hungary	Hungarian forint	a	2005	1993	B		Rolling	6		S	C	S
Iceland	Iceland krona	2005		1993	B		Rolling	6		G	C	S
India	Indian rupee	2004/05		1993	B		2005	6	A	G	C	S
Indonesia	Indonesian rupiah	2000		1993	P		2005	6	A	S	B	S
Iran, Islamic Rep.	Iranian rial	1997/98		1993	B	1980–2002	2005	6	A	S	C	G
Iraq	Iraqi dinar	1997		1968	B	1997, 2004	2005	6				G
Ireland	Euro	2005		1993	B		Rolling	6		G	C	S
Isle of Man	Pound sterling	2003		1968								
Israel	Israeli new shekel	2005		1993	P		2008	6		S	C	S
Italy	Euro	2005		1993	B		Rolling	6		S	C	S
Jamaica	Jamaican dollar	2007		1993	B			6	A	G	C	G
Japan	Japanese yen	2005		1993	B		2008	6		G	C	S
Jordan	Jordanian dinar	1994		1968	B		2005	6	A	G	B	S
Kazakhstan	Kazakh tenge	a	2000	1993	B	1987–95	2005	6	A	G	C	S
Kenya	Kenyan shilling	2001		1993	B		2005	6	A	G	B	G
Kiribati	Australian dollar	2006		1993	B			6		G		G
Korea, Dem. Rep.	Democratic People's Republic of Korean won			1968				6				
Korea, Rep.	Korean won	2005		1993	B		2008	6		G	C	S
Kosovo	Euro	2008		1993					A			G
Kuwait	Kuwaiti dinar	1995		1968	P		2005	6		S	B	G
Kyrgyz Republic	Kyrgyz som	a	1995	1993	B	1990–95	2005	6	A	S	B	S
Lao PDR	Lao kip	2002		1993	B		2005	6	P	S	B	
Latvia	Latvian lats	2000		1993	B	1987–95	Rolling	6	A	S	C	S
Lebanon	Lebanese pound	1997		1993	B		2005	6	A	G	B	G
Lesotho	Lesotho loti	1995		1993	B		2005	6	A	G	C	G

	Latest population census	Latest demographic, education, or health household survey	Source of most recent income and expenditure data	Vital registration complete	Latest agricultural census	Latest industrial data	Latest trade data	Latest water withdrawal data
Denmark	2011		ITR, 1997	Yes	2010	2008	2011	2009
Djibouti	2009	MICS, 2006	PS, 2002				2009	2000
Dominica	2011			Yes			2010	2004
Dominican Republic	2010	DHS, 2007	IHS, 2011		2012/13		2011	2005
Ecuador	2010	RHS, 2004	LFS, 2011		2013/15	2008	2011	2005
Egypt, Arab Rep.	2006	DHS, 2008	ES/BS, 2008	Yes	2010	2006	2011	2000
El Salvador	2007	RHS, 2008	IHS, 2010	Yes	2008		2011	2007
Equatorial Guinea	2002							2000
Eritrea	1984	DHS, 2002				2009	2003	2004
Estonia	2012		ES/BS, 2004	Yes	2010	2009	2011	2007
Ethiopia	2007	DHS, 2011	ES/BS, 2010/11			2009	2011	2002
Faeroe Islands	2011			Yes			2009	
Fiji	2007		ES/BS, 2009	Yes	2009	2008	2010	2000
Finland	2010		IS, 2000	Yes	2010	2009	2011	2005
France	2006[e]		ES/BS, 1994/95	Yes	2010	2009	2011	2007
French Polynesia	2007			Yes			2011	
Gabon	2003	DHS, 2012	CWIQ/IHS, 2005				2009	2005
Gambia, The	2003	MICS, 2010	IHS, 2010		2001/02	2004	2011	2000
Georgia	2002	MICS, 2005	IHS, 2009	Yes		2009	2010	2005
Germany	2011[e]		IHS, 2000	Yes	2010	2009	2011	2007
Ghana	2010	MICS, 2011	LSMS, 2005/06		2013/14	2003	2011	2000
Greece	2011		IHS, 2000	Yes	2009	2007	2011	2007
Greenland	2010			Yes			2011	
Grenada	2011	RHS, 1985		Yes	2012		2009	2005
Guam	2010			Yes				
Guatemala	2012	RHS, 2008/09	LSMS, 2011	Yes	2013		2011	2006
Guinea	1996	DHS, 2005	CWIQ, 2012				2008	2001
Guinea-Bissau	2009	MICS, 2010	CWIQ, 2010				2005	2000
Guyana	2012	DHS, 2009	IHS, 1998				2011	2000
Haiti	2003	DHS, 2012	IHS, 2001		2008		1997	2000
Honduras	2001	DHS, 2011/12	IHS, 2010		2013		2009	2006
Hungary	2011		ES/BS, 2007	Yes	2010	2009	2011	2007
Iceland	2011			Yes	2010	2005	2011	2005
India	2011	DHS, 2006	IHS, 2010		2011	2008	2011	2010
Indonesia	2010	DHS, 2012	IHS, 2012		2013	2008	2011	2000
Iran, Islamic Rep.	2011	DHS, 2000	ES/BS, 2005		2003	2008	2011	2004
Iraq	1997	MICS, 2011	IHS, 2007		2012		2009	2000
Ireland	2011		IHS, 2000	Yes	2010	2009	2011	1979
Isle of Man	2011			Yes				
Israel	2009		ES/BS, 2001	Yes		2008	2011	2004
Italy	2012		ES/BS, 2000	Yes	2010	2009	2011	2000
Jamaica	2011	MICS, 2011	LSMS, 2010		2007		2010	1993
Japan	2010		IS, 1993	Yes	2010	2007	2011	2001
Jordan	2004	DHS, 2012	ES/BS, 2010		2007	2009	2011	2005
Kazakhstan	2009	MICS, 2010/11	ES/BS, 2011	Yes			2011	2010
Kenya	2009	MIS, 2010; HIV/MCH SPA, 2010	IHS, 2005/06			2007	2010	2003
Kiribati	2010						2011	
Korea, Dem. Rep.	2008	MICS, 2009						2005
Korea, Rep.	2010		ES/BS, 1998	Yes	2000	2008	2011	2002
Kosovo	2011		IHS, 2009					
Kuwait	2010	FHS, 1996		Yes		2009	2009	2002
Kyrgyz Republic	2009	DHS, 2012	ES/BS, 2010	Yes	2002	2009	2011	2006
Lao PDR	2005	MICS, 2011/12	ES/BS, 2008		2010/11		1974	2005
Latvia	2011		IHS, 2008	Yes	2010	2009	2011	2002
Lebanon	1970	MICS, 2000		Yes	2011	2007	2011	2005
Lesotho	2006	DHS, 2009	ES/BS, 2002/03		2010		2009	2000

Primary data documentation

	Currency	National accounts						Balance of payments and trade			Government finance	IMF data dissemination standard
		Base year	Reference year	System of National Accounts	SNA price valuation	Alternative conversion factor	PPP survey year	Balance of Payments Manual in use	External debt	System of trade	Accounting concept	
Liberia	Liberian dollar	2000		1968	P		2005	6	A	S	B	G
Libya	Libyan dinar	1999		1993	B	1986		6		G		G
Liechtenstein	Swiss franc	1990		1993	B					S		
Lithuania	Lithuanian litas	2000		1993	B	1990–95	Rolling	6	A	G	C	S
Luxembourg	Euro	[a]	2005	1993	B		Rolling	6		S	C	S
Macedonia, FYR	Macedonian denar	1995		1993	B		Rolling	6	A	S		S
Madagascar	Malagasy ariary	1984		1968	B		2005	6	A	S	C	G
Malawi	Malawi kwacha	2007		1993	B		2005	6	A	G		G
Malaysia	Malaysian ringgit	2000		1993	P		2005	6	E	G	B	S
Maldives	Maldivian rufiyaa	2003		1993	B		2005	6	A	G	C	G
Mali	CFA franc	1987		1968	B		2005	6	A	S	B	G
Malta	Euro	2005		1993	B		Rolling	6		G	C	S
Marshall Islands	U.S. dollar	2004		1968	B					G		
Mauritania	Mauritanian ouguiya	2004		1993	B		2005	6	A			G
Mauritius	Mauritian rupee	2006		1993	B		2005	6	A	G	C	S
Mexico	Mexican peso	2003		1993	B		2008	6	A	G	C	S
Micronesia, Fed. Sts.	U.S. dollar	2004		1993	B							
Moldova	Moldovan leu	[a] 1996		1993	B	1990–95	2005	6	A	G	C	S
Monaco	Euro	1990		1993						S		
Mongolia	Mongolian tugrik	2005		1993	B		2005	6	A	G	C	G
Montenegro	Euro	2000		1993	B		Rolling	6	A	S		G
Morocco	Moroccan dirham	1998		1993	B		2005	6	A	S	C	S
Mozambique	New Mozambican metical	2003		1993	B	1992–95	2005	6	A	S		G
Myanmar	Myanmar kyat	2005/06		1968	P			6	E	G	C	
Namibia	Namibian dollar	2004/05		1993	B		2005	6		G	B	G
Nepal	Nepalese rupee	2000/01		1993	B		2005	6	A	G	C	G
Netherlands	Euro	[a] 2005		1993	B		Rolling	6		S	C	S
New Caledonia	CFP franc	1990		1993						S		
New Zealand	New Zealand dollar	2005/06		1993	B		2008	6		G	C	
Nicaragua	Nicaraguan gold cordoba	2006		1993	B	1965–95		6	A	G	B	G
Niger	CFA franc	1987		1993	P	1993	2005	6	A	S	B	G
Nigeria	Nigerian naira	2002		1993	B	1971–98	2005	6	A	G	B	G
Northern Mariana Islands	U.S. dollar			1968								
Norway	Norwegian krone	[a] 2005		1993	B		Rolling	6		G	C	S
Oman	Rial Omani	1988		1993	P		2005	6		G	B	G
Pakistan	Pakistani rupee	1999/2000		1993	B		2005	6	A	G	B	G
Palau	U.S. dollar	1995		1993	B					S		
Panama	Panamanian balboa	1996		1993	B			6	A	S	C	G
Papua New Guinea	Papua New Guinea kina	1998		1993	B	1989		6	A	G	B	G
Paraguay	Paraguayan guarani	1994		1993	P		2005	6	A	S	B	G
Peru	Peruvian new sol	1994		1993	B	1985–90	2005	6	A	S	B	S
Philippines	Philippine peso	2000		1993	P		2005	6	A	G	B	S
Poland	Polish zloty	[a] 2005		1993	B		Rolling	6		S	C	S
Portugal	Euro	2005		1993	B		Rolling	6		S	C	S
Puerto Rico	U.S. dollar	1954		1968	P					G		
Qatar	Qatari riyal	2001		1993	P		2005			S	B	G
Romania	New Romanian leu	[a] 2005		1993	B	1987–89, 1992	Rolling	6	A	S	C	S
Russian Federation	Russian ruble	2000		1993	B	1987–95	2008	6	P	G	C	S
Rwanda	Rwandan franc	2006		1993	P	1994	2005	6	A	G	C	G
Samoa	Samoan tala	2002		1993	B			6	A	S		G
San Marino	Euro	1995	2000	1993	B						C	G
São Tomé and Príncipe	São Tomé and Príncipe dobra	2001		1993	P		2005	6	A	S		G
Saudi Arabia	Saudi Arabian riyal	1999		1993	P		2005	6		S		G
Senegal	CFA franc	1999	1987	1993	B		2005	6	A	G	B	G
Serbia	New Serbian dinar	[a] 2002		1993	B		Rolling	6	A	S	C	G

   Front | User guide | World view | People | Environment

	Latest population census	Latest demographic, education, or health household survey	Source of most recent income and expenditure data	Vital registration complete	Latest agricultural census	Latest industrial data	Latest trade data	Latest water withdrawal data
Liberia	2008	MIS, 2011	CWIQ, 2007				1984	2000
Libya	2006						2010	2000
Liechtenstein	2010			Yes				
Lithuania	2011		ES/BS, 2008	Yes	2010	2009	2011	2007
Luxembourg	2011			Yes	2010	2009	2011	1999
Macedonia, FYR	2011	MICS, 2011	ES/BS, 2009	Yes	2007	2009	2011	2007
Madagascar	1993	MIS, 2011	PS, 2010		2006		2011	2000
Malawi	2008	MIS, 2012; LSMS, 2010/11	IHS, 2010/11		2007	2009	2011	2005
Malaysia	2010		ES/BS, 2009	Yes	2012	2008	2011	2005
Maldives	2006	DHS, 2009	IHS, 2010	Yes			2011	2008
Mali	2009	DHS, 2012	IHS, 2009/10				2010	2000
Malta	2011			Yes	2010	2008	2011	2002
Marshall Islands	2011							
Mauritania	2000	MICS, 2011	IHS, 2008				2011	2005
Mauritius	2011	RHS, 1991		Yes		2007	2011	2003
Mexico	2010	ENPF, 1995	LFS, 2010		2007	2007	2011	2009
Micronesia, Fed. Sts.	2010		IHS, 2000					
Moldova	2004	MICS, 2012	ES/BS, 2010	Yes	2011	2009	2011	2007
Monaco	2008			Yes				2009
Mongolia	2010	MICS, 2010	LSMS, 2011	Yes	2012	2008	2007	2009
Montenegro	2011	MICS, 2005/06	ES/BS, 2011	Yes	2010		2011	2010
Morocco	2004	MICS/PAPFAM, 2006	ES/BS, 2007		2012	2009	2010	2000
Mozambique	2007	DHS, 2011	ES/BS, 2008/09		2010		2011	2001
Myanmar	1983	MICS, 2009/10			2011/12	2003	2010	2000
Namibia	2011	HIV/MCH, 2009	ES/BS, 2009				2011	2002
Nepal	2011	DHS, 2011	LSMS, 2011		2012	2008	2011	2006
Netherlands	2011		IHS, 1999	Yes	2010	2008	2011	2008
New Caledonia	2009			Yes			2011	
New Zealand	2006		IS, 1997	Yes	2012	2008	2011	2002
Nicaragua	2005	RHS, 2006/07	LSMS, 2009		2011		2011	2001
Niger	2012	DHS, 2012	CWIQ/PS, 2008		2008	2002	2011	2005
Nigeria	2006	MICS, 2011	IHS, 2010		2007		2011	2005
Northern Mariana Islands	2010							
Norway	2011		IS, 2000	Yes	2010	2008	2011	2006
Oman	2010	MICS, 2012			2007		2011	2003
Pakistan	1998	DHS, 2012	IHS, 2008		2010	2006	2011	2008
Palau	2010			Yes				
Panama	2010	LSMS, 2008	LFS, 2010		2011	2001	2011	2000
Papua New Guinea	2011	LSMS, 1996	IHS, 1996				2004	2005
Paraguay	2012	RHS, 2008	IHS, 2011		2008	2002	2011	2000
Peru	2007	Continuous DHS, 2012	IHS, 2011		2012	2007	2011	2000
Philippines	2010	DHS, 2008	ES/BS, 2009	Yes	2012	2006	2011	2009
Poland	2011		ES/BS, 2010	Yes	2010	2009	2011	2009
Portugal	2011		IS, 1997	Yes	2009	2009	2011	2002
Puerto Rico	2010	RHS, 1995/96		Yes	2007	2006		2005
Qatar	2010	MICS, 2012		Yes		2006	2010	2005
Romania	2011	RHS, 1999	LFS, 2010	Yes	2010	2009	2011	2009
Russian Federation	2010	LSMS, 1992	IHS, 2010	Yes	2006	2009	2011	2001
Rwanda	2012	Special DHS, 2011	IHS, 2011		2008		2011	2000
Samoa	2011	DHS, 2009			2009		2011	
San Marino	2010			Yes				
São Tomé and Príncipe	2012	DHS, 2008/09	PS, 2009/10		2011/12		2010	1993
Saudi Arabia	2010	Demographic survey, 2007			2010	2006	2011	2006
Senegal	2002	Continuous DHS, 2012	PS, 2010/11		2011/12	2009	2011	2002
Serbia	2011	MICS, 2010	IHS, 2010	Yes	2012	2009	2011	2009

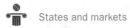 

Primary data documentation

	Currency	National accounts						Balance of payments and trade			Government finance	IMF data dissem- ination standard
		Base year	Reference year	System of National Accounts	SNA price valuation	Alternative conversion factor	PPP survey year	Balance of Payments Manual in use	External debt	System of trade	Accounting concept	
Seychelles	Seychelles rupee	2006		1993	P			6	A	G	C	G
Sierra Leone	Sierra Leonean leone	2006		1993	B		2005	6	A	S	B	G
Singapore	Singapore dollar	2005		1993	B		2005	6		G	C	S
Sint Maarten	Netherlands Antilles guilder			1993								
Slovak Republic	Euro	2005		1993	B		Rolling	6		S	C	S
Slovenia	Euro	a	2005	1993	B		Rolling	6		S	C	S
Solomon Islands	Solomon Islands dollar	2004		1993	B			6	A	S		G
Somalia	Somali shilling	1985		1968	B	1977–90			E			
South Africa	South African rand	2005		1993	B		2005	6	P	G	C	S
South Sudan	South Sudanese pound			1993								
Spain	Euro	2005		1993	B		Rolling	6		S	C	S
Sri Lanka	Sri Lankan rupee	2002		1993	P		2005	6	A	G	B	G
St. Kitts and Nevis	East Caribbean dollar	2006		1993	B			6		S	C	G
St. Lucia	East Caribbean dollar	2006		1968	B			6	A	S		G
St. Martin	Euro			1993								
St. Vincent and Grenadines	East Caribbean dollar	2006		1993	B			6	A	S	B	G
Sudan	Sudanese pound	1981/82[f]	1996	1968	B		2005	6	A	G	B	G
Suriname	Suriname dollar	1990		1993	B			6		G		G
Swaziland	Swaziland lilangeni	2000		1993	B		2005	6	E	G	B	G
Sweden	Swedish krona	a	2005	1993	B		Rolling	6		G	C	S
Switzerland	Swiss franc	2005		1993	B		Rolling	6		S	C	S
Syrian Arab Republic	Syrian pound	2000		1968	B	1970–2010	2005	6	E	S	C	G
Tajikistan	Tajik somoni	a	2000	1993	B	1990–95	2005	6	A	G	C	G
Tanzania	Tanzanian shilling	a	2001	1993	B		2005	6	A	G		G
Thailand	Thai baht	1988		1993	P		2005	6	A	G	C	S
Timor-Leste	U.S. dollar	2000		2008	P					G		G
Togo	CFA franc	2000		1968	P		2005	6	A	S	B	G
Tonga	Tongan pa'anga	2010/11		1993	B			6	A	G		G
Trinidad and Tobago	Trinidad and Tobago dollar	2000		1993	B			6		S	C	G
Tunisia	Tunisian dinar	1990		1993	B		2005	6	A	G	C	S
Turkey	New Turkish lira	1998		1993	B		Rolling	6	A	S	B	S
Turkmenistan	New Turkmen manat	a	2007	1993	B	1987–95, 1997–2007		6	E	G		
Turks and Caicos Islands	U.S. dollar			1993						G		
Tuvalu	Australian dollar	2005		1968	P					G		
Uganda	Ugandan shilling	2001/02		1968	B		2005	6	A	G	B	G
Ukraine	Ukrainian hryvnia	a	2003	1993	B	1987–95	2005	6	A	G	C	S
United Arab Emirates	U.A.E. dirham	2007		1993	P			6		G	B	G
United Kingdom	Pound sterling	2005		1993	B		Rolling	6		G	C	S
United States	U.S. dollar	a	2005	1993	B		2008	6		G	C	S
Uruguay	Uruguayan peso	2005		1993	B		2005	6	A	G	C	S
Uzbekistan	Uzbek sum	a	1997	1993	B	1990–95		6	A	G		
Vanuatu	Vanuatu vatu	2006		1993	P			6	E	G	C	G
Venezuela, R.B.	Venezuelan bolivar fuerte	1997		1993	B		2005	6	A	G	C	G
Vietnam	Vietnamese dong	1994		1993	P	1991	2005	6	A	G		
Virgin Islands (U.S.)	U.S. dollar	1982		1968						G		
West Bank and Gaza	Israeli new shekel	1997		1968	B			6		S	B	S
Yemen, Rep.	Yemeni rial	1990		1993	P	1990–96	2005	6	A	S	B	G
Zambia	Zambian kwacha	1994		1968	B	1990–92	2005	6	P	S	B	G
Zimbabwe	U.S. dollar	2009		1993	B	1991, 1998	2005	6	A	G	C	G

	Latest population census	Latest demographic, education, or health household survey	Source of most recent income and expenditure data	Vital registration complete	Latest agricultural census	Latest industrial data	Latest trade data	Latest water withdrawal data
Seychelles	2010		IHS, 2007	Yes	2011		2008	2005
Sierra Leone	2004	MICS, 2010	IHS, 2011				2002	2005
Singapore	2010	General household, 2005		Yes		2009	2011	1975
Sint Maarten	2001	Population Census, 2011						
Slovak Republic	2011		IS, 2009	Yes	2001	2009	2011	2007
Slovenia	2011b		ES/BS, 2004	Yes	2010	2009	2011	2009
Solomon Islands	2009		IHS, 2005/06		2012/13		2011	
Somalia	1987	MICS, 2006					1983	2003
South Africa	2011	DHS, 2003	ES/BS, 2010		2012	2009	2011	2000
South Sudan	2008		ES/BS, 2009					
Spain	2011		IHS, 2000	Yes	2010	2009	2011	2008
Sri Lanka	2012	DHS, 2006/07	ES/BS, 2010	Yes	2013	2008	2011	2005
St. Kitts and Nevis	2011			Yes			2011	
St. Lucia	2010	MICS, 2012	IHS, 1995	Yes			2008	2005
St. Martin								
St. Vincent and Grenadines	2011			Yes			2011	1995
Sudan	2008	SHHS, 2010	ES/BS, 2009			2001	2009	2005g
Suriname	2012	MICS, 2010	ES/BS, 1999	Yes	2008	2004	2011	2000
Swaziland	2007	MICS, 2010	ES/BS, 2009/10				2007	2000
Sweden	2011		IS, 2000	Yes	2010	2009	2011	2007
Switzerland	2010		ES/BS, 2000	Yes	2008	2007	2011	2000
Syrian Arab Republic	2004	MICS, 2006	ES/BS, 2004		1981	2009	2010	2005
Tajikistan	2010	LSMS, 2009	LSMS, 2009		2013		2000	2006
Tanzania	2012	AIS, 2011/12; LSMS, 2010/11	ES/BS, 2011		2007/08	2007	2011	2002
Thailand	2010	MICS, 2012	IHS, 2010		2013	2006	2011	2007
Timor-Leste	2010	DHS, 2009/10	LSMS, 2007		2012		2005	2004
Togo	2010	MICS, 2010	CWIQ, 2011		2011/12		2011	2002
Tonga	2006						2011	
Trinidad and Tobago	2011	MICS, 2011	IHS, 1992	Yes		2006	2010	2000
Tunisia	2004	MICS, 2011	IHS, 2010		2004	2006	2011	2001
Turkey	2011	DHS, 2003	LFS, 2009			2008	2011	2003
Turkmenistan	2012	MICS, 2011	LSMS, 1998	Yes			2000	2004
Turks and Caicos Islands	2012			Yes			2011	
Tuvalu	2012						2008	
Uganda	2002	DHS, 2011	PS, 2009/10		2008	2000	2011	2002
Ukraine	2001	MICS, 2012	ES/BS, 2009	Yes	2012/13	2004	2011	2005
United Arab Emirates	2010				2012		2008	2005
United Kingdom	2001		IS, 1999	Yes	2010	2009	2011	2007
United States	2010		LFS, 2000	Yes	2007	2008	2011	2005
Uruguay	2011	MICS, 2012	IHS, 2011	Yes	2011	2008	2009	2000
Uzbekistan	1989	MICS, 2006	ES/BS, 2003	Yes				2005
Vanuatu	2009	MICS, 2007			2007		2011	
Venezuela, R.B.	2011	MICS, 2000	IHS, 2011	Yes	2007		2011	2000
Vietnam	2009	MICS, 2010/11	IHS, 2010	Yes	2011	2000	2010	2005
Virgin Islands (U.S.)	2010			Yes	2007			
West Bank and Gaza	2007	MICS, 2010	IHS, 2009		1971	2009	2011	2005
Yemen, Rep.	2004	MICS, 2006	ES/BS, 2005			2006	2011	2005
Zambia	2010	DHS, 2007	IHS, 2010				2011	2002
Zimbabwe	2012	DHS, 2010/11	IHS, 2003/04				2011	2002

Note: For explanation of the abbreviations used in the table, see notes following the table.

a. Original chained constant price data are rescaled. b. Population data compiled from administrative registers. c. Latest population census: Guernsey, 2009; Jersey, 2011. d. The population censuses for 1986 and 1996 were based on a one-in-seven sample of the population, while that for 2006 was based on a one-in-ten sample of the population. e. Rolling census based on continuous sample survey. f. Reporting period switch from fiscal year to calendar year from 1996. Pre-1996 data converted to calendar year. g. Includes South Sudan.

• **Base year** is the base or pricing period used for constant price calculations in the country's national accounts. Price indexes derived from national accounts aggregates, such as the implicit deflator for gross domestic product (GDP), express the price level relative to base year prices. • **Reference year** is the year in which the local currency constant price series of a country is valued. The reference year is usually the same as the base year used to report the constant price series. However, when the constant price data are chain linked, the base year is changed annually, so the data are rescaled to a specific reference year to provide a consistent time series. When the country has not rescaled following a change in base year, World Bank staff rescale the data to maintain a longer historical series. To allow for cross-country comparison and data aggregation, constant price data reported in *World Development Indicators* are rescaled to a common reference year (2000) and currency (U.S. dollars). • **System of National Accounts** identifies whether a country uses the 1968, 1993, or 2008 System of National Accounts (SNA). • **SNA price valuation** shows whether value added in the national accounts is reported at basic prices (B) or producer prices (P). Producer prices include taxes paid by producers and thus tend to overstate the actual value added in production. However, value added can be higher at basic prices than at producer prices in countries with high agricultural subsidies. • **Alternative conversion factor** identifies the countries and years for which a World Bank–estimated conversion factor has been used in place of the official exchange rate (line rf in the International Monetary Fund's [IMF] *International Financial Statistics*). See *Statistical methods* for further discussion of alternative conversion factors. • **Purchasing power parity (PPP) survey year** is the latest available survey year for the International Comparison Program's estimates of PPPs. • **Balance of Payments Manual in use** refers to the classification system used to compile and report data on balance of payments. 6 refers to the 6th edition of the IMF's *Balance of Payments Manual* (2009). • **External debt** shows debt reporting status for 2011 data. *A* indicates that data are as reported, *P* that data are based on reported or collected information but include an element of staff estimation, and *E* that data are World Bank staff estimates. • **System of trade** refers to the United Nations general trade system (G) or special trade system (S). Under the general trade system goods entering directly for domestic consumption and goods entered into customs storage are recorded as imports at arrival. Under the special trade system goods are recorded as imports when declared for domestic consumption whether at time of entry or

on withdrawal from customs storage. Exports under the general system comprise outward-moving goods: (a) national goods wholly or partly produced in the country; (b) foreign goods, neither transformed nor declared for domestic consumption in the country, that move outward from customs storage; and (c) nationalized goods that have been declared for domestic consumption and move outward without being transformed. Under the special system of trade, exports are categories a and c. In some compilations categories b and c are classified as re-exports. Direct transit trade—goods entering or leaving for transport only—is excluded from both import and export statistics. • **Government finance accounting concept** is the accounting basis for reporting central government financial data. For most countries government finance data have been consolidated (C) into one set of accounts capturing all central government fiscal activities. Budgetary central government accounts (B) exclude some central government units. • **IMF data dissemination standard** shows the countries that subscribe to the IMF's Special Data Dissemination Standard (SDDS) or General Data Dissemination System (GDDS). S refers to countries that subscribe to the SDDS and have posted data on the Dissemination Standards Bulletin Board at http://dsbb.imf.org. G refers to countries that subscribe to the GDDS. The SDDS was established for member countries that have or might seek access to international capital markets to guide them in providing their economic and financial data to the public. The GDDS helps countries disseminate comprehensive, timely, accessible, and reliable economic, financial, and sociodemographic statistics. IMF member countries elect to participate in either the SDDS or the GDDS. Both standards enhance the availability of timely and comprehensive data and therefore contribute to the pursuit of sound macroeconomic policies. The SDDS is also expected to improve the functioning of financial markets. • **Latest population census** shows the most recent year in which a census was conducted and in which at least preliminary results have been released. The preliminary results from the very recent censuses could be reflected in timely revisions if basic data are available, such as population by age and sex, as well as the detailed definition of counting, coverage, and completeness. Countries that hold register-based censuses produce similar census tables every 5 or 10 years. Germany's 2001 census is a register-based test census using a sample of 1.2 percent of the population. A rare case, France has been conducting a rolling census every year since 2004; the 1999 general population census was the last to cover the entire population simultaneously. • **Latest**

demographic, education, or health household survey indicates the household surveys used to compile the demographic, education, and health data in section 2. AIS is HIV/AIDS Indicator Survey, DHS is Demographic and Health Survey, ENPF is National Family Planning Survey, FHS is Family Health Survey, HIV/MCH is HIV/Maternal and Child Health, IBEP is Integrated Survey on Population Welfare, LSMS is Living Standards Measurement Study Survey, MICS is Multiple Indicator Cluster Survey, MIS is Malaria Indicator Survey, NSS is National Sample Survey on Population Change, PAPFAM is Pan Arab Project for Family Health, RHS is Reproductive Health Survey, SHHS is Sudan Household Health Survey, and SPA is Service Provision Assessments. Detailed information for AIS, DHS, MIS, and SPA are available at www.measuredhs.com; for MICS at www.childinfo.org; and for RHS at www.cdc.gov/reproductivehealth. • **Source of most recent income and expenditure data** shows household surveys that collect income and expenditure data. Names and detailed information on household surveys can be found on the website of the International Household Survey Network (www.surveynetwork.org). Core Welfare Indicator Questionnaire Surveys (CWIQ), developed by the World Bank, measure changes in key social indicators for different population groups—specifically indicators of access, utilization, and satisfaction with core social and economic services. Expenditure survey/budget surveys (ES/BS) collect detailed information on household consumption as well as on general demographic, social, and economic characteristics. Integrated household surveys (IHS) collect detailed information on a wide variety of topics, including health, education, economic activities, housing, and utilities. Income surveys (IS) collect information on the income and wealth of households as well as various social and economic characteristics. Income tax registers (ITR) provide information on a population's income and allowance, such as gross income, taxable income, and taxes by socioeconomic group. Labor force surveys (LFS) collect information on employment, unemployment, hours of work, income, and wages. Living Standards Measurement Study Surveys (LSMS), developed by the World Bank, provide a comprehensive picture of household welfare and the factors that affect it; they typically incorporate data collection at the individual, household, and community levels. Priority surveys (PS) are a light monitoring survey, designed by the World Bank, that collect data from a large number of households cost-effectively and quickly. 1-2-3 (1-2-3) surveys are implemented in three phases and collect sociodemographic and employment data, data on the informal sector, and information on living conditions and household consumption. • **Vital registration complete** identifies countries that report at least 90 percent complete registries of vital (birth and death) statistics to the United Nations Statistics Division and are reported in its *Population and Vital Statistics Reports*. Countries with complete vital statistics registries may have more accurate and more timely demographic indicators than other countries. • **Latest agricultural census** shows the most recent year in which an agricultural census was conducted and reported to the Food and Agriculture Organization of the United Nations. • **Latest industrial data** show the most recent year for which manufacturing value added data at the three-digit level of the International Standard Industrial Classification (revision 2 or 3) are available in the United Nations Industrial Development Organization database. • **Latest trade data** show the most recent year for which structure of merchandise trade data from the United Nations Statistics Division's Commodity Trade (Comtrade) database are available. • **Latest water withdrawal data** show the most recent year for which data on freshwater withdrawals have been compiled from a variety of sources.

Exceptional reporting periods

In most economies the fiscal year is concurrent with the calendar year. Exceptions are shown in the table at right. The ending date reported here is for the fiscal year of the central government. Fiscal years for other levels of government and reporting years for statistical surveys may differ.

The **reporting period for national accounts data** is designated as either calendar year basis (CY) or fiscal year basis (FY). Most economies report their national accounts and balance of payments data using calendar years, but some use fiscal years. In *World Development Indicators* fiscal year data are assigned to the calendar year that contains the larger share of the fiscal year. If a country's fiscal year ends before June 30, data are shown in the first year of the fiscal period; if the fiscal year ends on or after June 30, data are shown in the second year of the period. Balance of payments data are reported in *World Development Indicators* by calendar year.

Revisions to national accounts data

National accounts data are revised by national statistical offices when methodologies change or data sources improve. National accounts data in *World Development Indicators* are also revised when data sources change. The following notes, while not comprehensive, provide information on revisions from previous data. • **Afghanistan.** National accounts data are sourced from the IMF and differ from the Central Statistics Organization numbers due to exclusion of the opium economy. • **Angola.** Based on IMF data, national accounts data have been revised for 2000 onward; the new base year is 2002. • **Australia.** Value added series data are taken from the United Nations National Accounts Main Aggregates, and gross national income is computed using Australian Bureau of Statistics data. • **Bhutan.** Data were updated recently using the government of Bhutan macroeconomic framework. • **China.** National accounts historical data for expenditure series in constant prices have been revised based on National Statistics Bureau data not previously available. • **Democratic Republic of Congo.** Based on IMF data, national accounts data have been revised for 2000 onward; the new base year is 2000. • **Republic of Congo.** Based on IMF data, national accounts data

Economies with exceptional reporting periods

Economy	Fiscal year end	Reporting period for national accounts data
Afghanistan	Mar. 20	FY
Australia	Jun. 30	FY
Bangladesh	Jun. 30	FY
Botswana	Jun. 30	FY
Canada	Mar. 31	CY
Egypt, Arab Rep.	Jun. 30	FY
Ethiopia	Jul. 7	FY
Gambia, The	Jun. 30	CY
Haiti	Sep. 30	FY
India	Mar. 31	FY
Indonesia	Mar. 31	CY
Iran, Islamic Rep.	Mar. 20	FY
Japan	Mar. 31	CY
Kenya	Jun. 30	CY
Kuwait	Jun. 30	CY
Lesotho	Mar. 31	CY
Malawi	Mar. 31	CY
Myanmar	Mar. 31	FY
Namibia	Mar. 31	CY
Nepal	Jul. 14	FY
New Zealand	Mar. 31	FY
Pakistan	Jun. 30	FY
Puerto Rico	Jun. 30	FY
Sierra Leone	Jun. 30	CY
Singapore	Mar. 31	CY
South Africa	Mar. 31	CY
Swaziland	Mar. 31	CY
Sweden	Jun. 30	CY
Thailand	Sep. 30	CY
Uganda	Jun. 30	FY
United States	Sep. 30	CY
Zimbabwe	Jun. 30	CY

have been revised for 1990 onward; the new base year is 1990. • **Croatia.** Based on official government statistics, the new base year for constant price series is 2005. • **Eritrea.** Based on IMF data, national accounts data have been revised for 2000 onward; the new base year is 2000. • **The Gambia.** Based on official government statistics, national accounts data have been revised for 2004 onward; the new base year is 2004. • **Guinea.** Based on IMF data, national accounts data have been revised for 2000 onward; the new base year is 2003. • **Hong Kong SAR, China.** Agriculture value added includes mining and quarrying. • **India.** The India Central Statistical Office revised historical data series both current and constant going back to 1960 with 2004–05 as the base. • **Jamaica.** Based on official government statistics, national accounts data have been revised for 2002 onward; the new base year is 2007. • **Kiribati.** Based on data from the Asian Development Bank, national accounts data have been revised for 2005 onward. • **Liberia.** Based on IMF data, national accounts data have been revised for 2000 onward; the new base year is 2000. • **Malawi.** Based on IMF data, national accounts data have been revised for 2003 onward; the new base year is 2007. • **Malaysia.** Based on data from the National Statistics Office, national accounts data in current prices have been revised for 2005 onward. • **Nicaragua.** Based on official government statistics, national accounts data have been revised for 1994 onward; the new base year is 2006. • **Palau.** Based on IMF data, national accounts data have been revised for 2007 onward. • **Rwanda.** Based on official government statistics, national accounts data have been revised for 1999 onward; the new base year is 2006. • **Samoa.** Based on IMF data, national accounts data have been revised for 2007 onward. • **Seychelles.** Based on official government statistics, national accounts data have been revised for 1976 onward; the new base year is 2006. • **Sierra Leone.** Based on official government statistics, national accounts data have been revised for 1990 onward; the new base year is 2006. • **Syrian Arab Republic.** Based on data from the Central Bureau of Statistics, national accounts data have been revised for 2003 onward. • **Togo.** Based on IMF data, national accounts data have been revised for 2000; the new base year is 2000. • **Tonga.** Based on data from the National Bureau of Statistics, national accounts data have been revised; the new base year is 2010/11. • **Tuvalu.** Based on IMF data, national accounts data for 2000 onward have been revised. • **United Arab Emirates.** Based on data from the National Bureau of Statistics, national accounts data have been revised for 2001 onward; the new base year is 2007.

Statistical methods

This section describes some of the statistical procedures used in preparing *World Development Indicators*. It covers the methods employed for calculating regional and income group aggregates and for calculating growth rates, and it describes the *World Bank Atlas* method for deriving the conversion factor used to estimate gross national income (GNI) and GNI per capita in U.S. dollars. Other statistical procedures and calculations are described in the *About the data* sections following each table.

Aggregation rules

Aggregates based on the World Bank's regional and income classifications of economies appear at the end of the tables, including most of those available online. The 214 economies included in these classifications are shown on the flaps on the front and back covers of the book. Aggregates also contain data for Taiwan, China. Most tables also include the aggregate for the euro area, which includes the member states of the Economic and Monetary Union (EMU) of the European Union that have adopted the euro as their currency: Austria, Belgium, Cyprus, Estonia, Finland, France, Germany, Greece, Ireland, Italy, Luxembourg, Malta, Netherlands, Portugal, Slovak Republic, Slovenia, and Spain. Other classifications, such as the European Union, are documented in *About the data* for the online tables in which they appear.

Because of missing data, aggregates for groups of economies should be treated as approximations of unknown totals or average values. The aggregation rules are intended to yield estimates for a consistent set of economies from one period to the next and for all indicators. Small differences between sums of subgroup aggregates and overall totals and averages may occur because of the approximations used. In addition, compilation errors and data reporting practices may cause discrepancies in theoretically identical aggregates such as world exports and world imports.

Five methods of aggregation are used in *World Development Indicators*:

- For group and world totals denoted in the tables by a *t*, missing data are imputed based on the relationship of the sum of available data to the total in the year of the previous estimate. The imputation process works forward and backward from 2000. Missing values in 2000 are imputed using one of several proxy variables for which complete data are available in that year. The imputed value is calculated so that it (or its proxy) bears the same relationship to the total of available data. Imputed values are usually not calculated if missing data account for more than a third of the total in the benchmark year. The variables used as proxies are GNI in U.S. dollars; total population; exports and imports of goods and services in U.S. dollars; and value added in agriculture, industry, manufacturing, and services in U.S. dollars.

- Aggregates marked by an *s* are sums of available data. Missing values are not imputed. Sums are not computed if more than a third of the observations in the series or a proxy for the series are missing in a given year.

- Aggregates of ratios are denoted by a *w* when calculated as weighted averages of the ratios (using the value of the denominator or, in some cases, another indicator as a weight) and denoted by a *u* when calculated as unweighted averages. The aggregate ratios are based on available data. Missing values are assumed to have the same average value as the available data. No aggregate is calculated if missing data account for more than a third of the value of weights in the benchmark year. In a few cases the aggregate ratio may be computed as the ratio of group totals after imputing values for missing data according to the above rules for computing totals.

- Aggregate growth rates are denoted by a *w* when calculated as a weighted average of growth rates. In a few cases growth rates may be computed from time series of group totals. Growth rates are not calculated if more than half the observations in a period are missing. For further discussion of methods of computing growth rates see below.

- Aggregates denoted by an *m* are medians of the values shown in the table. No value is shown if more than half the observations for countries with a population of more than 1 million are missing.

Exceptions to the rules may occur. Depending on the judgment of World Bank analysts, the aggregates may be based on as little as 50 percent of the available data. In other cases, where missing or excluded values are judged to be small or irrelevant, aggregates are based only on the data shown in the tables.

Growth rates

Growth rates are calculated as annual averages and represented as percentages. Except where noted, growth rates of values are computed from constant price series. Three principal methods are used to calculate growth rates: least squares, exponential endpoint, and geometric endpoint. Rates of change from one period to the next are calculated as proportional changes from the earlier period.

Least squares growth rate. Least squares growth rates are used wherever there is a sufficiently long time series to permit a reliable calculation. No growth rate is calculated if more than half the observations in a period are missing. The least squares growth rate, r, is estimated by fitting a linear regression trend line to the logarithmic annual values of the variable in the relevant period. The regression equation takes the form

$$\ln X_t = a + bt$$

which is the logarithmic transformation of the compound growth equation,
$$X_t = X_0 (1 + r)^t.$$

In this equation X is the variable, t is time, and $a = \ln X_0$ and $b = \ln (1 + r)$ are parameters to be estimated. If b^* is the least squares estimate of b, then the average annual growth rate, r, is obtained as $[\exp(b^*) - 1]$ and is multiplied by 100 for expression as a percentage. The calculated growth rate is an average rate that is representative of the available observations over the entire period. It does not necessarily match the actual growth rate between any two periods.

Exponential growth rate. The growth rate between two points in time for certain demographic indicators, notably labor force and population, is calculated from the equation

$$r = \ln(p_n/p_0)/n$$

where p_n and p_0 are the last and first observations in the period, n is the number of years in the period, and ln is the natural logarithm operator. This growth rate is based on a model of continuous, exponential growth between two points in time. It does not take into account the intermediate values of the series. Nor does it correspond to the annual rate of change measured at a one-year interval, which is given by $(p_n - p_{n-1})/p_{n-1}$.

Geometric growth rate. The geometric growth rate is applicable to compound growth over discrete periods, such as the payment and reinvestment of interest or dividends. Although continuous growth, as modeled by the exponential growth rate, may be more realistic, most economic phenomena are measured only at intervals, in which case the compound growth model is appropriate. The average growth rate over n periods is calculated as

$$r = \exp[\ln(p_n/p_0)/n] - 1.$$

World Bank Atlas method

In calculating GNI and GNI per capita in U.S. dollars for certain operational purposes, the World Bank uses the *Atlas* conversion factor. The purpose of the *Atlas* conversion factor is to reduce the impact of exchange rate fluctuations in the cross-country comparison of national incomes.

The *Atlas* conversion factor for any year is the average of a country's exchange rate (or alternative conversion factor) for that year and its exchange rates for the two preceding years, adjusted for the difference between the rate of inflation in the country and that in Japan, the United Kingdom, the United States, and the euro area. A country's inflation rate is measured by the change in its GDP deflator.

The inflation rate for Japan, the United Kingdom, the United States, and the euro area, representing

Statistical methods

international inflation, is measured by the change in the "SDR deflator." (Special drawing rights, or SDRs, are the International Monetary Fund's unit of account.) The SDR deflator is calculated as a weighted average of these countries' GDP deflators in SDR terms, the weights being the amount of each country's currency in one SDR unit. Weights vary over time because both the composition of the SDR and the relative exchange rates for each currency change. The SDR deflator is calculated in SDR terms first and then converted to U.S. dollars using the SDR to dollar *Atlas* conversion factor. The *Atlas* conversion factor is then applied to a country's GNI. The resulting GNI in U.S. dollars is divided by the midyear population to derive GNI per capita.

When official exchange rates are deemed to be unreliable or unrepresentative of the effective exchange rate during a period, an alternative estimate of the exchange rate is used in the *Atlas* formula (see below).

The following formulas describe the calculation of the *Atlas* conversion factor for year *t*:

$$e_t^* = \frac{1}{3}\left[e_{t-2}\left(\frac{p_t}{p_{t-2}} \Big/ \frac{p_t^{S\$}}{p_{t-2}^{S\$}} \right) + e_{t-1}\left(\frac{p_t}{p_{t-1}} \Big/ \frac{p_t^{S\$}}{p_{t-1}^{S\$}} \right) + e_t \right]$$

and the calculation of GNI per capita in U.S. dollars for year *t*:

$$Y_t^{\$} = (Y_t / N_t)/e_t^*$$

where e_t^* is the *Atlas* conversion factor (national currency to the U.S. dollar) for year *t*, e_t is the average annual exchange rate (national currency to the U.S. dollar) for year *t*, p_t is the GDP deflator for year *t*, $p_t^{S\$}$ is the SDR deflator in U.S. dollar terms for year *t*, $Y_t^{\$}$ is the *Atlas* GNI per capita in U.S. dollars in year *t*, Y_t is current GNI (local currency) for year *t*, and N_t is the midyear population for year *t*.

Alternative conversion factors

The World Bank systematically assesses the appropriateness of official exchange rates as conversion factors. An alternative conversion factor is used when the official exchange rate is judged to diverge by an exceptionally large margin from the rate effectively applied to domestic transactions of foreign currencies and traded products. This applies to only a small number of countries, as shown in *Primary data documentation*. Alternative conversion factors are used in the *Atlas* methodology and elsewhere in *World Development Indicators* as single-year conversion factors.

 Front | User guide | World view | People | Environment

Credits

1. World view

Section 1 was prepared by a team led by Eric Swanson. Eric Swanson wrote the introduction with input from Neil Fantom, Juan Feng, Masako Hiraga, Wendy Huang, Hiroko Maeda, Johan Mistiaen, Vanessa Moreira, Esther Naikal, William Prince, Evis Rucaj, Rubena Sakaj, and Emi Suzuki. Bala Bhaskar Naidu Kalimili coordinated tables 1.1 and 1.6. Masako Hiraga, Hiroko Maeda, Johan Mistiaen, Vanessa Moreira, and Emi Suzuki prepared tables 1.2 and 1.5. Mahyar Eshragh-Tabary, Masako Hiraga, Buyant Erdene Khaltarkhuu, Hiroko Maeda, Vanessa Moreira, and Emi Suzuki prepared table 1.3. Wendy Huang prepared table 1.4 with input from Azita Amjadi. Signe Zeikate of the World Bank's Economic Policy and Debt Department provided the estimates of debt relief for the Heavily Indebted Poor Countries Debt Initiative and Multilateral Debt Relief Initiative.

2. People

Section 2 was prepared by Juan Feng, Masako Hiraga, Hiroko Maeda, Johan Mistiaen, Vanessa Moreira, Emi Suzuki, and Eric Swanson in partnership with the World Bank's Human Development Network and the Development Research Group in the Development Economics Vice Presidency. Emi Suzuki prepared the demographic estimates and projections. The poverty estimates at national poverty lines were compiled by the Global Poverty Working Group, a team of poverty experts from the Poverty Reduction and Equality Network, the Development Research Group, and the Development Data Group. Shaohua Chen and Prem Sangraula of the World Bank's Development Research Group prepared the poverty estimates at international poverty lines. Lorenzo Guarcello and Furio Rosati of the Understanding Children's Work project prepared the data on children at work. Other contributions were provided by Samuel Mills (health); Maddalena Honorati, Montserrat Pallares-Miralles, and Claudia Rodríguez (vulnerability and security); Theodoor Sparreboom and Alan Wittrup of the International Labour Organization (labor force); Amélie Gagnon, Said Ould Voffal, and Weixin Lu of the United Nations Educational, Scientific and Cultural Organization Institute for Statistics (education and literacy); the World Health Organization Chandika Indikadahena (health expenditure), Monika Bloessner and Mercedes de Onis (malnutrition and overweight), Teena Kunjumen (health workers), Jessica Ho (hospital beds), Rifat Hossain (water and sanitation), Luz Maria de Regil (anemia), Hazim Timimi (tuberculosis), and Lori Marie Newman (syphilis); Leonor Guariguata of the International Diabetes Federation (diabetes); Mary Mahy of the Joint United Nations Programme on HIV/AIDS (HIV/AIDS); and Colleen Murray of the United Nations Children's Fund (health). Eric Swanson provided comments and suggestions on the introduction and at all stages of production.

3. Environment

Section 3 was prepared by Mahyar Eshragh-Tabary in partnership with the Agriculture and Environmental Services Department of the Sustainable Development Network Vice Presidency of the World Bank. Mahyar Eshragh-Tabary wrote the introduction with suggestions from Eric Swanson. Other contributors include Esther G. Naikal and Karen Treanton of the International Energy Agency, Gerhard Metchies and Armin Wagner of German International Cooperation, Craig Hilton-Taylor and Caroline Pollock of the International Union for Conservation of Nature, and Cristian Gonzalez of the International Road Federation. The World Bank's Agriculture and Environmental Services Department devoted generous staff resources.

4. Economy

Section 4 was prepared by Bala Bhaskar Naidu Kalimili in close collaboration with the Sustainable Development and Economic Data Team of the World Bank's Development Data Group and with suggestions from Liu Cui and William Prince. Bala Bhaskar Naidu Kalimili wrote the introduction with suggestions from Eric Swanson. The highlights section was prepared by Bala Bhaskar Naidu Kalimili, Maurice Nsabimana, and Olga Victorovna Vybornaia. The national accounts data for low- and middle-income economies were gathered by the World Bank's regional staff through the annual Unified Survey. Federico M. Escaler, Mahyar Eshragh-

Credits

Tabary, Bala Bhaskar Naidu Kalimili, Buyant Erdene Khaltarkhuu, Maurice Nsabimana, and Olga Victorovna Vybornaia updated, estimated, and validated the databases for national accounts. Esther G. Naikal prepared adjusted savings and adjusted income data. Azita Amjadi contributed trade data from the World Integrated Trade Solution. The team is grateful to Eurostat, the International Monetary Fund, the Organisation for Economic Co-operation and Development, the United Nations Industrial Development Organization, and the World Trade Organization for access to their databases.

5. States and markets

Section 5 was prepared by Federico Escaler and Buyant Erdene Khaltarkhuu in partnership with the World Bank's Financial and Private Sector Development Network, Poverty Reduction and Economic Management Network, and Sustainable Development Network; the International Finance Corporation; and external partners. Buyant Erdene Khaltarkhuu wrote the introduction with input from Eric Swanson. Other contributors include Alexander Nicholas Jett (privatization and infrastructure projects); Leora Klapper (business registration); Federica Saliola and Joshua Wimpey (Enterprise Surveys); Carolin Geginat and Frederic Meunier (Doing Business); Alka Banerjee, Trisha Malinky, and Michael Orzano (Standard & Poor's global stock market indexes); Gary Milante and Kenneth Anya (fragile situations); Satish Mannan (public policies and institutions); James Hackett of the International Institute for Strategic Studies (military personnel); Sam Perlo-Freeman of the Stockholm International Peace Research Institute (military expenditures and arms transfers); Christian Gonzalez of the International Road Federation, Zubair Anwar and Narjess Teyssier of the International Civil Aviation Organization, and Marc Juhel and Hélène Stephan (transport); Vincent Valentine of the United Nations Conference on Trade and Development (ports); Azita Amjadi (high-tech exports); Vanessa Grey, Esperanza Magpantay, and Susan Teltscher of the International Telecommunication Union; Torbjörn Fredriksson and Diana Korka of the United Nations Conference on Trade and Development (information and communication technology goods trade); Martin Schaaper of the United Nations Educational, Scientific and Cultural Organization Institute for Statistics (research and development, researchers, and technicians); and Ryan Lamb of the World Intellectual Property Organization (patents and trademarks).

6. Global links

Section 6 was prepared by Wendy Huang with input from Evis Rucaj and Rubena Sukaj and in partnership with the Financial Data Team of the World Bank's Development Data Group, Development Research Group (trade), Development Prospects Group (commodity prices and remittances), International Trade Department (trade facilitation), and external partners. Wendy Huang and Evis Rucaj wrote the introduction, with substantial input from Eric Swanson. Azita Amjadi (trade and tariffs) and Rubena Sukaj (external debt and financial data) provided substantial input on the data and tables. Other contributors include Frédéric Docquier (emigration rates); Flavine Creppy and Yumiko Mochizuki of the United Nations Conference on Trade and Development and Mondher Mimouni of the International Trade Centre (trade); Cristina Savescu (commodity prices); Jeff Reynolds and Joseph Siegel of DHL (freight costs); Yasmin Ahmad and Elena Bernaldo of the Organisation for Economic Co-operation and Development (aid); Ibrahim Levent and Maryna Taran (external debt); Gemechu Ayana Aga and Ani Rudra Silwal (remittances); and Teresa Ciller of the World Tourism Organization (tourism). Ramgopal Erabelly, Shelley Fu, and William Prince provided technical assistance.

Other parts of the book

Jeff Lecksell of the World Bank's Map Design Unit coordinated preparation of the maps on the inside covers. Alison Kwong and William Prince prepared *User guide* and the lists of online tables and indicators for each section. Eric Swanson wrote *Statistical methods*, with input from William Prince. Federico Escaler and Leila Rafei prepared *Primary data documentation*. *Partners* was prepared by Alison Kwong.

Database management

William Prince coordinated management of the World Development Indicators database, with assistance from Liu Cui and Shelley Fu in the Data Administration and Quality Team. Operation of the database management system was made possible by Ramgopal Erabelly in the Data and Information Systems Team under the leadership of Reza Farivari.

Design, production, and editing

Azita Amjadi and Alison Kwong coordinated all stages of production with Communications Development Incorporated, which provided overall design direction, editing, and layout, led by Meta de Coquereaumont, Jack Harlow, Bruce Ross-Larson, and Christopher Trott. Elaine Wilson created the cover and graphics and typeset the book. Peter Grundy, of Peter Grundy Art & Design, and Diane Broadley, of Broadley Design, designed the report.

Administrative assistance, office technology, and systems development support

Elysee Kiti provided administrative assistance. Jean-Pierre Djomalieu, Gytis Kanchas, and Nacer Megherbi provided information technology support. Ugendran Machakkalai, Shanmugam Natarajan, Atsushi Shimo, and Malarvizhi Veerappan provided software support on the Development Data Platform application.

Publishing and dissemination

The Office of the Publisher, under the direction of Carlos Rossel, provided assistance throughout the production process. Denise Bergeron, Stephen McGroarty, Nora Ridolfi, and Janice Tuten coordinated printing, marketing, and distribution. Merrell Tuck-Primdahl of the Development Economics Vice President's Office managed the communications strategy.

World Development Indicators mobile applications

Software preparation and testing were managed by Shelley Fu with assistance from Prashant Chaudhari, Ying Chi, Liu Cui, Ghislaine Delaine, Neil Fantom, Ramgopal Erabelly, Federico Escaler, Buyant Erdene Khaltarkhuu, Sup Lee, Maurice Nsabimana, Parastoo Oloumi, Beatriz Prieto Oramas, William Prince, Virginia Romand, Jomo Tariku, Malarvizhi Veerappan, and Vera Wen. Systems development was undertaken in the Data and Information Systems Team led by Reza Farivari. William Prince provided data quality assurance.

Online access

Coordination of the presentation of the WDI online, through the Open Data website, the World Databank application, the new table browser application, and the Application Programming Interface, was provided by Neil Fantom and Soong Sup Lee. Development and maintenance of the website were managed by a team led by Azita Amjadi and including Alison Kwong, George Gongadze, Timothy Herzog, Jeffrey McCoy, and Jomo Tariku. Systems development was managed by a team led by Reza Farivari, with project management provided by Malarvizhi Veerappan. Design, programming, and testing were carried out by Ying Chi, Shelley Fu, Siddhesh Kaushik, Ugendran Machakkalai, Nacer Megherbi, Shanmugam Natarajan, Parastoo Oloumi, Manish Rathore, Ashish B. Shah, Atsushi Shimo, Maryna Taran, and Jomo Tariku. Liu Cui and William Prince coordinated production and provided data quality assurance. Multilingual translations of online applications were provided by a team led by Jim Rosenberg in the World Bank's External Affairs department.

Client feedback

The team is grateful to the many people who have taken the time to provide feedback and suggestions, which have helped improve this year's edition. Please contact us at data@worldbank.org.